The professionals praise *Will My Kid Grow Out of It?*

"Known for her no-nonsense straight talk, Dr. Forrest has worked with hundreds of families to help them navigate the complex maze of the children's mental health system. From the premature baby to the seventeen-year-old going on twenty-five, she can help you sort through what you need to know to successfully understand children's issues."

> —KEVIN ROBERTSON, MBA, executive director of Miracle Babies

"In a clear, even-handed way, Dr. Forrest sorts out myth from fact and shows how best to support and advocate for children."

> —WILLIAM PERRY, PhD, professor of psychiatry and director of the Division of Clinical Psychiatry, University of California, San Diego

"Dr. Forrest does an incredible job condensing complex volumes of information into a very useful resource with sensitivity and real-world common sense. Anyone interested in prevention and children should read this book."

> —RUSS NEWMAN, PhD, JD provost, Alliant International University and former executive director of the Practice Directorate of the American Psychological Association

"Dr. Forrest is a trusted ally, an expert on your team, for any parents with concerns about mental health issues in their child. Her supportive and direct explanations of prevalent mental disorders in youth and the value of early intervention give parents the tools to successfully navigate the mental health system to help their child."

> —LISA MILLER, PhD, professor and director of Clinical Psychology, director of the Spirituality and Mind-Body Institute, Teachers College, Columbia University

Will My Kid Grow Out Of It?

A Child Psychologist's
Guide to Understanding
Worrisome Behavior

BONNY J. FORREST, JD, PhD

ISBN 978-1-61374-762-9

Diagnostic criteria where listed are reprinted with permission from the Diagnostic and Statistical Manual of Mental Disorders, Fifth Edition, (Copyright ©2013). American Psychiatric Association. All Rights Reserved.

Library of Congress Cataloging-in-Publication Data

Forrest, Bonny Jo.
  Will my kid grow out of it? : a child psychologist's guide to understanding worrisome behavior / Bonny J. Forrest.
    pages cm
  Summary: "A parental road map to navigate a child's mental health Helping parents determine whether their child's behavior is typical for the age or, possibly, a sign of something more serious they should look into, Will My Kid Grow Out of It? uses lay terms and concrete examples to aid adults in establishing if their child may have a commonly diagnosed issue such as ADHD, depression, a learning disability, and others; where to go to get help; how to get support from schools and the medical community; and what questions to ask along the way. Each chapter expands on a specific set of behaviors that may be problematic by listing types of problems, possible diagnoses, the types of treatments that have been found to be effective, discussions of the pros and cons of alternative treatments, and typical medications. The book provides readers with access to a free interactive online screening tool and Project SKIP. Extensive ancillary resources—such as an overview of child brain development, organizations and hotlines for families, a list of commonly used medications for mental health, and a glossary—are also included"— Provided by publisher.
  Includes bibliographical references and index.
  ISBN 978-1-61374-762-9 (paperback)
  1. Child psychology. 2. Behavioral assessment of children. 3. Parenting. I. Title.

BF721.F644 2014
155.4'13—dc23

2014018309

Cover and interior design: Andrew Brozyna, AJB Design, Inc.
Interior illustrations: Frank Corl

Printed in the United States of America
5 4 3 2 1

Contents

Author's Note

IN WRITING THIS book, I have drawn extensively on my experience as a clinician and a researcher. But any work that covers such a wide range of topics is deeply indebted to the vast amount of research and clinical experience that medical and mental health professionals have made available to other professionals and to the public. Wherever possible, as my citations show, I have tried to draw on the best available information about diagnoses and treatments and to provide the most widely accepted criteria for identifying and assessing the problems children may have. I often cite two or three sources when providing symptoms or criteria for a disorder. Many of these checklists or warning signs are commonly used in the offices of mental health professionals and are widely available on the Internet. My descriptions are intended to be as comprehensive as possible in summarizing and giving appropriate credit to those original sources.

None of this is to say that you should accept anything in this book as a truth that will never change. I have not covered every possible diagnosis nor is this book a substitute for professional advice. Our understanding of how children develop, and of their behavioral and mental health issues, is changing quickly—in some cases, dramatically. Throughout the book, I encourage you to educate yourself further about any issue your child faces, and to be energetic in questioning the professionals with whom you work about the latest research and developments in diagnosis and treatment.

In all the case examples used in this book, names and identifying information have been changed. Some of the examples are composites of my experiences with more than one family.

Regarding gender pronouns, rather than writing "he or she" or "him or her" every time I refer to an individual child, I use feminine pronouns in the book's first half and male pronouns in the second half.

Finally, throughout this book I have included Internet addresses for some of the best, most trusted sources of children's mental health information on the Web. Those links often change, however. As of the date of publication of this book they all worked. The most up-to-date information can always be found at my website, www.AskDrForrest.com. You may also reach me through social media on Facebook at Dr. Bonny Forrest, on Twitter @DrBonnyForrest, or via my blog at www.AskDrForrest.com.

Project SKIP

I AM PLEASED to provide readers with free access to my web tool Project SKIP: Screening Kids for Intervention and Prevention (www.projectskip.com), which screens children for social-emotional, cognitive, and developmental issues. Use the code BOOK1 to access the site. Please note that *the screening is not a diagnosis or a definitive assessment of your child.* It is simply one tool among many to help you determine whether you need to seek professional help for your child. Many others are described in this book, where you will also learn more about how and when to best use Project SKIP.

Introduction

PERHAPS A TEACHER has told you that your child's behavior is not quite right—she's just a little too energetic in the classroom and can't sit still long enough to focus on a lesson. Or you have begun to worry that your child isn't progressing as quickly as other children. Or you simply need reassurance after seeing a news headline that has set your heart racing and your mind fast-forwarding to all the problems that can affect a child:

"Autism Boom: An Epidemic of Disease or of Discovery?"

"ADHD Drug Shortage Pushes Parents to Seek Substitutes"

"The Childhood Obesity Epidemic: Health Crisis or Social Construction?"

Whatever your reason for picking up this book, you're probably asking yourself questions such as these:

- Will my child grow out of this?
- Is there really a problem, or should I stop worrying?
- Will she do better in school if she just tries harder and I force her to do her homework?
- I'm getting conflicting advice. Whom should I trust?
- I'm looking for help and run into obstacles at every turn. What can I do?
- Does our child really need medication?

For parents who have concerns about their child, what can be scariest is feeling that you are alone—trying to sort through a lot of information, not all of it reliable; having to trust "experts" whom you're not sure you really trust; and, perhaps, asking for support from schools or agencies that are understaffed and underfunded.

Over the years, I have worked with thousands of families, from those who had already been given a diagnosis and were struggling to find an effective treatment to those who were still searching for answers about their child's puzzling behavior. What did all of these parents have in common? They all needed help to get their bearings in the midst of all the information available to them, all the choices facing them, and all the complications of dealing

1

with schools or mental health systems when their children needed support. More than anything, they needed help in asking the right questions.

In your journey to find the answers and support you need, this book can be your first partner. It will help you understand your child's behavior, find the right professionals, and advocate effectively for her when she needs support. It describes a step-by-step process, complete with tools and resources, to support you in taking control of your child's welfare. Along the way, I provide lists of "typical" symptoms of disorders most commonly identified in children by clinicians, answer the common questions I encounter from families, and translate the relevant scientific research into easily accessible terms. As an attorney and psychologist who has advocated for children with special needs for many years, I am well equipped to show you how to negotiate with your child's school if that becomes necessary. This book is no substitute for a long-term partnership with a professional you trust, but it can guide you through the system as you search for the best advice and support.

Some of you may come away from the book reassured that you have nothing to worry about. Some of you may decide that your child's behavior or development deserves a closer look from a professional. Making the decision to take that closer look is courageous. There is pressure for every child to succeed. If the professional finds something wrong, what will that mean for your child? Americans still have a prejudice against those with developmental or mental health issues, especially because troubled teenagers splash across the news in such horrible cases as the stabbings by a Pennsylvania high school student in 2014 and the Columbine school shootings in 1999. Only recently have many successful people—Richard Branson, Charles Schwab, Catherine Zeta-Jones, Keira Knightley, and Danny Glover, to name a few—come out publicly to say that they have struggled with emotional disorders or had learning disabilities while growing up.

The Importance of Early Intervention

However anxious you may feel about that first step to consult a professional, it can be very important to take it. As you will see throughout the book, my experience has taught me that *early intervention is the key to better outcomes.* This point is critical. If you suspect your child is not progressing, or a teacher or caregiver suggests there could be an issue, you should seek answers regardless of how scary you find the questions. Better to seek a professional view than to wait or ignore the issue. If there is something wrong, a prompt intervention will increase the odds of a better outcome for your child.

Here is an example from my practice that underlines the importance of early intervention. One reason for this book is to help you learn from the experiences of other parents, and I will be sharing these stories throughout the book.

Andrew

Andrew was only three, and small for his age. He had been born prematurely, and he constantly struggled to catch up. At his preschool, his teacher described periods during which he zoned out, staring into space, and seemed unresponsive to her requests. He would frequently play by himself away from other kids and, if left to his own devices, he would wander around the play area in circles. More recently, he would melt down into crying fits if the teacher said no to him or if he were forced to wait. His parents wanted to know if I should do an assessment now or if they should wait to see if he grew out of his behavior.

Fortunately, they chose to find out if Andrew had a problem. An assessment discovered that he was having multiple small and brief seizures that affected his behavior. He was started on medication to control the seizures and now has caught up to his peers in both his physical and social development, especially in his ability to interact with kids his own age. (As later chapters discuss, medication is by no means the right solution for every issue, but it worked for Andrew because of the nature of his problem.)

Andrew's story was straightforward: his parents were able to find out what was wrong and what to do about it quickly. For many parents, though, the journey to find answers and help can be agonizingly frustrating. As a series in the *Los Angeles Times* highlighted a few years back, parents can have difficulties getting solid answers to their questions even when dealing with apparently qualified professionals. That's because not all professionals, even doctors and psychologists who deal with children, are trained to diagnose and treat the full range of children's developmental issues, and some do not normally look for them. In fact, although *one in seven* children has some form of developmental disability, *fewer than half* the pediatricians in the country screen children for these disorders.

The journey can often be frustrating for another reason as well: it can be difficult to accurately diagnose developmental problems in children, especially young children. For example, autism, which is so much in the news, can be very tricky to diagnose in younger children. Although there is a gold-standard instrument for evaluating a child's behavior in relation to the symptoms of autism (Autism Diagnostic Observation Schedule [ADOS]), it does not provide a diagnosis of autism. It only reports how a child's social and communication abilities rate in relation to other children the same age who have an autism spectrum disorder (ASD).

Despite the difficulties some parents encounter in their journey to seek help for their child, I would offer a word of encouragement and optimism: my experience has taught me that, even if your child faces serious difficulties, it is important that neither you nor anyone else in her life set your expectations for her future too low. Here is another story to underscore that point.

Emily

When I first saw Emily it was clear that something needed to be addressed. Sitting in my office with a 1960-something tie-dyed shirt, long frizzy hair, and horn-rimmed glasses, Emily could say hello but not engage in a back-and-forth conversation. Her parents were seeking help for her academic issues. Emily was an eighth grader in an extremely rigorous academic environment, and, for the first time, was starting to fall behind her peers. After two days of intense testing, I confidently announced to the family my diagnosis of Asperger's syndrome. (Asperger's syndrome used to be a separately diagnosed autism spectrum disorder characterized by significant difficulties in social interaction, with restricted and repetitive patterns of behavior and interests but relatively normal intelligence and linguistic skills.)

Imagine my surprise when they said, "We know." The parents had figured this out themselves. They wanted her to succeed beyond a label and the expectations for failure that came with that label. So they had made the conscious choice long before they saw me to have Emily be successful on her own terms, no matter what her doctor said she might be capable of. They did not disclose the diagnosis to her or anyone else and therefore were not limited by the confines of what the diagnosis was usually taken to mean for her development. We designed an intervention plan for Emily to get her up to par at school, and she went on to graduate with excellent grades and attend the college of her choice.

I learned a lot from that clinical moment, as I have from all my patients, about understanding a family's expectations, their fears about a diagnosis or label, and the importance of providing alternative information for families who want to push the boundaries of the traditional definitions provided by the mental health system. I have pondered how best to use clinical information to guide intervention and school planning for many years, and this book is in part a result of that effort.

How Does This Book Work?

In these pages I will guide you through the process of deciding whether to seek help for your child and will discuss the dilemmas you may encounter once you make that decision, as you start navigating the children's mental health care system. The next two chapters advise you on how to make the decision to seek help and how to think about diagnoses and overcome worries about their ramifications. Chapters 3 to 11 address specific disorders or clusters of disorders. Each chapter provides a list of symptoms that can help you decide if you should seek help, information about how a diagnosis is reached, a brief synopsis of the latest research when relevant, a summary of some of the most effective treatments, and notes from my personal experiences. The final chapters will help you understand the types of mental health professionals and general treatments available and give you specific questions to ask; help you navigate mental health, school, and state systems to get help for your child; and provide answers to commonly asked questions. Throughout this process, you can contact me at any time directly through my website, AskDrForrest.com, for additional help and support.

Parents want healthy and happy kids who prosper. It is very hard to hear that your child's development might be delayed or at risk. As a result, some treatments claim to be an easy fix. I wish I could offer quick answers, no hard times, and a magical pill with no side effects. But no one can. Indeed, if someone claims to, run the other way! Instead, what this book offers you is my guidance crafted by years of practice, working with families who have been where you are. What I wish most for you is the peace of mind you deserve in knowing that you are doing everything you can to make your child successful.

Adelia

Not all stories have happy endings. The ones that haunt me are the ones in which I could not make a connection with the parents to persuade them to seek the help their child needed.

When I first started my private practice as a clinical psychologist in New York City, I received a call from a young mother. She had been told by her daughter's teacher that her seven-year-old, who wasn't talking, might be "retarded." The mother brought her daughter, Adelia, in to see me for several days of testing. Not talking and not able to sit with me to complete many tests, Adelia was very delayed for her age. What little testing I was able to do didn't rely on her nonexistent language skills and indicated that she had well-below-average intelligence. More important, perhaps, she was not able to sit still for any amount of time, and I could see immediately why the teacher had been concerned. The teacher followed up with me and said that what she saw in school was a child with profound delays in language and communication of any sort. Many days Adelia would run around the classroom aimlessly or sit by herself pulling on her hair or rocking back and forth.

In an attempt to see Adelia in a variety of settings, I offered to see her at home and school. Her mother was opposed because she didn't feel it was necessary, a sign that she might not be ready to hear what was really up with her child. Over four days I saw Adelia in my office and tried to engage her so I could understand her behavior and her world. Over time, it became clear to me that Adelia's delays in adapting to her environment and low intelligence qualified her for the shorthand term for this constellation of symptoms: developmental or intellectual disability.

When I tried to explain this to her mother, she became infuriated with me and left my office without the results of her daughter's tests or any of the recommendations I had tried to make for treatment to increase Adelia's daily functioning.

It is so difficult to deliver this sort of information to a parent about their child. I try to stay focused on strengths and to explain that a diagnosis is just shorthand through which medical professionals communicate. It doesn't equate to their child's potential or worth. But Adelia's mother forbade me from working with the school or even speaking with them. I wasn't able to say the things that Adelia's mom needed to hear, and Adelia's mom wasn't ready to hear what I had to say. To this day I wish that I could have found a better way to communicate my concerns, a way through which the mother could have heard me. I still wonder what happened to Adelia.

Even in the case of a disability as severe as Adelia's, early intervention can make the difference between independence or dependence as an adult. The latest research shows that early intervention, even for children with autism, can alleviate many of the effects of the disorder—for example, by creating better social skills and speech and language skills. I hope Adelia's parents found the help they needed, even if they did not find it through me.

I share this story with you not only to stress again the importance of early intervention, but also to demonstrate the importance of finding a professional with whom you can connect, communicate easily, and build a long-term relationship. Not every relationship succeeds, and not necessarily because either party is at fault. But there are many professionals who will work with you patiently and persistently, applying their clinical expertise in a manner that is humane and caring. That attitude, in combination with true expertise rather than superficial knowledge, matters most. You should keep looking until you find a professional who will be your trusted partner through the entire process.

Finally, I urge you not to let terms like "professionals," "diagnoses" or "the mental health system" scare you or prevent you from reading on. Medical, psychological, and educational professionals who may be beneficial to your child include specialists of all kinds at all levels of intervention, from meetings with your school's reading specialist or social worker to help from an occupational therapist to regular sessions with a psychologist or anything in between.

Part I

"Is That Normal?"

1

Where to Start When Your Child's Behavior Is Troubling You

IF YOU HAVE noticed any of the following behaviors in your child, they may have you worrying that things are not quite "normal."

Children of Elementary School Age

- exhibits unusual sleep patterns
- persistently refuses to go to school
- attends school regularly, does homework, but still gets bad grades
- is constantly worried or anxious, or is more fearful than others her age
- throws frequent temper tantrums for no apparent reason
- never slows down
- is disorganized, or can concentrate for only a short time
- frequently resists or opposes authority figures, more so than other children of the same age
- feels the need to stay in rigid routine; repeatedly washes hands or insists on things being "just so"
- is delayed in reaching developmental milestones (see appendix A)
- does not seem to understand social norms; cannot make friends or understand the feelings or behavior of others

Preteens and Adolescents

- is isolated from friends and family
- has an intense fear of becoming obese despite normal body weight, or otherwise has an unusually poor self-image

- opposes or defies authority figures in ways that often lead to truancy or breaking the law
- abuses alcohol, drugs, or tobacco
- behaves promiscuously
- cuts or otherwise intentionally injures herself
- expresses unusually strange thoughts or feelings
- hears voices

How do you know how seriously to take these behaviors? While some of them are clear signs that something is wrong, others may seem like nothing more than a particularly intense phase of normal kid behavior. How can you tell if you should consult a professional, at least for reassurance if not for help?

Here is a straightforward process for tackling that question.

First, consider whether your child's early development is or has been different from the milestones described in appendix A. Read through the chapters in Part II to see if any of the symptom lists describe your child's behavior. If you think you find a match, rather than relying only on your impressions and your memory, take notes about what you observe over time and refer to this chapter's guide on duration, intensity, and overall impact as well as the information on charting behaviors given here to decide if you should take the next steps.

Next, log on to www.ProjectSKIP.com and conduct a screening for your child using the code BOOK1. Again, I want to stress that the online screening is not a diagnosis or a definitive assessment of your child; it is simply an initial step.

Finally, using your notes and the results of the screening, and armed with questions and information you find in this book, talk to your doctor, psychologist, or mental health professional. In that conversation, you will discuss in depth the behaviors that are worrying you and what to do next.

Is This Serious?

There are five guidelines that I suggest parents, teachers, pediatricians, and others consider when assessing the seriousness of a child's emotional, social, or behavioral issues:

- the symptom's duration and intensity and its overall impact on the child
- the symptom's impact on other areas of the child's development
- the symptom's impact on the family
- the age at which the symptoms develop and how they change with time
- the advisability of early intervention

And, of course, an obvious question is whether the behavior is so serious that you clearly have to ask for help immediately.

I will explain these guidelines by applying them to the cases of two different children who were both struggling in school.

Emma and Donna

Emma was a seven-year-old who was in first grade. She had resisted going to school for more than a year. Even though she had recently begun talking about school in a positive way, saying that she liked her teachers and classmates, she began each day with the same refusal. She simply did not want to get on the school bus. If her parents insisted, Emma would cry, scream, and start to shake uncontrollably. Otherwise, she was cooperative, affectionate, and kind with her siblings and parents.

Although her morning tantrum often resulted in one of her parents driving her to school, once at school she was able to leave her parent comfortably and was not afraid to go to class. She would be slow to warm up to teachers, however, and would stand a bit at a distance simply to watch them when she first met them in the morning. During the day, if called upon, she was often silent at first and then gradually became more engaged and responded to what they had to say. But this pattern was improving. She began taking less and less time to become responsive in the mornings and began to often answer immediately when called on in class. Within an hour of arriving at school, she participated actively in games or lessons. She had made friends and interacted with those friends regularly. The trip home on the bus was uneventful, more like the behavior of other children her age.

Donna was another seven-year-old who had also resisted going to school for more than a year. She would not ride the bus at all and would have a full tantrum if her parents even suggested that she ride it. In addition, Donna had a number of other behavioral difficulties. She frequently wet her bed, and needed to follow a very specific bedtime routine that had to be restarted from the beginning if it were interrupted. She had particular difficulties when she had to move from one activity to another in school, such as moving from quiet time to circle time. She would often become anxious about small changes in her routine, such as a slightly late dinner or not being able to wear her favorite dress several days in a row.

Donna's parents felt overwhelmed by her behavior and were at a loss for what to do. At school, Donna would cry and scream when the parent who dropped her off tried to leave. Once her school day finally started, she participated in most school activities, but she tried to avoid those—such as circle time—that involved a group. She played with only a few children, and often ordered them around or hit them.

Let's see how the guidelines above apply to Emma and Donna. Overall, Emma's struggles with riding the bus to school in the morning were clearly less extensive than Donna's. But let's consider more closely the duration, intensity, and overall impact of the symptoms in each of these children, and also how the symptoms changed over time.

Duration

Each girl had been having difficulties for about a year at a time when they were entering the first grade and therefore facing a longer school day with greater expectations. First grade often brings with it stresses that cause behavioral changes. Nevertheless, the duration of the symptoms warrants being taken seriously. I would rate both girls' difficulties an 8 on a symptom scale of 1 to 10, with 1 being mild and 10 being severe.

Intensity

Donna's tantrums were certainly more intense than Emma's. They happened frequently, often twice a day, and they happened across settings.

Her parents were at a loss about what to do.

Overall Impact

Emma's difficulties certainly caused some difficulty in the morning, but they had not as yet changed the family's schedule beyond forcing them to drive her to school more often than they wanted to. Once at school, Emma's day proceeded relatively normally. Her teachers didn't need to invest special effort in her or make special arrangements for her. Outside school, her days were relatively normal.

By contrast, Donna was having multiple problems in multiple areas—with friends, siblings, teachers, and family—and her problems were having a substantial impact on her parents' lives and her teacher's classroom. Her parents were also starting to experience consequences at their jobs because they were often late or had to leave early to pick Donna up from school again. Her teachers invested a great deal of time in trying to make things easier for her so that she could participate more actively in the classroom and in creating plans to help her progress. And there were no signs of improvement that indicated they would be able to end those efforts any time soon.

Progress over Time

Next, let's look at the impact of the symptoms on Emma's and Donna's development—in particular, on their "developmental trajectory," the rate at which they were growing as compared to a normal path for children their age.

First, was the refusal to transition from the house to school in the morning a specific issue, or was it part of a larger set of problems affecting the child more generally? Emma's refusal was a troubling but isolated issue; she was not struggling in other areas of her development. Donna, on the other hand, was struggling in several areas, especially in her relationships with her parents, teachers, and peers. Her habit of avoiding group activities at school reinforced the impression that she had difficulty relating to other children or adults, and that this pattern was starting to affect her ability to learn in school.

Second, what was the child's developmental trajectory? Emma was making progress in separating from her parents and participating in school activities. She had taken steps toward mastering this new developmental task, such as being able to describe to her teachers what upset or scared her. In contrast, while Donna had made some progress in a few areas, such as learning to play more with other children without hitting them, she had not been making as much progress as she should have been across the board: separating in the morning, joining in group activities, and having fewer periods of being upset at school. In fact, she was lagging further and further behind her peers.

Here is a snapshot of our measures:

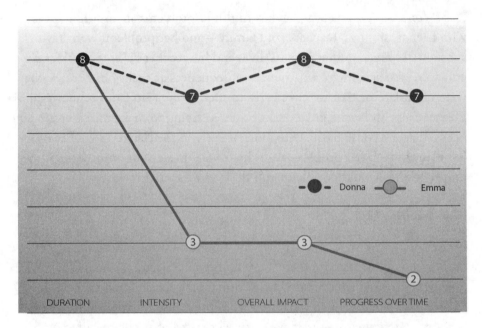

These guidelines provide an objective, careful way of confirming—or contradicting—your initial impression that your child may need help or may just be going through a phase. Donna clearly needs a full and careful professional evaluation, the sooner the better. For Emma, especially given the value of early intervention if there is an underlying issue, I would advise an initial screening even though her problems are less severe and she is improving. There is no downside to a screening. It will either provide reassurance or identify an issue that warrants a closer look through a fuller evaluation. Assuming the screening shows no underlying issues, the next step could simply be to see if the family's pediatrician or a mental health professional has advice about helping her to emerge from this phase.

While these guidelines should help you decide if your child's behaviors warrant an evaluation, there is no clear-cut test for making that decision. If you're uncertain, consult a professional to discuss the next steps. It's far better to err on the side of learning more, rather than simply hoping for the best.

Some Things Need Immediate Attention

Certain behaviors should cause parents to seek immediate help for their children. These include:

- expressing serious thoughts about hurting themselves or other children
- engaging in extremely risky behavior (e.g., threatening another child with a knife or other weapon)
- experiencing significant physical symptoms such as chronic headaches or self-mutilation
- using drugs or alcohol in a way that interferes with their schoolwork, changes their habits significantly, or is otherwise disruptive (some experimentation with drugs or alcohol is typical)
- sleeping excessively or displaying energy to the point that it disrupts a normal daily function, such as running around the house at night instead of sleeping or being unable to get out of bed to go to school

Charting the Problem

In addition to using the guidelines described, parents and mental health providers frequently find it helpful to chart a child's behavior to understand it more thoroughly. Ask the following questions when observing your child, then write down the answers each day for a week or more. Take them with you when you consult the professional.

- Where does the behavior occur?
- During what activities does the behavior occur?
- What is the time of day when the behavior occurs?
- Who or what kind of person is around when the behavior occurs?
- What things happen just before the behavior occurs?

- What things happen during the behaviors?
- What happens right after the behavior?

What Is an Evaluation?

A psychological evaluation can take several forms. The simplest, which is usually called an assessment or screening rather than an evaluation, typically involves a single interview with a psychologist or other mental health professional, with the goal of beginning to learn about a child and any problems she might have.

In contrast, a full evaluation typically involves several sessions. It begins with the initial assessment meeting but then involves several psychological tests. It also usually includes interviews with parents and teachers, and perhaps with others who play a major role in the child's life, as well as a review of any relevant documents, such as school reports or the results of previous evaluations. It may also include a school observation. In most cases, the parents will be present at the initial meeting, but you may be asked to allow the therapist to talk to or test the child alone after the first session. During that first session, you and your child will need to consent to the questions the child will be asked.

There are many types of psychological tests, and they can be used to explore a range of issues—for example, emotional health, intelligence (IQ), potential learning disabilities, or potential psychological problems. Psychologists are generally the most qualified to use and interpret psychological test results, so tests should be conducted or at least supervised by a licensed psychologist, even if they are actually administered by someone in training who isn't yet licensed. It takes years of training and a wealth of expertise to know which tests to give, how to interpret their results, and how to combine the results with all the other information about a child to reach conclusions and decide upon next steps. Anyone you go to, psychologist or not, should be well trained in the use of these instruments.

Because the evaluation can take different forms and use different tests, if your child is to be evaluated, you should ask what, specifically, the evaluation will involve and the reasons why each test was chosen.

Final Thoughts

Over the years I have had parents complain that, when they sought help because their child was delayed in talking, crying too much, or displaying some other behavior that concerned them, the professional told the parent, wrongly, that the child would simply grow out of it. Evaluating child development, especially in infants, is a tricky business; professionals are identifying many issues far earlier than they used to, thanks to advances in science, but they can all make mistakes in diagnoses. There are no definitive blood tests that can tell us if a child has a particular mental health issue or not, and kids' symptoms exist on a spectrum from mild to more severe. A good evaluation requires time and the use of interviews, standardized measures, thoughtfulness, and clinical judgment. Clinicians may differ in the result that they reach, but they should not differ in the process they use to make those clinical judgments. They should always take parents' concerns seriously and take enough time to adequately evaluate your child. If you don't feel a professional has done that, you should seek a second opinion.

In addition, there are things you can do right now to shore up your children's mental and emotional health:

- Show your love and your concern for their health and well-being.
- Be aware of their changing needs as they develop.
- Provide dependable care, be consistent in your use of discipline, and avoid severe punishments.
- Listen to their worries and anxieties and take them seriously.
- Encourage them to talk about their feelings and to work through difficulties.
- Praise them and celebrate their accomplishments.
- Comfort them when they are unhappy or worried.
- Spend time with each of your children individually.
- Work on projects and take part in activities together.
- Don't involve them in your own problems or arguments.
- Seek help early if your child's behavior or mental health is beginning to worry you.

2

Diagnosis, Stigma, and the Clinician's Manual

ALTHOUGH A GROWING number of people now understand that mental health and other developmental issues are diseases of the brain, just as arthritis or diabetes are diseases of the body, there remains a stigma attached to mental health issues that prevents many people from seeking treatment that could help them lead better lives. This seems to be the case for children especially because parents don't want their child "labeled," particularly if they worry that others may blame them for their child's problems.

My answer to this is twofold. First, you need to act now. Failing to seek help early usually leads to one of two results. Either you continue to worry needlessly, when an evaluation might provide reassurance. Or the symptoms become worse and more difficult and expensive to treat—and, sometimes, the odds of a successful outcome shrink.

Second, a diagnosis is only a shorthand term for a cluster of symptoms. It doesn't doom your child to anything, and it doesn't predict the future. A diagnosis should be a tool to help you and your team guide treatment and get insurance coverage. It is not a scientific fact, like the makeup of a water molecule. The definitions of diagnoses, and the criteria for choosing a diagnosis, have changed over time because mental health researchers and clinicians still have a lot to learn. Any diagnostic manual is only as good as the clinician applying it (more on this follows), and no diagnosis determines how successful a treatment will be. That's why you need to ask the right questions of your professional and persist until you get answers that satisfy you.

Introducing the topic to your child can be difficult, but I find that most children, even teens, are surprisingly receptive to getting help if the topic is approached in a nonjudgmental and supportive manner. For example, when children are younger you can talk about going to the doctor to help them with their "worries" or with "learning" or "feelings," or to "help us understand how to give you more support with friends." As children get older, they often see the mental health professional as someone who will listen to them in a way their parents might not. You can tell them that they don't have to tell anyone—not even you—about what they say to the treatment provider.

I never recommend that parents misrepresent what is happening. Be honest with your children and tell them that you are seeking help from someone who is a "brain doctor" (for younger kids) or a "mental health specialist" (for older children). Finally, reassure them you are there to support them, that this is all about making them more successful, happier, or less frustrated, and that the treatment professional is going to be dedicated to that task along with you.

Diagnoses and the DSM: Why They Matter

Before you get into part II and learn about possible diagnoses for various groups of behaviors, it's helpful to know just how clinicians arrive at these diagnoses. Throughout this book I refer to the DSM, the shorthand term for *The Diagnostic and Statistical Manual of Mental Disorders*. It is the guide that mental health professionals use to diagnose mental health disorders in adults and children. The DSM covers a huge array of disorders, ranging from eating disorders to learning problems to schizophrenia. It describes the symptoms of each disorder, including the symptoms that distinguish it from similar disorders, and provides other useful information, such as data about how commonly a disorder occurs.

The DSM is revised periodically, and the latest revision—the DSM-5—was released in 2013. The newest release has been fraught with controversy in part because many professionals are concerned that the revisions, which include broader descriptions of some diagnoses, will lead to more children (and adults) being diagnosed with disorders unnecessarily, and as a result overmedicated. Partly in response, the National Institutes of Mental Health (NIMH) announced that it will begin to explore other classifications of mental health diseases.

Overdiagnosis and overmedication are undeniably important issues for parents to be aware of, but the utility of the DSM is essential. Additionally, a formal diagnosis from the DSM is usually necessary for reimbursement from an insurance company and for treatment to begin. Whether or not you choose to share with others that your child has received a diagnosis, it will often help you to get the support and services you want for your child. Recognize, however, that definitions of mental disorders change as research develops, many disorders are difficult to diagnose, and professionals may disagree about a diagnosis. The key is to proceed with caution and to ask questions. Throughout this book, I have noted cases in which there is controversy surrounding a diagnosis. Here is a case that illustrates my own diagnostic process and thinking.

Thomas

Thomas was a delight and still very young at three. His family was one of the first I had the great fortune of working with when I opened a private practice. When I walked into my office for our first meeting, Thomas was already hard at work in my waiting room. He had collected all of my business cards and those of my colleagues and had carefully arranged them in his own card case.

His parents were extremely nurturing and supportive of his growth and curiosity, but also very concerned about his lagging speech and social skills. With all of the press about autism, they came to my office worried that Thomas might be autistic since compulsive behaviors, such as his card collecting, when coupled with speech delay, can be a sign of an autism spectrum disorder.

After a very short time in my office, Thomas warmed to me, eventually sitting in my lap to help me play with the toys that I kept in the closet. He took great pleasure in doing things with me: blowing bubbles, playing with blocks, and watching me let a balloon filled with air fly around the room, shrieking, "Do it again! Do it again, Dr. Bonny!"

On more formal written and behavior tests, Thomas did very well when he didn't have to rely on using words, and he was very engaged with me. Autism is defined in part by impaired social interaction and communication as well as by restricted and repetitive behavior, and children with autism frequently have difficulty interacting with others. The fact that Thomas made good eye contact with me and was laughing and looking at things to get me to enjoy them with him throughout our sessions together suggested he wasn't autistic.

Instead, Thomas's language delays were causing him to gravitate toward activities that he could do on his own, such as the business card collecting—something semisocial that didn't require him to use words. Even at such a young age, Thomas was aware of his speech difficulties and told his parents and me he talked "funny." I suggested that the school and his parents support him through increased intensive speech therapy and keep a close watch on his social skills. Over time, he flourished, and he is now doing quite well both academically and socially.

What to Know and Ask About a Diagnosis

Below are some important questions to ask clinicians about their diagnostic decision-making:

- What are the factors they considered in making the diagnosis?
- Why did they make the decision they made?
- What other diagnoses did they consider, if any?
- What are the consequences for your child if they are wrong?

It is also important to make sure the clinician is taking the time to do a thorough assessment and is focusing on the best intervention rather than only making a diagnosis. In Thomas's case above, I spent substantial time getting to know him in addition to conducting a formal assessment, and I could explain why I reached my conclusion in a way that satisfied his parents. Most important, I prescribed an intervention, and I made it clear that I expected his parents to continue to follow up with me.

If a diagnosis is a close call, I will always err on the side of giving the diagnosis so we can arrange for the appropriate intervention, with the instruction to the parents to evaluate their child's progress in six months. As a clinician, my thought process is that it is better to intervene and reassess in six months than not to intervene at all, because early intervention makes such a critical difference in the course of many disorders.

Throughout your search for answers, you should trust your instincts and persist if you are not getting what you need or, conversely, if you believe someone is diagnosing too quickly and superficially. If someone tells you not to worry but you're still worried, your instincts are telling you something. While it is important not to overreact, it is also important to trust your gut. The parents in the following case did just that, with a positive outcome.

Fred

A mother, father, and their son Fred entered my office, anxious, as all parents are, to find some answers. Fred was eight and could not control his behavior at school. He would wander down the hallways, fail to finish tasks, and disrupt the class and school lunchroom by making noises that made the other kids laugh. In fact, he was so disruptive that he had been forced to sit at lunch by himself, looking at the wall in the lunchroom, in sight of the other kids.

At eight, all children are active, but for Fred, sitting still for any length of time was just too difficult. He would giggle and wriggle and make small clicking sounds in his throat. Fred was like a little train chugging around a track with no brakes. He wanted to hold still, but that just wasn't possible for him. Fred was smart, however, and he was able to do things with me in our more formal examination using pencil-and-paper tests that were beyond his grade level—as long as he could pay attention long enough to take the tests or complete a task when I asked.

Fred's wonderful parents came to our evaluation center after they had already seen a number of health providers. They had been told that Fred just needed to pay better attention and that they should be more effective in disciplining Fred's inappropriate behavior. But, certain in their own instincts as parents, they kept searching for answers.

After several days of testing with Fred and watching him in the classroom, I determined that Fred had more than one issue: Tourette syndrome (TS), attention deficit hyperactivity disorder (ADHD), and obsessive-compulsive disorder (OCD). As I discuss in chapter 6, these conditions can sometimes show up together. TS, although scary sounding, is simply the presence of motor and vocal tics, or hiccuplike movements or sounds, that persist for more than a year. ADHD is a sort of distracted behavior that leads to the inability to pay attention to something for a sustained period. OCD is the persistent presence of thoughts or behaviors that cause discomfort and can even, for example, make a person unable to leave their house. I will describe these conditions in more detail in the chapters that follow (chapter 5 for ADHD and chapter 6 for OCD and Tourette's).

Fred's parents, very concerned for his future, insisted he be treated like any other kid in the classroom. However, his parents, school personnel, and I needed to put supports in place so he could learn like other kids. Because his parents didn't want to put him on medication to help him focus, we designed a program that would support him as he learned new habits and behaviors that allowed him to prosper in the classroom and socialize at lunch. This program involved giving him rewards for paying attention and for focusing over increasingly longer periods of time.

Over the course of several years, his parents ultimately decided to put him on medication when the demands of the classroom increased in later grades, but his teachers, parents, and I constantly monitored his progress and revised his program to meet his needs. Fred graduated from high school with great grades and went on to college. Most important, he is a great person leading a full life who has triumphed over his learning difficulties.

Many parents take their children to be evaluated at the first sign of a problem and receive an "all clear" from the professional. I'm glad Fred's parents trusted their guts and kept searching for answers. If you think there is something a little off with your child's behavior and the answers you receive don't satisfy or make sense to you, get a second opinion. Good professionals will often differ in opinion and few mental health tests are definitive. That's why persistence is so important. In Fred's case, his parents' instincts changed the course of his illness.

Part II

Common Concerns and Possible Diagnoses

3

Infant and Preschool Mental Health: Even Babies Get the Blues

RESEARCHERS AND CLINICIANS' understanding of the mental health and development of infants and preschoolers—including the problems that can affect even very young children and the evidence-based, non-pharmaceutical treatments that can help children who are experiencing problems—is constantly growing and evolving.

The Importance of the First Years

Extensive research has shown that the *first three years* of the child's life have a profound impact on later development, including scholastic performance and the ability to form relationships with others. By the age of three, the brain will have grown to about 80 percent of its adult size, and to 90 percent by the age of five. In the last ten years, in part due to the invention of new technologies such as magnetic resonance imaging (MRI) that allow professionals to look inside the brain without being invasive, researchers have learned a remarkable amount about how the brain develops in a child's early years.

Infant mental health researchers now know that, although most of the brain's cells are present at birth, the connections and strengths of the signals sent from cell to cell depend on children's early environment, and especially on the behavior of their primary caregivers and their attachment to them (see appendix A). In these early years, what matters most is a foundation of supportive relationships that allows a child to feel secure and confident as she explores her world. These relationships with sensitive caregivers are the most important factor in determining a child's ability to be successful later in life.

In my own practice, I constantly see the long-lasting impact that our earliest relationships have on us.

The field of infant and preschool mental health is devoted to understanding these early caregiving relationships and how they interact with the environment and biology to affect the mental health and development of young children. Selma Fraiberg, a social worker in the 1950s who pioneered the idea that infants had a social and emotional life that should be understood, first defined *infant mental health* as the healthy social and emotional development of a child from birth to three years. This definition has been adopted by the national organization Zero to Three, made up of professionals dedicated to working with and advocating for children under age three. As of late, however, the definition has been expanded to include children under the age of six, an expansion supported by a growing field of research and practice.

In addition, infant and preschool mental health specialists are now learning more about how some of a mother's experiences during pregnancy—especially extreme stress—can affect the fetus's developing brain and, by extension, an infant or toddler's behavior. It makes sense to begin our discussion there, at the beginning.

Stress During Pregnancy and the Developing Brain

Most prospective parents know that what a mother ingests during pregnancy—too much alcohol, for example, or toxins in the environment such as lead—can affect the fetus. However, mental health researchers now know that there can be other effects that arise from less physical causes. To understand how this occurs, a basic understanding of genetics is important.

Genes are the building blocks, inherited from your family, that provide the instructions for building your brain and body. However, those instructions result not only from the genes themselves, but also from how the genes are expressed as they issue the instructions. That expression can be influenced by environmental factors—not only physical factors, but also experiential ones such as stress. As a result, those factors can change the form in which the genetic inheritance affects the brain of the developing fetus. Epigenesis is the process by which genes interact with the environment in ways that affect the legacy that is passed on to offspring, and the effects of epigenesis on fetal development have been discovered in many brain functions.

In this context, new research is very clear: if a mother is too stressed during pregnancy, it can affect her baby. For example, thirty-eight women who were directly exposed to the World Trade Center attacks were the subject of a study conducted by researchers at the Traumatic Stress Studies Division of the Mount Sinai Medical Center in New York. The study found, first, that the women who had developed symptoms of post-traumatic stress disorder (PTSD) had significantly lower levels of the stress hormone cortisol than those who had not developed PTSD. Stress hormones such as cortisol are chemicals produced by the body in situations that might be perceived as potentially dangerous. A lower level of stress hormones can be associated with a greater susceptibility to stress because the cortisol released in response to stress inhibits other stress-induced biological responses. As a result, reduced cortisol levels permit an extended release of other chemicals and biological processes during trauma that increase stress.

One year later, children of the women who had developed PTSD also had lower levels of cortisol than children born to the other mothers. Additionally, children whose mothers who were in their third trimester of pregnancy at the time of the attack had children with the most readily apparent reductions in cortisol. This research suggested that a mother's PTSD can affect her child's biological makeup in utero. In fact, the researchers, Rachel Yehuda and her colleagues at Mount Sinai, then went on to show that children of women whose mothers were in the second or third trimester when exposed to trauma from 9/11 exhibited an increased stress response to new situations.

Yehuda's work, along with other studies, suggests that offspring can be left with epigenetic marks from traumatic experiences prior to birth. For example, another study has found a similar correlation between PTSD in Holocaust survivors and the cortisol levels of their offspring. And researchers from the University of Pennsylvania have reported that epigenetic markers can be transmitted through two generations of mice, suggesting that the effects of trauma may linger for more than one generation.

The Importance of Attachment in Shaping Brain Development

Once a child is born, the process of developing attachment with a mother or other caregiver begins. This period is one of the most crucial in the child's development. Early interactions between infants and their caregivers shape the infant brain's development, because these interactions can strengthen the internal brain connections that will support the behaviors children should develop as they mature. Since the 1950s, there has been a great deal of research into the impact of these early interactions on people's long-term growth and development. Perhaps the most important message from the research is that an infant typically needs to build an attachment to at least one primary caregiver if her social and emotional development is to be normal.

Attachment is the bond that develops between a child and a parent or other caregiver who is a consistent, supportive presence, especially in the period between six months and two years. It is not just about feeding the child or playing with her, although it often involves those activities and many other specific ones. An attached relationship is one that assures the child of the consistent presence of a person to whom they can safely return once they begin to explore the world around them and who, when necessary, will be a haven of safety and a source of comfort.

The most commonly cited signs that this attachment is forming include the following:

- newborn: scans parent's face, increasing eye contact
- 6 weeks: begins to smile and coo responsively
- 4 months: begins to be aware of strangers
- 7 months: may become anxious around strangers
- 9 months: has anxiety if separated from the attachment figure; turns to that person for comfort when distressed

Why is attachment so important? The research suggests that a caregiver's responses to the child, and the pattern of interaction between them, create what are in effect internal models that guide the child in navigating other relationships, affecting her perceptions, emotions, thoughts, and expectations during those relationships. For example, if the child cries and the caregiver comforts her, the child learns that asking for help will result in soothing or feeding. If the child is not cared for when she cries, she learns instead that her needs may not be met and that expressing a need or discomfort may do no good.

The caregiver can also help the infant learn to verbalize a need. For example, when a child is sad, a caregiver who says, "You are sad because you lost your toy. I am sorry," helps a child learn to verbalize her upset and handle frustration, rather than just crying or having a tantrum. In this way, the parent is teaching the child how to use language to express needs and emotions, as well as modeling behavior: "This is what you do when you are mad or angry or sad." You can imagine how learning to express emotions in a calm and thoughtful way might be a skill that is critical for later success in life!

Through these experiences, the child gradually begins to feel competent and effective, and the internal brain connections that form the biological basis for those self-regulatory skills are reinforced (see appendix A).

The most prolific researcher in the field of attachment has been John Bowlby, a psychiatrist who published a three-volume study entitled *Attachment and Loss* in 1969. Another important researcher was developmental psychologist Mary Ainsworth, who emphasized the caregiver's role as a "secure base" for the child. Over the years, Ainsworth and other researchers described four basic attachment patterns in infants, based on the nature of the connection between the infant and the caregiver: secure attachment, avoidant attachment, ambivalent or resistant attachment (sometimes called anxious attachment), and disorganized attachment.

Research that follows children over time has shown that a secure and consistent attachment with a loving primary caregiver acts as a protective factor against social and emotional risk. In contrast, the lack of a secure attachment (the avoidant and ambivalent/resistant patterns) has been proven to be a risk factor for later development. And the fourth pattern, disorganized attachment, is recognized as a powerful predictor for serious mental health issues in children. Children with disorganized attachments are more vulnerable to the negative effects of stress, have problems controlling negative emotions, and are therefore prone to screaming or tantrums in school, and display hostile or aggressive behaviors toward adults and peers.

Not surprisingly, disorganized attachment is overrepresented in groups of children who are victims of maltreatment. Indeed, nearly 80 percent of maltreated infants have a disorganized attachment to their caregivers. In some situations, however, disorganized attachment can develop as a result of the primary caregiver's depression. A mother who is depressed will be less attentive or attuned to her infant's needs, more likely to fail to respond to her cues, and

Infant and Caregiver Behavior Patterns Before the Age of 18 Months		
Attachment Pattern	**Child**	**Caregiver**
Secure	A secure relationship is characterized by an adult's sensitivity and responsiveness to the infant's needs. The infant uses the primary caregiver as a base from which to explore the rest of her environment. When scared or confronted with something new, the child will return to the caregiver for comfort.	In this relationship the caregiver responds to the child's needs with appropriate affect and actions, and with consistency. The child learns that the parent or other caregiver is a source of comfort and security.
Avoidant	The avoidant relationship arises from interactions in which the caregiver is unable to acknowledge or model for the child the display or processing of emotions. Instead, the caregiver discourages emotion and encourages the child to stop crying or to comfort herself.	Because the caregiver is unable to provide the child comfort when she is experiencing intense emotions, the child will often turn instead to strangers for comfort, treating them no differently than the caregiver—but unable to be comforted by them either.
Ambivalent/ Resistant	This relationship is characterized both by an inability to use the caregiver for comfort and by a display of ambivalence or in frustration when with the caregiver. (In this type of relationship the caregiver often responds only to extreme pleas for comfort.) The child will often seek the caregiver but then display inconsistent or frustrated behaviors in the caregiver's company.	If the caregiver is inconsistent in responding to the child, then the child's reactions to the caregiver will become mixed, often alternating between seeking the caregiver and responding angrily to being reunited.
Disorganized	This relationship is characterized by fear and automatic avoidance by the child. The child learns that the caregiver is not to be trusted and is often the source of negative interactions. As a result, the child will often freeze up or turn away from the caregiver.	This is the form of attachment most often associated with child abuse.

even, when engaged with her, more intrusive and controlling. Studies have also found that an infant whose caregiver is depressed has a shorter attention span, has less motivation to master new tasks, experiences elevated heart rates and levels of cortisol (the stress hormone), and has reduced activity in the right front of her brain. (The right frontal part of the brain has been found to be most closely associated with attention and emotional processing.) Over time, the lack of social experience can have an impact on brain development, resulting in reduced overall size and the loss of important neural connections.

To complicate matters, although these four patterns are very useful for understanding a child's development, none is recognized as a clinical diagnosis. In the DSM-IV, the formal diagnosis that opened the door to payment from insurers for treatment was called reactive attachment disorder. In the DSM-5, a new diagnosis, disinhibited social engagement disorder, has been added and, as a result, the definition of reactive attachment disorder has changed. These diagnoses are now part of a much larger category of stress- and trauma-related disorders and, for the first time, the DSM-5 provides criteria for diagnosing post-traumatic stress syndrome in very young children.

Two Mental Health Issues in Young Children: Reactive Attachment Disorder and Depression

A full discussion of all the possible mental health issues in this age group is beyond the scope of this book. I discuss two issues here that I have treated with some frequency in my practice. The first is reactive attachment disorder, a particularly difficult disorder to treat. It is infrequently diagnosed in children but often a consideration in children who have been adopted after spending time in institutional settings. The second is depression, which is frequently not considered as a possible issue in the smallest children.

Reactive Attachment Disorder

The DSM-5 changed the formal framework for diagnosing this type of disorder to inhibited and disinhibited, but I find the descriptions of the disorder that preceded the change to be the most useful in understanding a child's behavior, because they are the same descriptions that have guided research and treatment for many years.

The Causes

This disorder develops because a child's basic needs for comfort, affection, and nurturing aren't met, and she therefore fails to establish the strong, supportive bond with a parent or other caregiver as described earlier. The condition often has serious consequences because it may permanently change the child's growing brain, and in turn hurt her ability to establish relationships in adulthood. Although there are no accurate statistics about how many children have reactive attachment disorder, according to the data summarized by the Mayo Clinic it typically arises from an unusually unsupportive or abusive environment, such as:

- institutional care
- frequent changes in foster care or caregivers
- extreme neglect, either intentionally or as a result of inexperienced and overwhelmed parents
- prolonged hospitalization
- extreme poverty
- physical, sexual, or emotional abuse
- forced removal from a neglectful or abusive home
- postpartum depression suffered by the baby's mother
- parents who have a mental illness, anger management problems, or drug or alcohol issues

Not all children who emerge from these environments will have the disorder, however, and some who are particularly resilient go on to develop healthy relationships in their lives. And, although the disorder is a lifelong condition, treatments including those described later in this chapter can provide substantial help.

The Symptoms

Reactive attachment disorder begins in the early years, and the first signs may appear as early as infancy. The Mayo Clinic lists the following signs:

- withdrawn, sad, and listless appearance
- failure to smile

- lack of the normal tendency to follow others in the room with her eyes
- failure to reach out when picked up
- no interest in playing peekaboo or other interactive games
- no interest in playing with toys
- engaging in self-soothing behavior, such as rocking or self-stroking
- calm when left alone

In toddlers and older children, symptoms may include:
- withdrawing from others
- avoiding or dismissing comforting comments or gestures
- acting aggressively toward peers
- watching others closely but not engaging in social interaction
- failing to ask for support or assistance
- obvious and consistent awkwardness or discomfort
- masking feelings of anger or distress

In adolescents:
- alcohol or drug abuse

As the disorder continues, the signs may fall into either an inhibited or a disinhibited pattern of behavior (although some children may demonstrate both patterns). Children with an *inhibited pattern* avoid relationships with almost everyone, often because as infants they never formed a healthy bond with any caregiver. In contrast, children with a *disinhibited pattern* seek attention from almost everyone, including strangers, often as a result of having moved among several caregivers, with no single, stable presence.

In the DSM-5, the new diagnosis of disinhibited social engagement disorder is used to describe children who are at least nine months old and who exhibit—in the context of what their culture finds appropriate—inappropriate or overly familiar behavior with strangers. In essence, it is an undiluted form of the disinhibited behavior described above. Most very young children with secure attachments have an appropriate hesitancy to go to strangers, but disinhibited kids may rush to hug everyone and show no reticence among strangers.

Depression

Until recently, mental health professionals paid little attention to depression (or anxiety) in children under the age of six. But depression and anxiety, as well as some of the other mental health issues described elsewhere in this book, can now be reliably diagnosed in children under six and, in fact, in children as young as three. In addition, researchers are learning more about the course of depression in very young children. For example, in 2009, a research team led by Joan Luby, a researcher and clinician, studied a group of preschoolers aged three to six that included seventy-five (of 306 children enrolled in the study) who were diagnosed with major depression. Each child received up to four mental health exams during the two-year study. After two years, among those children who were initially depressed, 64 percent were still depressed or had a recurrent episode of depression six months later, and 40 percent still had problems. Overall, at all four exams, nearly 20 percent of them had persistent or recurrent depression. Depression was most common in children whose mothers were also depressed, had other mood disorders, or who had experienced a traumatic event such as the death of a parent or physical or sexual abuse. The study provides evidence: little kids can and do get depressed.

Getting Help: Assessment and Diagnosis

The most frequently used handbook for early childhood mental health is the *Diagnostic Classification of Mental Health and Developmental Disorders of Infancy and Early Childhood* (DC-0-3R), which was originally published in 1995 by Zero to Three: National Center for Infants, Toddlers, and Families, the world's largest infant/toddler/early childhood professional organization. Developed by leading experts worldwide, this manual guides those who are trained to work with infants, children, and their families in assessing and diagnosing children under three.

The DC-0-3R has been translated into ten languages, and it has been or is being adopted in more than a dozen states in America by agencies that provide services for children. It does not replace the American Psychiatric

Association's DSM-5, or the World Health Organization's International Classification of Diseases, Ninth Revision (ICD-9), which is more frequently used by researchers outside the United States. (Revision 11 is actually in development now, but in the United States mental health professionals are still using an earlier version for diagnosis.) However, the DC-0-3R provides an alternative classification system for diagnosis that focuses specifically on earlier childhood and the family.

You need to know about these resources because you should make certain that the mental health professional whom you consult has training in diagnosing children this young and is using the best resources to help them better understand your child's behavior. In this age group, assessment and diagnosis differ from those for children six and older. For both groups, however, assessment and diagnosis are connected but different processes—in essence, clinicians assess individuals but diagnose problems, not people. Let's explore each of these processes separately.

Assessment

In younger children, assessment should be an ongoing process because little children grow and change so rapidly. A "snapshot" assessment is not very helpful and, in fact, can be misleading and do more harm than good. Assessment for this age group should be seen as an ongoing dialogue between the caregiver and mental health professional during which the assessment is constantly updated and refined.

In addition, the assessment of a young child should consider two more factors:

- All infants and young children differ in development, including their motor, sensory, language, affective (emotional development), and cognitive skills.

- These skills develop in the context of relationships with parents, other family members, teachers, and childcare workers. In turn, the family exists within the context of community and culture. A good assessment looks at the impact of all of these factors on a child's life.

All assessments at any age should use multiple pieces of information, including standardized behavioral scales, from multiple sources. Additionally, an assessment ideally is based on several hours spent directly with the child as well as interviews with the parent and any other caregivers, including teachers. It should also include a direct observation of the child and family during the family's usual interactions. I insist on time with the child in both the home and my office.

The assessment leads to a profile or report of the child's strengths and weaknesses, including overall abilities to navigate her everyday world successfully, in comparison to the developmental expectation for children of a similar age. The report also identifies potential targets for intervention and suggests successful strategies for intervention and treatment.

Diagnosis

As a mental health professional who works a great deal with children of this age group, I know it is important for parents to understand that clinicians diagnose and classify only problems, not individuals. The assessment should precede the diagnosis—and without it, the diagnosis alone is of minimal benefit to the child and family. However, a diagnosis is important for several reasons. It can give the family much-needed financial support by triggering insurance payments or access to state-funded programs. It also becomes an efficient way for mental health care providers to communicate with each other.

Most important, a diagnosis helps clinicians decide how to intervene, because it allows us to employ targeted interventions that have proven effective for children with similar specific difficulties. The diagnosis can also help us decide how to recognize and track progress. For example, if a child as young as three is diagnosed with an autism spectrum disorder, depression, or anxiety, early intervention can alleviate the symptoms. At times progress can seem slow, but tracking the number of words a child learns or the number of social interactions she has while in an intervention program designed for this disorder can help us understand her progress.

Many well-intentioned professionals have asked me whether clinicians should avoid "labeling" kids this young. My answer is simple: these kids are already being labeled from a very young age, and not in a way that will be helpful to getting them on the right path. In a nationwide study, a former teacher of mine at Yale University Child Study Center, Walter Gilliam, found an alarming rate of expulsion among our youngest children: preschools were expelling youngsters at three times the rate of public schools. In state-supported programs, the expulsion rates ranged widely from zero expulsions per thousand students in Kentucky to more than twenty-one per thousand in New Mexico.

Boys are being expelled from state-supported preschools four and a half times as frequently as girls. African American preschoolers are five times as likely as Asian Americans to be expelled and twice as likely as white or Latino children. Twice as many five-year-olds are expelled as four-year-olds. The most frequent behaviors resulting in expulsion are aggressive actions toward other children, such as pulling hair, biting, or kicking.

A lack of support for children with behavioral issues at this early age can lead parents and teachers to label a child as a troublemaker or failure even before she enters kindergarten. Additionally, the evidence continues to mount that little kids in this age group can be reliably diagnosed with many of the same issues that adults experience, including depression and anxiety. Early treatment can prevent later suffering.

Treatments

A number of treatments have been found to be effective for young children. These are detailed in appendix B. However, in the earliest years, the child/ parent relationship and the family are paramount in development. Given the importance of the relationship between the child and caregiver, it follows that an intervention targeting the child's relationships is crucial to better treatment and outcome. As a result, at this young age many of the interventions focus on the relationship with the primary caregiver.

Perhaps the most important workshops I give these days are for parents to learn better parenting skills (see AskDrForrest.com for a schedule). I have also led a number of early intervention programs that rely on various intervention strategies. The best two have been the Incredible Years curriculum and Child-Parent Psychotherapy.

Incredible Years

The Incredible Years curriculum is a set of comprehensive classes for children (beginning at birth and continuing up to age ten) and their parents and teachers. The classes are designed to promote emotional and social competence and to prevent or treat children's behavioral and emotional problems. In all of the training components, facilitators use videotaped scenes to encourage group discussion, problem solving, and sharing of ideas. Parents may decide on their own to join a program or be referred by a professional. Either way, I recommend these workshops highly and would spend some time researching their availability in your community. A recently developed workshop in this series is for all parents who want to sharpen their parenting skills.

Child-Parent Psychotherapy

Child-parent psychotherapy (CPP) is a treatment for children from birth through age five who are experiencing serious behavior, attachment, or mental health problems, including post-traumatic stress disorder (PTSD), usually as a result of a traumatic event. (The event may be, for example, a traumatic accident, the death of a parent, sexual abuse or other maltreatment, or exposure to domestic violence.) The treatment aims to support the relationship between a child and her caregiver as a means of repairing the child's sense of safety and attachment and, eventually, improving the child's emotional, intellectual, and behavioral functioning.

The specific methods used in the treatment depend on the type of trauma and the child's stage of development. For example, treatment with infants focuses on helping parents understand how their interaction with the child may affect her functioning and development. Older children and toddlers participate more actively, and the sessions often involve the child and parents playing together as a means of improving communication between them. If a parent also has a history of trauma that interferes with his or her ability to respond to the child in ways that support her optimal growth, the therapist helps the parent understand what is happening and helps the parent respond to the child's needs differently.

Final Thoughts and Recent Research

Children mature in an environment filled with both risk and protective factors that affect their mental health. Risk factors are only that: they increase the odds that something negative will happen, but they do not necessarily lead to mental health problems. Conversely, protective factors can act as buffers, lessening the impact of risks and increasing the likelihood that children will experience positive mental health.

Risk factors can be environmental, biological, or psychological. For example, they can include genetics; a family history of mental illness, abuse, or neglect; stress; poor physical health or injury; exposure to violence; poor nutrition; exposure to toxins or illegal substances; the bad influence of peers; and repeated spanking. (Although children absolutely need appropriate forms of discipline and limit-setting, research has shown that consistent spanking makes them more aggressive.) Protective factors can include stable, two-parent families; warm, caring parents who use authoritative parenting styles; intelligence; a positive temperament; and access to resources in the community.

The greater number of risk or protective factors, the greater likelihood they will influence a child's mental health either negatively or positively. A recent study yielded some surprising and fascinating results in this regard. Dr. Hallam Hurt at the University of Pennsylvania has been investigating the impact of cocaine in a group of children since 1989. During the 1990s, when I was in graduate school, stories of "crack babies" and the damage that the drug did to fetuses were plentiful.

Of the 224 babies originally in Hurt's study, she continued to follow 110. For this group, she recently reported some unexpected findings. On a number of tests for qualities such as intelligence, there were no significant differences between the children exposed to cocaine and the other children enrolled in the study for comparison. Although one brain area linked to attention skills did function differently in the drug-exposed children, that difference did not result in any clinically significant behavior.

The study's most important finding, however, was that environmental factors, especially those associated with poverty, mattered a great deal. In fact, poverty was a more powerful risk factor for inner-city children than exposure to cocaine during pregnancy. Other researchers have found similar results (although some evidence does suggest that cocaine-exposed children have more difficulty regulating their reactions to stress). Many of the children in the study had seen violence, including seeing people arrested or shot; some (sadly and almost unbelievably) had seen a dead body. Children with a higher exposure to violence were more likely to show signs of depression and anxiety and to have lower self-esteem. On the other hand, protective factors—especially a nurturing home with affectionate and stimulating caregivers—made a positive difference.

Studies such as this are further evidence that we need to come together in this country to enact policies and programs that support the development of our children, especially those who live in stressful environments that increase the risk of mental health problems. Aside from its impact on the children, it would save money in the long run.

4

Delayed, Different, Not Fitting In: Does My Child Have an Autism Spectrum Disorder?

Adam

Adam was an adorable four-year-old. His smile was bright, and he approached adults cautiously but readily. Some of his language and social skills were a little delayed, however, so his preschool teacher put him in a class with three-year-olds because he played more readily with younger kids with similar abilities. Over the course of the year, as he grew to know the other children in the class, the teacher reported improvement: he was participating more in story time and approaching other kids to play rather than sitting on the sideline and watching all of the time.

Adam's development had otherwise been normal (for example, crawling, walking, and sitting up on par with others his age) but, in some areas of language, he still lagged developmentally behind where his six-year-old brother had been at the same age. For example, he misused pronouns, such as saying "you" or "he" for "I." There were some other worrisome behaviors as well: he frequently preferred to play with parts of toys, such as the wheels on a truck, rather than engage in making up a story about the entire toy. When he ran he leaned forward on the balls of his feet and flapped his arms, behaviors that are characteristic of an autism spectrum disorder (ASD).

Adam's mother had seen a television program on autism and wondered if some of Adam's behaviors—such as the flapping, poor social skills, and delayed language—meant that he was autistic. Given those symptoms, some professionals might have given Adam a diagnosis of autism. After a full evaluation, however, I decided in consultation with his parents and school personnel that he was not autistic. Instead, the behaviors that concerned his mother arose primarily from his language delays. He seemed to want to play with other children, but he lacked the language skills to do so. In contrast, children with ASD typically don't show that interest. His flapping and other behaviors seemed a result of his isolation and an attempt at self-stimulation. And, finally, he had improved over the course of the last few months of my observation at a greater rate than I would have expected had he been autistic.

But this diagnosis didn't mean at all that Adam's mother had been wrong to bring him for an assessment. In fact, that intervention made all the difference. His parents and I decided that Adam would benefit from structured play groups, in which social skills are taught to children through modeling and coaching, as well as from some extra language intervention. The county that was paying for services under its early intervention program would pay for only one thirty-minute language session a week, but his parents chose to supplement that with an additional two and a half hours per week.

Several years later, Adam has caught up with his peers developmentally and now has a number of friends his own age. His mother is convinced that the early intervention and extra support resulted in his excellent progress.

Although different studies have produced differing data, all the recent data indicate that more children are being diagnosed with autism spectrum disorders. For example, a study published by the Centers for Disease Control in 2013 found that, in 2011–12, one in seven children had a developmental disability, including an autism spectrum disorder, and one in fifty had been diagnosed with autism compared to one in eighty-six in 2007. The increase was seen in every age group, and in boys but not girls. Another study, published by the CDC's Autism and Developmental Disabilities Monitoring (ADDM) Network in 2012, found that one in every eighty-eight children had been diagnosed with autism, a relative increase of 23 percent from 2006 and 72 percent from 2002. The most recent statistic in 2014, from the ADDM, is one in every sixty-eight. The studies' results differ because they collect data in different ways, but the overall trend is clear.

Some of the increase probably results from improvements in diagnosing ASDs rather than from an actual increase in the disorder. In fact, the 2013 study attributed much of the increase to the diagnosis of children who had milder symptoms and, as a result, had not previously been diagnosed as having an ASD. But it is unlikely that the magnitude of increase is attributable to better diagnosis alone.

Yet, despite the increased focus on ASDs, clinicians, schools, and parents are still not doing a good enough job identifying it in early childhood. The research shows that fewer than 40 percent of children with ASDs are diagnosed before they enter school. Because an enormous amount of growth takes place in the first five years of a child's life, it is critical that we do a better job of identifying children with ASDs (and other developmental delays) when they are younger and treatments can be more effective.

Types of Problematic Behaviors

Typically, when parents are concerned that their child may have an ASD, it is because the child is not interacting with them as they hoped or because a secondary caregiver (a preschool teacher or day-care provider) has similar concerns. These concerns warrant attention because children with an ASD frequently, though not always, have language delays and, most important, have a delay in social skills or communication. For example, they may not respond when their name is called, smile back at others, or engage in the type of give-and-take that typically defines most social interactions.

More specifically, as summarized by the Centers for Disease Control and Prevention, here are some important red flags that should lead you to ask for an evaluation promptly. Your child:

- does not respond to her name by twelve months of age
- does not point at objects to show interest (point at an airplane flying overhead) by fourteen months
- does not play pretending games (such as feeding a doll) by eighteen months
- avoids eye contact and wants to be alone
- has trouble understanding other people's feelings or talking about her own feelings

- has delayed speech and language skills
- repeats words or phrases over and over (echolalia)
- gives answers that are unrelated to the questions
- gets upset by minor changes in routine
- has obsessive interests
- flaps her hands, rocks her body, or spins in circles
- has unusual reactions to the way things sound, smell, taste, look, or feel

Diagnosing ASDs

ASDs are one category of developmental delays. A developmental delay can occur in one or many areas, including motor, language, social, or cognitive abilities. However, developmental delay is a diagnosis based on strict guidelines and an ongoing delay in the developmental process. If your child is temporarily lagging behind in reaching her developmental milestones, that is not called a developmental delay. It is very hard to determine if a delay is temporary. Parents most often compare a child to a sibling or another child they know, but those comparisons may not be the best measure. For more detailed information about developmental milestones based on researchers' understanding of how a child's brain develops, please turn to appendix A.

If you have concerns about your child's delay in reaching developmental milestones, it is critical that you take your child to a professional right away. Better safe than to delay intervention if there is a problem (and better for your peace of mind to know if there isn't a problem). You can also use the evidence-based screeners for children's developmental issues at www.ProjectSKIP.com, which will provide an initial screening to help you to decide whether to arrange a more detailed, in-depth assessment. One of the screeners, the Social Communication Questionnaire or SCQ, specifically targets the types of issues that arise in children with ASDs. You can access it using the code BOOK1 (you will need this code to access the screening after you register).

ASDs, a subtype of developmental delays, involve delays in multiple areas of development. The diagnosis includes a range of disorders, including autism or Asperger's syndrome. You may have heard them referred to separately, and professionals may still talk about them individually, but the DSM does not name them separately any longer. Kids with an ASD have differences in the development of their thinking, language, and behavior and, most noticeably, their social skills. These differences typically appear before age three and can be diagnosed in some cases in children as young as twelve months.

For a diagnosis of an ASD, a child must have a specified number of symptoms in two areas:

- social interaction and communication (such as answering to her name, making eye contact, playing with others, and sharing enjoyment)

- restricted and repetitive range of behaviors, activities, and interests with stereotypic or repetitive movements and behaviors that have no meaning

Thinking about ASDs can be scary. But what is really scary is not knowing, and that is why you need a good mental health professional as a partner. Remember, a diagnosis is just a shorthand label that clinicians use to communicate with each other about how to intervene. It also tells you about strengths and weaknesses, but it does not always equate to your child's potential or predict their future.

Social (Pragmatic) Communication Disorder

DSM-5 added a new diagnostic category for children who suffer from some of the same social deficits as children with autism, but for whom the social deficits are the result of deficits in the "pragmatic"—that is, the social—use of language and communication. For example, they have trouble understanding social rules and nonverbal communication. If those communication deficits affect your child's ability to engage in age-appropriate social or academic activities, then you should consult your mental health professional to help determine whether your child has social (pragmatic) communication disorder.

There are a number of genetic disorders that affect development that I do not discuss in detail in this book, such as Down syndrome, Angelman syndrome, Turner syndrome, and fragile X. In most cases, these require specialized diagnostic procedures.

Evidence-Based Treatments

Once you have settled on a diagnosis and ruled out other possible causes, it is time to pursue treatment. Three main approaches to treating ASDs exist: educational, medicinal, and behavioral. (Educational or school interventions are covered separately in chapter 13.) Unfortunately, medication therapy for children with ASDs is still developing. Before considering medication—or any form of therapy—I encourage you to work with someone who has had a lot of experience treating children with an ASD, someone who is willing to answer your questions and who will tell you what evidence exists to support each type of treatment. (See the resources in the back of this book, under University Centers for Excellence in Developmental Disabilities and NIH Autism Centers, for state-by-state listings of ASD treatment centers.)

The best support in the research favors behavioral treatment in combination with intensive communication training. Following are the most commonly used behavior therapies.

Applied Behavior Analysis (ABA)

This form of treatment takes a research-based approach—based on an understanding of what does or doesn't lead to new behaviors or skills in children—to shape everyday behaviors. To a behaviorist, the social skills absent in an ASD can be taught, just as a child would learn a foreign language or other new skill.

As research has repeatedly shown, ABA techniques can help individuals with an ASD develop specific skills that improve their abilities to communicate, develop relationships, and play with others, as well as to care for themselves and, eventually, to learn in school, succeed at work, and go on to lead full and productive lives. The research has also shown that, if a child with ASD participates in an individualized early intervention program that makes intensive use of several ABA techniques, the results can be very good.

One of the primary tools used in ABA is discrete trial training, or DTT. DTT is conducted using intensive drills. The drills will clearly prompt or guide a very specific behavior, and the child receives reinforcement for proper responses. For example, the therapist will tell the child, "Come here"—a direct and easily understood prompt—rather than saying "I want you to come here, please." Then the therapist rewards the child when she responds. Initially, the therapist uses a simple reward that the child will want (such as candy, although it should of course not become a regular diet). Eventually, some specific techniques are used to teach children to respond to other types of reinforcement, such as praise or breaks. To be effective this work should be intensive. The recommended amount is at least twenty-five hours per week.

Two other forms of therapy—behavior therapy and pivotal response therapy (PRT)—use the major principles of ABA but vary the approach.

Behavior Therapy

Behavior therapy is often a comprehensive approach that is carried out as much as possible in every setting, in every available moment. Typically, it focuses on negative behaviors such as aggression or lack of social interaction. Its goal is to increase the child's engagement in positive or socially reinforcing activities such as playing nicely with other children—for example, approaching another child with a toy, asking the child to play, sharing the toy, and engaging in back-and-forth play. These steps would first be tackled one by one and then all brought together to form a smooth social interaction with another child.

Frequently, a therapist will begin with a functional behavior assessment, which is a structured observation of a child's behavior to determine what conditions or events immediately precede an undesirable behavior. The goal is to determine its causes, or what might be rewarding or reinforcing it. For example, if your child frequently melts down in class, what happens right before the meltdown? Is the meltdown preceded by a task that is too difficult for the child or involves something she doesn't understand? Does the child then get individual attention from the teacher, so that she comes to expect one-on-one attention if she has a meltdown? Intervention will involve removing both the cause, in this case the frustrating task, and the reinforcing behavior, the teacher's attention.

Pivotal Response Therapy (PRT)

PRT focuses on critical, or pivotal, behaviors that in turn affect a wide range of other behaviors. The primary pivotal behaviors are a child's initiation of communications with others and her willingness to engage in those communications. They are pivotal because they are critical for smooth social relations, but often they are the very skills that are weak or nonexistent in a child with an ASD.

Unlike the methods of teaching used in ABA, which targets individual behaviors, PRT is directed at the full repertoire of a child's behavior in a situation—for example, all aspects of a social encounter including approach, eye contact, responding to a smile from another person, and processing a social cue. In contrast to DTT's highly structured method of teaching specific behavioral skills, PRT uses a less structured, more play-based format, using discrete drills as they are needed. The goal is to improve communication skills, play skills, and, more generally, all social behaviors, to help the child monitor her own behavior and to decrease disruptive or self-stimulatory behaviors. PRT relies heavily on motivational strategies, such as varying tasks and rewarding attempts to perform new behaviors. The child plays a crucial role in determining the activities and objects on which the therapy will focus, because they should be the ones that she prefers to be a part of her everyday interactions.

Popular Alternative Treatments and Misconceptions

Understandably, given the limited number of effective treatments for ASDs and the lack of a single well-documented and noncontroversial cure, some parents have turned to alternative therapies. (Even the use of the word *cure* is controversial: while there are some reports of "recovering" from the symptoms, even in those cases many of the overall difficulties seem to remain.) Before parents consider trying a new, unproven treatment for their child, they need to be aware of its potential costs, both emotional and financial, and weigh any potential benefits against costs and risks.

Hyperbaric Chambers

Hyperbaric oxygen chambers deliver high concentrations of oxygen quickly. During the procedure, the child enters a small closed chamber. The physician then raises the level of atmospheric pressure and increases the oxygen level in the air to 100 percent. Hyperbaric oxygen therapy is believed to reduce oxidative stresses, which are changes seen in living organisms in response to excessive levels of oxidants and free radicals in the environment. It also has anti-inflammatory effects, which some believe will increase blood flow and decrease inflammation in an autistic child's brain.

While there have been several clinical trials, the results—excepting the study described below—have been inconclusive, and there is still very little scientific support for use of the hyperbaric chamber for the treatment of ASDs. Moreover, the cost of this therapy is quite high.

To date, only one study has received widespread attention. Researchers looked at fifty-six children aged two to seven who had varying degrees of an ASD. Each received forty hour-long treatments, estimated to cost from $100 to $900 per session. The twenty-six children in the control group had the atmospheric pressure increased by 3 percent, while thirty of the children had the pressure in the chamber increased by 30 percent. Researchers found that 8 percent in the control group had increased functioning, while 30 percent of the children who received the treatment reported greatly increased overall functioning, receptive language, social interaction, and eye contact.

While the treatment may hold some promise, I think it is far too expensive and as of yet too poorly understood to be of benefit for most families, given the inconclusive results of other studies.

Gluten-Free Diets

Researchers have not found that keeping the proteins in wheat, barley, rye, and dairy out of the diet of children with an ASD improves their behavior. As a result, most doctors do not recommend gluten- or lactose-free diets as a form of therapy for an ASD.

However, there are widespread anecdotal reports that families who have avoided foods containing gluten and casein have seen positive effects. In fact, it has been reported that nearly one in three children with an ASD is now given a gluten-and-casein-free diet in an effort to reduce the symptoms of autism such as poor attention span. TV personality Jenny McCarthy has been one the most vocal parents advocating for this treatment and claims her son's ASD symptoms improved when she switched his diet. Afterward, she said, he spoke in complete sentences and made eye contact with her for the first time.

These anecdotal reports are not to be ignored, but the research still does not back them up. Researchers at the University of Rochester Medical Center in upstate New York put the gluten-and-casein-free diet to one of the most stringent tests to date. They looked at fourteen children between the ages of two and a half and five and a half years old with ASD and without celiac disease or allergies to milk and wheat. The study was done in stages. First, they removed gluten and casein from the children's diet. Next, after four weeks, the children were randomly given either gluten or casein or both or a placebo through a carefully measured snack. Finally, parents, teachers, and a research assistant were questioned about the child's behavior before and after the snacks were eaten. No effect on behavior was found. The evidence for the use of gluten-free diets is inconclusive at best.

Chelation Therapy

Proponents of chelation therapy believe that ASD is caused by exposure to mercury, which has been widely used as a preservative in vaccines (but now has largely been removed). The therapy involves administering drugs—or chelating agents—to remove heavy metals from the body. It is most frequently used successfully when children have been exposed to high levels of lead. Because it also removes low-level mercury from the body, however, supporters say it cures ASD. But there's no evidence of a link between mercury exposure and ASD, and chelation therapy has not been found to be an effective ASD treatment. It can also have dangerous side effects, including potentially fatal liver and kidney damage. Current research does not support the use of chelation therapy in the treatment of ASD.

Questions to Ask Treatment Providers

Part of your job as an equal partner in the diagnostic and treatment process for your child is to ask questions, as well as to make certain that your child's providers have all the information they need to help you make decisions about your child's care. In the case of an ASD, here are some questions you should ask your team of professionals.

How Many Children with Autism Spectrum Disorders Have You Seen?

ASD is a complex diagnosis. Particularly in younger children, it is very difficult to determine if a child is less social because she lacks interest in social interactions or has poor language skills. As a result, training and experience—seeing large numbers of children over time—are key for clinicians who deal with ASD.

Before 2000, most treatment providers saw very few children with ASD, in part because few providers were trained to recognize it and parents didn't recognize the symptoms themselves. Today, most providers are much more familiar with the criteria used to diagnose an ASD and other developmental delays. However, there is no substitute in clinical psychology or child psychiatry for seeing a number of patients with varying disorders to understand how the wide variations in a disorder may present themselves. Most important, seeing many children over time specifically for mental health disorders helps hone diagnostic accuracy.

Find out how many children the professional has assessed for developmental or mental health issues, where the person trained, and if they specialized in children's issues while they were in training. At a minimum, make certain the person you work with has trained on the ADOS, the gold-standard assessment instrument for an ASD, and is licensed by the state in which you live to give you a diagnosis. (See also chapter 12, Licensure and Training.)

How Can I Take Advantage of Early Intervention Services?

You will want to enroll your child in your state's mandated early invention program right away. You can find your state's early intervention services through the links provided in the resources section under "Early Childhood." States' early intervention programs offer a variety of services, and all of them will help set up an individualized program for your family called an Individual Family Service Plan (IFSP). It is critical that you start an intervention plan as soon as possible and make sure it includes lots of one-on-one interactions with your child (from both the provider and your family).

The next two questions will allow you to explore more generally the professional's knowledge about and attitudes toward ASD.

What Evidence Is There That Children "Recover" from an ASD?

Although it is generally thought that ASD is a lifelong illness, and speaking about recovery from an ASD is still regarded as controversial within the field, different research has found that between 3 and 25 percent of children lose their ASD diagnosis and enter the normal range of cognitive, adaptive, and social skills. One well-designed study from a group of researchers with whom I am familiar has found particular evidence to support this notion. In that study, predictors of recovery included relatively high intelligence, the ability to understand communication from others, the ability to imitate language and movements, and motor development—but not the overall severity of the symptoms. The predictors also include earlier diagnosis and a diagnosis of *pervasive developmental disorder—not otherwise specified*, a diagnosis that was available under previous editions of the DSM but has now been folded into the diagnosis of ASD. On the other hand, the presence of seizures, intellectual disability, and genetic syndromes are unfavorable signs for improvement.

Well-designed research studies have reported the highest rate of recovery came about after the use of behavioral techniques such as the ABA and DTT, methods described previously in this chapter. Even with improvement, residual difficulties or symptoms usually remain, such as difficulties with more advanced communication or attention, or tics, depression, and fears.

Final Thoughts: What Causes ASD?

A developmental delay can have many different causes: for example, genetic causes such as Down syndrome, or complications during pregnancy or birth, such as prematurity or infection. Often, however, the specific cause is unknown, and such is the case with ASD. The theory about vaccines has been shown to be false to the satisfaction of almost all of the scientific community, and the effect of environmental factors has not been proved conclusively.

ASD is most likely caused (like many other disorders), in my opinion, by some interaction of biology and environment. Let's discuss this interplay. First, it is clear that biology, and genetics in particular, play huge roles in all diseases, and ASD is not likely an exception to that fact. The preliminary studies suggest that, in most cases, something happens biologically to a fetus during pregnancy. Although researchers aren't certain what that something is yet, it likely involves a number of genes and not just one. Second, strong environmental factors, such as large exposure to toxic chemicals, such as lead or chemicals found in flame retardants, can affect brain development before birth.

Risk Factor	No Biological Risk	Biological Risk
No Environmental Risk	ASD doesn't occur	ASD may or may not occur depending on the nature of the biological risk or degree of genetic involvement
Environmental Risk	ASD may or may not occur depending on the nature or toxicity of the environmental risk	ASD occurs

Since biology and environment can both affect brain development, it is likely that a complex relationship between biology and environment creates the conditions in which ASD manifests. For example, if a child is exposed to a genetic risk from a parent who carries that genetic risk and the child is also exposed to some toxin or other environmental risk during pregnancy, the child may be more likely develop an ASD. The genetic risk, when coupled with the environmental risk, creates the optimal conditions for the disorder to occur. Conversely, if there is neither a biological nor environmental risk, an ASD isn't likely to develop. At this point in the research, however, it's not clear what specific genetic or environmental factors create the greatest risk. The search is ongoing.

The cases in which there is only a biological or an environmental risk, without exposure to the other factor, may turn out to be the most perplexing for scientists to explain. Because these cases occur rarely, large studies don't help us to understand them. Nor can those studies capture the individual variations of additive exposure to the types of risks. As a result, researchers and clinicians can only wonder whether, if someone is not at risk biologically, an extreme environmental exposure could still cause an ASD to develop. Conversely, if there is a biological risk—especially if, say, both parents carry a genetic risk—would it take just a very slight environmental exposure for an ASD to occur?

In April of 2014 researchers at the University of California, San Diego School of Medicine and the Allen Institute for Brain Science gave us an important new clue in understanding the origins of ASD. The study analyzed genes in the post-mortem tissue of brains of children with and without autism. The researchers found that the brains of children with autism all had similar patterns of disrupted development in their cortex: key genetic markers were absent from very specific layers of cells in the brain. These disruptions (reportedly the size of a pencil eraser) occurred in localized patches instead of broad distributions across the brain. Those localized faulty cell layers, and their specific locations (the front and sides of the brain in areas responsible for attention, planning, and speech), led researchers to conclude that the faulty development of these cell layers means that ASD begins in prenatal life. Most likely, the researchers hypothesized, ASD begins in the second trimester of pregnancy when organization of the cortex occurs. Additionally, the faulty genetic patches also give us an indication of why early intervention works. If intervention is started soon enough, the brain may be able to rewire itself to compensate for the faulty areas.

If the research is not yet definitive about the causes of ASD, it also hasn't produced clarity about another question: is the increase in the diagnosis of ASD primarily because professionals are identifying it more accurately, or because the disorder itself has actually increased in incidence?

Medical and health professionals are certainly recognizing and diagnosing ASDs more often, and the numbers are being inflated by the somewhat subjective nature of the diagnosis and its usefulness for obtaining treatment services. Parents sometimes feel forced to ask for an ASD diagnosis as one of the few means of obtaining much-needed in-school services (see chapter 13). Additionally, as clinicians, we have very few diagnoses to use when a child is delayed socially and needs some form of support. In the past, clinicians would not diagnose these kids at all; they were simply seen as eccentric or introverted. Now they are diagnosed with an ASD, which at least means they can receive needed services. Because early intervention is so critical, many professionals correctly err on the side of giving the diagnosis to a very broad spectrum of behaviors in order to open the door to interventions.

However, it's unlikely that this is the whole story. The rise in chemicals to which kids are exposed in the environment, perhaps coupled with an increase in genetic risk factors, probably also play a role in the increase. That opinion isn't yet fully based on hard evidence, but it seems to reflect the trend of current research.

5

Overactivity and Inattentiveness: Does My Child Have ADHD?

Emily

When Emily came to see me with her parents, she had just turned thirteen and entered the seventh grade. Only two months into the first semester, she was already starting to fall behind. Although she spent several hours a night in her room, she usually emerged without her homework finished. Her parents had grounded her and taken away many of her privileges, such as activities after school and phone calls with friends, but this didn't seem to motivate her to get her work done.

Her teachers thought she was friendly and cooperative but simply not very interested in learning. When her mother and father brought her to see me, they said they had both had difficulties in school when they were children, but they had just worked harder to get through the curriculum.

Emily and I met alone for the second session. Before she and I started doing pencil-and-paper tests to determine if she had a learning issue (see chapter 10), I asked her what she thought the problem might be. Emily explained that she wanted to do her work but would often find herself just staring off into space. By the time she could bring herself to focus, sometimes as much as an hour had passed. Then she would start reading an assignment or working on her math, only to find herself staring off into space again. The same thing, she explained, often happened at school as well. She would stare out the window or her mind would wander. Not surprisingly, her grades suffered.

After testing, I settled on a diagnosis of ADHD-Inattentive Type. (I will define the types shortly.) Then, after they read the studies I discuss in this chapter, Emily's parents put her on a trial of medications, and her parents, teachers, and I worked together to come up with behavioral strategies that would help her to become more successful at home and at school. These included introducing a behavioral reward program at home for studying and doing chores and also working with her teacher to reduce distractions in the classroom. After the school year, Emily was able to take medication breaks in the summer. She is now a successful college student.

Emily didn't look like what most parents envision when they think their child has ADHD, or attention deficit hyperactivity disorder. (In the DSM-5, the term ADHD is used in place of ADD, attention deficit disorder.) But, in fact, the disorder manifests itself in a variety of ways, and Emily looked and acted like many young girls with ADHD. ADHD takes three forms, each of which is separately diagnosed: a child can be hyperactive and impulsive, inattentive, or both. For a formal diagnosis, these symptoms must be present before the age of twelve. Whatever form the disorder takes, like many other mental health issues it can be treated quite effectively.

The diagnosis of ADHD has become quite controversial in the last few years. Some say clinicians are overdiagnosing it, some say parents and clinicians are just noticing it more, and still others think that there are environmental factors at work that are causing an increase. The truth is probably somewhere in the middle: as with autism spectrum disorders, an interaction between the environment and genetics may well be causing an increase in the disorder, but it also seems clear that it is overdiagnosed in younger kids. That is why parents need to educate themselves about it and learn how to ask the right questions of their mental health professional.

What Are the Warning Signs?

Does your child:

- frequently miss details or make careless mistakes in schoolwork?
- have difficulty staying focused and become easily distracted?
- fail to follow through on instructions, even if she understands them, and fail to finish schoolwork?
- have difficulty organizing tasks and activities?

- only pay attention to those things she likes or is interested in?
- often fidget or squirm?
- run around or climb on things in situations when this is inappropriate?
- seem always on the go or unable to be calm when appropriate?
- talk excessively or interrupt others?
- have difficulty waiting for her turn?

None of these individual signs means that your child has ADHD, but if they are serious or persistent, ADHD may well be a possibility that you should investigate.

What Is ADHD?

ADHD is a condition involving certain portions of the brain that help us put the brakes on our behavior and inhibit our desire to get up and move around—and, therefore, help us pay attention. Studies show that the areas of the brain affected by ADHD allow us to solve problems, plan ahead, understand others' actions, keep focused, and control our impulses.

I explain it in the following way to parents who bring their children for an ADHD assessment. Imagine the brakes in your car aren't working. Could you stop? Of course not. For kids with ADHD, the portion of the brain that puts on the brakes doesn't work; it is smaller and doesn't have "brake fluid." In order to help a child put the brakes on so they can pay attention, treatment professionals, parents, and teachers have to give them other tools that will help them with their inattentiveness or impulsivity.

What Are Its Symptoms?

The primary symptoms of ADHD as summarized by the NIMH are inattention, hyperactivity, and impulsivity. (More recently, some have hypothesized that a "sluggish cognitive tempo" in children is yet a separate disorder of attention.) Although some children will show primarily one type of ADHD symptoms, many may exhibit a combination of different types (for example, both hyperactive and inattentive).

Children with *inattention* get bored with a task in a few minutes unless it is something they really enjoy. As a result, they find it difficult to organize and complete a task or to learn something new. They often forget to write down a school assignment or to bring home what they need for homework. An inattentive teen has trouble focusing, often makes careless mistakes, forgets things, struggles to follow instructions or process information, or skips from one activity to another without completing any schoolwork. Such children can frequently be mistaken for daydreamers. However, when they are doing something they really like (such as playing a video game), these same children can focus for hours!

Hyperactivity is the constant impulse to move around even when it is inappropriate—for example, during dinner or during story time in school. Even while sitting, hyperactive children will squirm, fidget, tap their pencil on a desk, or find a moving part on a chair to play with. They may also talk continually in school to their classmates or teacher. They have great difficulty with tasks that require them to be quiet or focused. A teenager who is hyperactive will feel the need to be constantly on the go.

Impulsive children may be very impatient. They may blurt out inappropriate remarks without regard to the consequences or others' feelings, and they frequently display their emotions immediately and without any restraint. They also act without considering the consequences of their actions—that is, they won't think, *If I hit this other kid, it will make me feel better, but it will get me in trouble.* Children suffering from impulsivity also find it hard to wait for things they want or take turns, as is often required at school. Impulsive teenagers make choices that have an immediate result and frequently have difficulty working toward larger and more gratifying rewards if they are long-term. It's not that they don't want to wait; they can't. They don't have any brakes to stop their impulses.

Like Emily, some children with ADHD are mainly inattentive. They seldom act hyperactively or impulsively, but they are distracted by the slightest thing in the environment, such as movement outside a window or the child sitting in front of them. Even though an inattentive child with ADHD may not be focusing on the assignment, they still appear to be working. As a result, teachers and parents can easily miss the symptoms of inattention or dismiss such children as unmotivated to learn or lacking in discipline or drive. Inattentiveness is easier to miss in a child than the constant interruption by a child who is hyperactive or impulsive. But it is just as serious a problem, especially for girls who tend to act out less and instead tend to be seen as daydreamers or just as poor students.

Children with ADHD need the right supports to help them focus for longer periods of time, control their behavior, think about consequences, and go more slowly—and to feel better about themselves so that they can function at home, in school, and in life.

What Is *Not* ADHD?

Most children occasionally find that they are easily distracted or have trouble finishing tasks. To be diagnosed with ADHD, however, a child must have behaviors that appear before age twelve and continue persistently for at least six months. The symptoms must also create very real difficulties in at least two areas of the child's daily life: the classroom, the playground, home, the community, or social settings.

If a child seems impulsive or hyperactive or frequently fails to follow the rules at home but not elsewhere, or if the behaviors occur only in the classroom, the problem might not be ADHD. If a child's schoolwork or relationships are not impaired by their behaviors, a child who shows some symptoms would not be diagnosed with ADHD. A general physician, pediatrician, or mental health professional should use a checklist to diagnose ADHD, and they should get feedback from both parents and teachers before giving a diagnosis. In a recent study I conducted, I found that parents and teachers very rarely see the same sorts of behaviors in kids, given that the demands on kids are often so different at home than they are at school.

ADHD and Sleep Disorders

Some think that many children diagnosed with ADHD have a sleep disorder instead. Children need routine bedtimes and a good deal of sleep (eight to twelve hours a day for school-aged children, depending on age). One of the first questions I ask parents when they come to see me with concerns about their child's attention is how much sleep she is getting.

Many of the symptoms of ADHD are similar to symptoms children have when they don't get enough rest, and a number of studies show that there is a lot of overlap between sleep issues such as obstructive sleep apnea and ADHD. For example, one study found that children with obstructive sleep apnea had more behavior problems—including inattention and hyperactivity—as well as communication problems and aggressiveness. They also had more learning difficulties. Those findings were reinforced by another large-scale study of more than eleven thousand children from the age of six months. The study found that children with sleep-disordered breathing were significantly more likely to show signs of hyperactivity, had trouble interacting with peers, and had conduct issues including aggressiveness and a failure to follow appropriate rules. Among that group, the youngest children were, by age seven, more likely to have developed behavioral problems like those observed in ADHD.

To further complicate the picture, sleep problems continue to be significantly underdiagnosed in children. Researchers found that fewer than one in five pediatricians had received any training in sleep disturbances in children, and fewer than one in six felt confident about offering advice to parents about their child's sleep. Not surprisingly, the study also revealed that their lack of confidence was well founded: most could not answer questions about sleep disorders in children correctly.

Treatments: Medication and Behavior Therapy

Overall, there are not a large number of gold-standard research studies in child psychology. The studies are often small or not able to rule out all factors that may influence a treatment's success. The exception is in the treatment of ADHD, for which a number of excellent studies have been conducted. They provide very useful guidance—but, unfortunately, there is no simple answer that defines the best treatment for everyone.

Using Medication: What the Research Shows

In the 1990s, the National Institute of Mental Health funded a long-term study—the Multimodal Treatment Study of ADHD—to compare the most well-established and widespread treatments for children with ADHD. The initial phase studied 597 children, aged 7 to 9.9 years, with ADHD-combined type—that is, children who showed symptoms of both inattentive and hyperactive or impulsive ADHD types. The children were randomly assigned to one of four treatments: medication management (meds), behavior modification (behavior), meds and behavior combined (combined), and routine community care (community), which is what a typical pediatrician or local mental health professional would provide for treatment. (Community treatment varies greatly, and can include such steps as instituting a formal behavioral support system and parent training, or removing distracting stimuli from the child's classroom or study area at home.) At the end of the fourteen-month treatment phase, the researchers found that all four groups had experienced improvement—but with significant differences in the rate of improvement, especially in some areas.

Both the combined and meds treatments produced significantly more improvement than the behavior and community treatments. On the whole, the combined and meds groups did not differ significantly, but on several specific measures the combined group did better than the behavior or community groups, whereas the group treated with only meds did not. Those measures included oppositional/aggressive symptoms as rated by parents, internalizing symptoms (that is, depression or anxiety for which the symptoms are less obvious or disruptive), social skills as rated by teachers, parent-child relations, and reading achievement. I know a number of the researchers involved in this study and I trust the results of this work.

The study's bottom line: in the short term, treating a child with ADHD with behavioral therapy and medication is likely your *best and most effective* option for children over the age of six, although carefully crafted medication management maintained through fourteen months can even be superior to the combination of medications and behavior therapy in some specific cases for children over the age of six. For younger children (as mentioned in chapter 3) behavior therapy is usually the best course.

As children get older, the picture becomes more complicated. The NIMH study continued to follow the same children. In 2007, it published new results about how they were doing three years after the study began and almost two years after the fourteen-month treatment phase had ended. At that point, the children who had received only meds in the initial phase seemed to be doing no better than the others. (In fact, those who had taken medication for the entire three years were shorter and weighed less.) Then, in 2009, NIMH reported the results of another follow-up study with the same children, this time after eight years, which seemed to confirm that result, and led the *Washington Post* to publish a front-page article headlined "Debate Over Drugs for ADHD Reignites: Long-Term Benefit for Children at Issue." As the article reported, this follow-up found no differences among the four original treatment groups, either in their symptoms or how they were functioning. Although most of the children who were medicated at the fourteen-month end point were no longer taking medication eight years later, they were functioning no worse than children who were still medicated.

The results were not clear-cut, however, in part because the researchers no longer randomly assigned the children to the differing types of treatments, a change that affects the study's scientific rigor. After the first fourteen months of the first study, the children's treatment depended on their parents' choices among the treatments available in their communities: some children in the medicated groups stopped taking medication, and some in the behavior group started medication. The researchers also discovered that many in the community group had been taking medication all along, although without the same management as those in the medicated groups.

So Should My Child Use Medications or Not?

In my practice, parents often worry about using medications to treat their child for ADHD. Often, they fear that a child is just being medicated rather than assisted. This is an issue where my understanding has come full circle.

When I went back to school in 1994 to get my PhD, I thought most kids were overmedicated. During my training, however, I had the great fortune of practicing with some incredible psychiatrists, pediatricians, neurologists, and family medicine doctors, all of whom can write prescriptions (and some who were researchers involved in the studies I have described here). I never saw one of them take prescribing medications to children lightly. They did so with caution and careful consultation with the family. And this last part is key: regular monitoring of medications and their impact on your child is critical for their use and success.

If your child had diabetes, you would give them insulin. Why is taking medicine to assist the brain different? Parents often think that a child only needs to try harder or to work harder, but children with ADHD cannot improve just by trying harder. I respect parents' wishes and, if they don't want to try medication, I will help their children just with therapy. However, most of the parents who have decided first to choose therapy alone tell me that they wish they had also tried medication sooner. If medication allows a child who is struggling in school to focus, they can learn more easily and catch up in a subject in which they are having difficulty. As one of the authors of the NIMH study said, medications buy parents and clinicians time to teach youngsters behavioral strategies to combat inattention and hyperactivity.

Over the long term, however, children need to rely on those newly learned skills, not solely on drugs. As another of the study's coauthors said, "If you want something for tomorrow, medication is the best, but if you want something three years from now, it does not matter.... If you take medication long-term, beyond three years, I don't think there is any evidence that medication is better than no medication."

So what does this mean for you? There is no general rule about the treatment that works best for everyone. Instead, the treatment should be crafted for the specific child. For some children, medication will be more effective initially because behavioral therapy takes longer to have an effect. For others with milder symptoms, therapy alone may be enough. Even when medication is advisable, it should still not be a substitute for behavioral strategies.

If you try medication, you will know pretty quickly if the medicine works. If it doesn't or if you don't like a side effect, such as tiredness, then, in consultation with the prescriber, you can take your child off the medicine. I also recommend to parents that they fill out a checklist premedicine and postmedicine to see if there is an objective change in behavior. To help, you can use www.ProjectSKIP.com, which will guide you through a checklist of various symptoms that should decrease over time. You can also take breaks from the medicine over holidays or in the summer—when the rigors of schoolwork will not affect your children—though you must be sure to talk with your prescriber first.

Ultimately, as the parent, you are in control, and you will be the one to monitor the use and effects of medication most closely. Whichever treatment you choose, its effectiveness must be reviewed periodically and adjusted to meet your child's individual needs, and you will need to communicate regularly with your child's mental health team.

Behavior Therapy

Behavior therapy for kids with ADHD is usually essential in helping them pay attention and control impulsivity and hyperactivity. Most frequently, this therapy involves establishing a behavioral reward system that involves the child, the parents, and the teacher. Children with ADHD tend to respond well to reward systems, but only if they are well designed in the ways I will describe.

What works as a reward? In my practice, I often create charts with points for good behavior or for completing tasks that the parent rates as most important. (See the resources section, under "Attention Deficit Hyperactivity Disorder," for a link to free behavioral rewards charts that you can use at home.) Once the child has accumulated a certain number of points, the reward can be anything—within reason—that will motivate her in the short term, such as allowing an extra half hour of TV or playing a video game. I once designed a plan around a fishing tackle box that gave lures and tackle pieces to a child interested in fishing. Rewards should always be keyed to what your child likes. Be creative. You can rotate different types of rewards and tailor them to your child.

Here are some other tips for designing a rewards system:

- Give points for simple behaviors, even if other children don't need rewards to behave in those ways. Good examples are responding happily to a change in plans or asking for something in a respectful tone as opposed to having a meltdown.

- Try to avoid rewards of food or expensive items. Food should be less about comfort and more about nutrition. I also don't like to see parents getting into the habit of giving large gifts for behavior that should be part of being a good citizen of the house.

- Small rewards earned in the short term tend to work better than large rewards offered in the long term. I often give a small reward for three points of a possible total of five in a day. In addition, you can give the child cumulative points for specific behaviors. As the child accumulates the points, she can use them for larger tangible rewards, such as a special book or more daily time on the computer.

- Be consistent and follow through with rules and expectations. Children with ADHD respond to disappointment with much greater frustration than others. That response is part of their makeup, not something they should be blamed for—though they can learn to control it.

Other Activities

In addition to using a well-designed behavioral reward system, if children have attention problems, parents should also be on the lookout for physical activities—such as tennis or swimming or martial arts such as tae kwon do—that hold their attention and don't provide downtime for the mind to wander.

Meditation is also proving to be an effective tool for improving attention. It is often used as part of a group of self-verbalization or self-regulation strategies that have been shown to be highly effective in working with kids with ADHD. Self-regulation describes methods children can be taught to help them monitor and manage their behavior, and thus to decrease off-task behaviors or increase positive behaviors.

One important component of self-regulation is a steady stream of prompt feedback. With the help of a parent, teacher, or therapist, the child looks back at what has happened in the classroom or at home so that, if necessary, she can try to change her pattern of responding (i.e., inhibit an automatic response) in the future. For children with ADHD, the feedback should be immediate and frequent. For example, one child's mother obtained a small, discreet light box for his desk at school. His teacher would press a small device when she saw him off-task, which would cause the box to light up (only he could see it) and remind him to stop, assess what he was doing, and get back on task.

ADHD in the Classroom

Even if a parent is successful in managing a child's behavior at home, difficulties often arise at school. As I described with Emily, inattention is a major factor in low academic performance. It can cause children to forget homework, miss assignments, and fail to complete their homework. In addition, while children with ADHD often enjoy and do well with tasks that are short and intense, they often struggle with longer projects when no one is helping them to stay focused. They also have difficulties with tasks, such as math problems, that require a sequential set of steps, because they may miss an essential piece of the process.

There are many useful methods for helping ADHD kids in the classroom that should be discussed with their teachers. Some of these methods are quite simple: for example, having them sit in the front of the classroom and providing visual reminders or checklists, such as a list to carry in their backpacks.

Perhaps most important, to be effective, behavioral interventions for ADHD take a lot of time. Although most treatment providers see children once a week in their offices, that alone may not be enough to teach a child with ADHD the new skills that she needs. Something more intensive may be needed. For example, an intensive summer treatment program for children and adolescents that runs for seven or eight weeks, for eight to nine hours a day, has been found effective in helping children with ADHD learn to interact more appropriately with other children and their teachers. Some effective community programs run for five weeks for six hours a day.

Final Thoughts

In July 2013, as reported in the *Los Angeles Times*, the Food and Drug Administration approved a device that analyzes brain activity to help confirm a diagnosis of ADHD. The device, essentially an electroencephalogram, or EEG, and a computer program (neuropsychiatric EEG-based assessment aid, or NEBA), measures and analyzes two frequency bands of electrical pulses related to brain activity. The FDA based its decision on a 2006 study of 275 children and adolescents, but it emphasized that NEBA was intended to be used in conjunction with other clinical information. The FDA's decision has been controversial given that research since that study has cast doubt on the diagnostic accuracy of these two EEG frequency bands, called theta and beta waves.

To add to the confusion surrounding the diagnosis of ADHD, in March of 2014, one of the highly regarded psychologists involved in the original MTA study, Stephen Hinshaw, published a book with a renowned health economist, Richard Scheffler, called *The ADHD Explosion: Myths, Medication, Money, and Today's Push for Performance*. They make a convincing case that the rise in ADHD diagnoses can be tied to the increase in legislation that links student test performance to funding. Children who are diagnosed with ADHD frequently get greater support in the classroom, which can increase test scores. Children who perform better on tests increase the school's performance on standardized measures. Conversely, some states allow students with an ADHD diagnosis to be taken out of the testing pool altogether, so that they will not lower overall school performance on standardized measures.

For me, the bottom line is that you need teacher and parent ratings of behavior and a good clinician to diagnose ADHD. A thorough evaluation requires a good developmental history, parent and teacher objective checklists of symptoms, and school observations. Once your child is diagnosed, careful monitoring and follow-up is essential. If you have the money and can afford the extra test, great, go ahead and get it. But, given the current research, I would not base a diagnosis of ADHD on a single test.

6

Anxiety, Fear, Stress, and Obsessive-Compulsive Behaviors: Does My Child Worry Too Much?

Caroline

To her parents and teachers, Caroline seemed a typical eight-year-old: she wanted to spend more time playing with friends but still loved being at home with her parents and brother and sister. She was starting to enjoy learning how to play soccer and had begun a collection of toy horses. Her grades at school were good and, other than a few comments about sometimes daydreaming during math, her teachers seemed pleased with her work. She had a number of friends in class and wanted to spend more time with them outside of school.

Unfortunately, however, her daily routine at home had become so long that it left her little time for much other than homework, dinner, and getting ready for bed. By the time she and her parents came to see me just after her eighth birthday, her nightly bedtime ritual—placing her brush and clothes in just the right order on her chair, brushing her teeth, and combing her hair again—had expanded from about an hour to more than ninety minutes. Her morning rituals had also grown so considerably that it now took her three hours each morning to get up, get dressed, eat breakfast, and leave for school.

When she woke up, she would first comb her hair exactly three hundred times with her special brush that had its own tidy place on her dresser. Once she was out of bed, just getting to the bathroom was a long path because she would avoid stepping on any cracks inside the house. This meant she could not even step on the hardwood floor on the way to the bathroom, which resulted in an elaborate detour through the upstairs floor of their home.

But that was only part of Caroline's morning routine. Once in the shower, she needed to complete an elaborate washing pattern that included a certain number of scrubs with a bar of soap; specific patterns of rinsing off, starting with her head and down to her toes in circular rhythmic motions that needed to be done twenty times each; and toweling off her body parts in a specified order. Her clothes were all free of tags and could not be scratchy. Once out of her room, already almost two and a half hours into her day, she would come downstairs—but she needed to land on certain parts of each stair in a certain order.

Not surprisingly, she was beginning to butt heads with her mother over the length of her rituals, and the result was that her day usually started with a shouting match between the two of them. Her mother told me, "Caroline needs to just move faster." Although her father seemed somewhat more relaxed about the morning routine, he frequently was stuck taking Caroline to school at the last minute because she would miss the bus while still in the bathroom.

None of this, neither the routines nor the pressure from her mother, seemed to bother Caroline very much. This wasn't surprising, since many kids who have adopted these sorts of obsessive-compulsive disorder (OCD) behaviors simply incorporate them into their lives and aren't bothered by the way the rituals change their daily schedules. Essentially, the behaviors mean more to them than the changes. Caroline did not seem concerned that her days were starting earlier and earlier. When I asked her about this, she didn't understand what the big deal was about getting up earlier, even at 4:00 AM, as long as it involved only her and she could set her own alarm.

What had started as careful attention to hygiene had become an elaborate set of anxiety-driven rituals and compulsions. If Caroline did not complete these rituals successfully, she would become frozen with frustration and tension. For example, if she got to brush stroke 237 and then lost her place in counting the strokes because she was interrupted by something, such as her mother calling to her, she would have to start again at the beginning. And, if she was interrupted while descending the stairs just so, she would need to return to the beginning of her day, starting again with her brushing ritual. Whenever she was interrupted, she would become flushed in the face and unable to move for a minute or so until she could retrace her ritual in her head and then start over.

While she was retracing her physical movements in her mind, if her mother further interrupted, Caroline would become impatient, often shouting back and frantically moving to begin the complicated routine again. Her mother, attempting to avoid a meltdown and at a loss for how to make Caroline move faster, would give in and be forced to wait for her daughter to begin again and complete the entire ritual—all while she attempted to pack her other two children off to school and get ready for her own job, which was quite demanding.

To help Caroline, I used exposure therapy, a type of cognitive behavioral therapy (CBT) (described later in this chapter), to alleviate her anxieties. This first entailed working with her in my office to help her understand the physical signs of anxiety. For example, she could feel her heart start to race when she couldn't brush her hair or was interrupted.

Once Caroline and I identified what anxiety felt like, I taught her how to relax, which involved making a relaxation tape so she could listen to music and imagine her favorite place to go in the summer with her family. For her, it was the beach. She took the tape home and listened to it daily while visualizing the beach and focusing on what her body felt like when she was at the beach and relaxed. I also taught Caroline some deep-breathing techniques, such as taking three deep belly breaths.

In addition, she and I made a list of all the situations in which she became anxious, such as when she didn't brush her hair three hundred times, stepped on a crack, or landed on one of the stairs in the wrong place. Then we ranked the anxiety-producing thoughts and behaviors on a scale of one to ten: brushing got a ten because not brushing her hair made her the most anxious, and the stairs got a three.

Next, I went to Caroline's house very early in the morning, and she and I started with the stairs—the least anxiety-producing behavior—because that would be the easiest for Caroline to tackle. As she descended the stairs and I stood at the bottom, we talked through the beach scene and had her step on each step without worrying about where on the step she actually landed. When she started to get anxious we would work through her visualization of the beach or do deep breathing until she could continue. We did this for almost an hour the first time and repeated the process for three sessions until she could do it on her own.

She and I then went on to deal with the next-scariest thing on her anxiety list, until we got all the way through her morning routine. Eventually, she could brush her hair in less than two or three minutes, and her morning routine decreased to just about an hour. She could sleep much later and go to bed later, and her relationship with her mother improved greatly since they were no longer arguing about her getting out the door in the morning.

Anxiety, OCD, and Stress-Related Disorders in Children and Adolescents

There are three major types of intensive worries that produce dysfunctional behaviors or stress: anxiety disorders (excessive anxiety or fear and the related behavioral disturbances), obsessive-compulsive and related disorders (Caroline had obsessive-compulsive disorder, or OCD), and trauma- and stress-related disorders. Until recently, the DSM placed anxiety and OCD on the same spectrum of disorders; however, the latest edition separates them to emphasize that many of the treatments are separate. I am discussing them together because anxiety, OCD, and stress all produce behaviors in kids that are somewhat similar: they think or worry about things in excess.

Anxiety Disorder

About 8 percent of teens aged twelve to eighteen have an anxiety disorder. According to the NIMH, the disorder typically emerges around age six, although the latest version of the DSM places that age later. (A specific form of the disorder, separation anxiety disorder, is most common in kids under six.) It appears that girls are more at risk for an anxiety disorder than boys, although it is still up for debate whether this difference results from a biological difference or a cultural difference in the way we as a culture raise girls.

Unfortunately, the numbers have been on the rise. Five to eight times more high school and college students meet the criteria for an anxiety disorder diagnosis than did half a century ago. Sadly, of those teens with an identifiable anxiety issue, only 18 percent receive mental health care and even fewer younger children are properly diagnosed. Their parents often think that their children are just shy, that they will outgrow their fears, or that it is something they have to live with and accept.

What Is Anxiety?

Anxiety is the body's normal reaction to stress, and some anxiety is good. From an evolutionary point of view, anxiety helped us identify what was important to pay attention to, such as a predator or enemy, in order to survive. It can alert us to dangerous situations, make us more aware of the environment around us, cause us to focus on the task at hand, and even compel us to get things done, such as studying for a test. This good anxiety can also manifest as the tension—almost a sense of anticipation and excitement—that you feel in your body when you start something new. Whatever its cause, anxiety can take the physical form of an increased heartbeat or sweating or a general uneasiness or a tensing of muscles.

In small children, some caution and even fearfulness is typical and, in fact, healthy. Preschool-aged children want to touch, taste, smell, and hear things for themselves and frequently do so by putting anything and everything in their mouth. They are eager to learn through experiencing and doing. As they experience more, they become more fearful of certain things and less fearful of others, based on their previous experiences and the information and reassurances they get from the adults around them. Common fears include, for example, a fear of new places and experiences, separation from parents or siblings, or trying new foods. Those are all normal anxieties during this period.

When Should I Do Something About My Child's Anxiety?

In general, anxiety can be a positive coping mechanism, but when anxiety becomes excessive and irrational, it can become a disabling condition. For one example, someone who checks that things are turned off too many times may be late for work. For another, although thinking about hygiene was good for Caroline, the extremes to which she took that concern made it almost impossible for her to get through her day. When you are trying to understand whether such behavior is "normal," it becomes a question of degrees.

If a child's worries or fears or thoughts become obsessive-compulsive—so strong and overwhelming that, as in Caroline's case, she becomes unable to do even simple things that others kids can do with ease—then clearly things aren't normal. If your child can't get to sleep for hours every night because she worries about monsters in the room, that clearly calls for help. But what if your child describes monsters entering her room for a few nights and only for a half hour, or she runs back to check on her toys a few times before she leaves for school in the morning? Surely that's normal, isn't it? So when does her behavior start to become an issue? The most important test is whether the behavior starts to interfere with your child's normal daily activities and keeps her from doing things she would otherwise normally do. If the behavior is pervasive, excessive and accompanied by physical edginess, that's when you, as a parent, should consult a mental health professional.

Types of Problematic Behaviors

Does your child:

- feel jittery with butterflies inside or restless?
- complain of stomach pain, headaches, and/or dizziness?
- worry too much, brood over things, or feel very nervous?
- feel as though most situations will end badly?
- resist going to school or social functions?
- frequently do things in a certain way, repeatedly?
- have unusual fears for her age?

The Roots of Anxiety in the Brain

Recent studies on brain function have used neuroimaging, which takes a picture of the inside of the brain while someone is having a thought. These studies have demonstrated that children with anxiety disorders show greater activity in the areas of the brain associated with fear and emotional regulation.

For example, a 2008 study from the NIMH involved fourteen adolescents with significant anxiety about social situations, as well as fourteen other adolescents. All were told that they were going to participate in Internet chat rooms, chatting with another adolescent with whom the participant wanted to chat and who wanted to chat with him or her. To choose chat mates, participants divided photographs into less desirable and more desirable groups. They were told that those whose photos they reviewed would find out how the participants rated their desirability. Then the participants were themselves photographed and told that those who would receive their photographs would rate how interested they were in chatting with the participants.

After two weeks, the participants underwent functional magnetic resonance imaging (fMRI) scans of their brain activity while looking at pictures of the other adolescents they had rated. While the scan was taking place, they were asked how they thought the peers had rated them in return. When the participants anticipated ratings from peers whom they had rated as less desirable, an anxiety-provoking situation, the results were illuminating. The anxious adolescents showed increased activity in the amygdala, a place located deep in the brain that triggers a fear or anxiety response and alerts the rest of the brain that a threat is present. The increase was much greater than in the other group of adolescents.

Similarly, another 2008 study funded by the NIMH found that when the participants looked at angry faces so briefly that they had little awareness of seeing them, youth with generalized anxiety disorder (GAD) also had overreactions in the amygdala—the more severe the disorder, the greater the overreaction. When the amygdala overreacts, it signals fear repeatedly—when, in fact, the cause of the fear may not be present at all. The result is that, for children who worry too much, the portion of their brain that regulates or modulates fear won't turn off or keeps turning on more than in other kids their age.

Types of Anxiety Disorders

We will look at four types of anxiety disorders and their symptoms separately:

- generalized anxiety disorder
- social anxiety disorder
- panic disorder
- specific phobias

Generalized Anxiety Disorder

Symptoms of a generalized anxiety disorder include worrying too much for too long, which results in excessive fearfulness, nervousness, or uneasiness. Kids with GAD find it difficult, if not impossible, to stop worrying, even after making a brave effort. They're often easily annoyed or irritated, and they can seem impatient and edgy. They can also have difficulty focusing for long periods of time or maintaining their train of thought. Physical symptoms of generalized anxiety disorder include feeling tired or worn out, difficulty sleeping, and tight or sore muscles.

Although children with generalized anxiety disorder are often successful in many aspects of their lives, such as school and friendships, their accomplishments seldom seem to be enough to make them happy. They may feel that five friends aren't enough, or worry that they offended the latest person they met and this person won't like them. They will always find something, such as an A– on a test instead of an A, to make them worry that they are not good enough.

If any of these signs of generalized anxiety disorder persist in your child for more than a few months, a full evaluation (described in chapter 1) is in order. Your child may need some short-term therapy, medication, or both. This disorder is not uncommon, and it is very treatable.

If, however, your child worries more about specific social situations, keep reading.

Social Anxiety Disorder

It is normal for everyone to be somewhat nervous around others, especially when meeting new people or speaking in front of a group of strangers. But this nervousness can be magnified in children. Some children are terrified of every new encounter with a potential friend their own age or too afraid to deliver a simple report in front of the class. In a social context, these children focus on every imperfection: for example, they wonder if other children saw that they had a hair out of place or a smudge of dirt on their jeans. They constantly worry that they will look stupid, weird, or out of sync with their peers. It is only when these children are safe at home with friends and family that they can relax and engage in normal social interactions.

Children who worry too much in social situations may have social anxiety disorder. The signs include extreme anxiety when meeting or interacting with someone new, excessive distress when speaking in front of a group, avoidance of situations that require interactions with unfamiliar people, and extreme misery when having to perform in a social or school situation. If these social worries persist for longer than a few months and interfere with your child's ability to perform at school or in sports or to engage in typical social activities, you should seek an evaluation.

Again, this disorder is very treatable. I once treated a young girl who was so afraid of getting up in front of her class that she became unable to deliver reports and was in danger of flunking her English class, despite otherwise being an A student. With exposure therapy, as described with Caroline and expanded upon hereafter, she was able to get through her fear of public speaking and thrive in class. With treatment, a child can prosper and escape the pain that anxiety can cause.

Panic Disorder

A panic attack is a sudden episode of intense fear that triggers physical reactions, such as difficulty breathing, when there is no real danger or apparent cause. Panic attacks typically begin without warning. They can strike at almost any time: at the beginning of giving a report, before a big track meet, when faced with a first school dance. I frequently see children in my practice who have attacks when confronted with tests in school. But panic attacks can even appear during activities that were once pleasurable, such as in the midst of a birthday party for a close friend.

The symptoms of panic attacks have many variations, including sweating, a sense of impending doom or danger, rapid trembling, and a pounding heart, but they usually are the worst within the first ten minutes. Children often cannot put into words the experience of the attack. They can simply say that they couldn't move or had extreme difficulty breathing.

Children often have one or two isolated panic attacks before the problem goes away, perhaps when a stressful situation ends. But if a child has recurrent, unexpected panic attacks and spends long periods in constant fear of another attack, they may have a condition called panic disorder. Although panic attacks can often be dismissed as nerves or stress over a big event, they should be recognized as a real medical condition. Panic attacks unchecked or uncontrolled by effective treatment can significantly affect a child's academic career and well-being. With the right treatment, however, these kids can be just fine and avoid a lot of unnecessary suffering.

Specific Phobias

A phobia is an intense but irrational fear of something that actually poses no threat. Phobias can be tied to animals, a person's surroundings, blood or injury, and a wide range of other triggers. For example, some of the more common specific phobias involve closed spaces (claustrophobia), heights (acrophobia), escalators (escalaphobia), insects (entomophobia), water (hydrophobia), flying (pteromerhanophobia), dogs (cynophobia), and injuries involving blood (hemophobia). A fear of wide-open spaces (agoraphobia) is treated separately in the DSM. These phobias have a root in reality: that is, they are exaggerations of what most people can feel. Fearing bugs and blood and all that other stuff isn't crazy and can be self-protective. Many of us get dizzy looking down into the Grand Canyon and step back from the edge, which is not a bad impulse. In the film *North by Northwest*, the scene in which a plane attacks Cary Grant's character in an open cornfield plays on our fear of being vulnerable in the open, and Hitchcock's genius was that he extended our normal anxieties into nightmares of waking life.

A lot of these conditions, at heart, are wholly human and even helpful. It's only when they get out of whack and become obstructive to the point where your child won't or can't participate in school or social activities that they become problematic.

Specific phobias usually appear in childhood or adolescence and tend to persist into adulthood. Their causes are not well understood, but there is some evidence that the tendency to develop certain fears may run in families. The good news is that, once again, exposure therapy can be quite helpful.

If it is easy to avoid the thing or situation that triggers the phobia—for example, by riding the elevator rather than taking the escalator at the mall— parents may not seek help because they don't see the phobia as a problem. But behind each fear is usually a larger issue that applies to more than one situation in a child's life—for example, a fear of the dentist might really be a fear of germs. Even if it is a more general phobia, it can still be treated easily and effectively.

Obsessive-Compulsive Disorders

Up to 3 percent of children and adolescents have OCD. For them, obsessions are recurrent and persistent thoughts and mental images (such as a violent scene in one's head) or impulses (such as wanting to brush your hair over and over). Compulsions are repetitive behaviors or rituals such as hand washing, hoarding, or checking. Obsessive-compulsive disorder (OCD) is defined as the presence of recurrent, intense obsessions or compulsions that are time-consuming, cause significant distress, or interfere with daily functioning, such as making friends or going to school.

Obsessions and compulsions often look different depending on a child's age. For example, in children around six, obsessions can take the form of fears that a family member may be harmed. The child may check compulsively to make certain a parent is all right. In older children or teens, these fears are often self-focused—for example, fears about germs or diseases that they may contract. As a result, they often feel compelled to wash their hands repeatedly. The unwanted thought of the germs or disease is the obsession, and the behavior, the act of washing one's hands repeatedly, is the compulsion.

Once again, the good news is that most children with obsessions or compulsions can be treated effectively with a combination of psychotherapy and medications.

OCD, ADHD, and Tourette Syndrome

There is some evidence of a link, at least in some children, among OCD, ADHD, and Tourette syndrome. Tourette syndrome (TS), which is quite rare, is a more severe form of tic disorder. Tics are rapid, repetitive movements or vocal utterances. They may be motor tics, such as finger-snapping, touching, or other abrupt and sudden movements, or vocal tics, such as clicking noises or repetitive throat-clearing. Tics can be chronic and continue throughout childhood, or they can be transient and last less than a year. In Tourette's, motor and vocal tics occur many times a day and last for more than a year. The average age at which the syndrome appears is seven, and it peaks at eleven. While children with TS may develop ADHD, the two disorders are considered separate conditions. Tourette's affects only .05 to 3 percent of children.

At least one large study of the genetics of TS has reinforced the possibility that underlying biology, or common genes, ties together TS, OCD, and ADHD, thus explaining why they are frequently seen together. That doesn't mean all patients with Tourette's also have OCD and ADHD, but one-third of children with TS in that study had all three sets of symptoms. If your child exhibits OCD behaviors, it is important that an evaluation also consider the symptoms of ADHD and TS because the treatments and medicines will be guided by the entirety of a child's symptoms (for example, a stimulant for ADHD treatment may or may not be the best medicine for treating tic symptoms).

Post-Traumatic Stress Disorder

Post-traumatic stress disorder (PTSD) is a severe form of an anxiety disorder that can develop after an extremely traumatic event in a child's life. Children and teens may have PTSD if they have lived through an event that badly hurt them or someone else, or in which someone was killed, or that was violent and frightening, such as a horrific car crash or a fire—even if the child only observed the violence. Sexual or physical abuse can also result in PTSD.

According to the US Department of Veteran's Affairs National Center for PTSD, of those children and teens who have experienced a trauma, 3 to 15 percent of girls and 1 to 6 percent of boys develop PTSD. Rates of PTSD are higher for certain types of trauma survivors. For example, nearly 100 percent of children get PTSD if they see a parent killed or if they witness a sexual assault. PTSD develops in 90 percent of sexually abused children, 77 percent of children who see a school shooting, and 35 percent who see violence in their neighborhood.

More generally, three factors have been shown to raise the chances that children will develop PTSD:

- how severe the trauma is
- how the parents react to the trauma
- how close or far away the traumatic event was

These factors can interact, of course. Even if a child has gone through severe trauma, her PTSD symptoms may be less severe if her parents demonstrate that they are less upset and provide a lot of support.

To complicate the picture, the symptoms of PTSD take on a different appearance depending on the age at which the trauma occurs. For example, younger children might reenact part of the trauma in their play—for example, by acting out shooting games after they witnessed a traumatic shooting. Or they might assume that the traumatic event was preceded by signs that it was going to happen, and they keep on looking for those signs as a signal of future trauma. Although some PTSD symptoms in teens—such as fear and helplessness—begin to mirror those found in adults, teens are more likely than younger children or adults to show impulsive and aggressive behaviors.

Evidence-Based Treatments

In general, anxiety, OCD, and stress or trauma disorders are treated effectively with cognitive behavioral therapy or exposure-based approaches (with or without medications). The choice of a specific treatment depends on your child's specific issue and the treatment you and your child feel most comfortable with. Here are some of the options.

Treatments for Anxiety

CBT Treatment

One major study, the Child/Adolescent Anxiety Multimodal Study (CAMS), completed in 2010, found that high-quality cognitive behavioral therapy—when used with and even without medication—effectively reduced symptoms in children with separation anxiety disorder and social phobia and improved their daily lives. Its results have also been reflected in other studies. For example, a smaller study published in 2007 found that a form of therapy called social effectiveness therapy for children (SET-C) was more effective than medicine in reducing anxiety in children. According to the study's authors, SET-C includes individual and group therapy sessions, plus a type of exposure therapy (such as the therapy I used with Caroline) that reduces a child's social anxiety while simultaneously improving her social skills.

In that study, the children were provided with twelve weeks of treatment, either SET-C, medication, or a placebo pill. (Medications commonly used to treat social phobias in children include antidepressants such as fluoxetine and other selective serotonin reuptake inhibitors.) Many more of the children assigned to the SET-C group responded to the treatment: 79 percent, as compared to 36 percent treated with medicine alone and 6 percent treated with placebo. In addition, immediately after the twelve-week program, 53 percent of the SET-C group no longer met the criteria for social phobia, as compared to 21 percent of the medicine group and 3 percent of the sugar pill group.

One year after the program, the children who had responded to SET-C or medication retained their reduced levels of anxiety at about the same rate. However, SET-C also helped children improve their daily well-being and social skills, suggesting that it has a more wide-ranging positive effect than medication alone.

Coping Cat

One of the most effective treatments for childhood anxiety disorders, Coping Cat is a type of cognitive behavioral talk therapy that helps children understand their anxiety and develop coping strategies for situations that provoke it. According to the Promising Practices Network, the program first helps children to recognize and clarify their anxious feelings and the physical reactions those feelings provoke. Using a workbook, the therapist guides children to understand how they behaved during situations in which they felt anxious and to understand how they might behave differently in the future. They then are guided to develop a coping plan. For example, they might be helped to change their self-talk—that is, the interior dialogue we all conduct with ourselves—from talk that heightens anxiety into an inner dialogue that instead helps us to cope with anxiety.

The Coping Cat program teaches skills like those taught in all cognitive behavioral therapies, but focuses on presenting them in a way that is specifically suited to the child's stage of development. In addition, to increase the child's motivation for continuing the treatment, the Coping Cat program emphasizes positive reinforcement, focusing on accomplishments and teaching children to reward themselves as they improve on coping with their anxiety.

In the early sessions, the therapist asks the child to describe situations in which she becomes anxious and the physical sensations (such as a stomach-ache) that she feels as her anxiety takes over. These sessions help children learn how to identify anxiety at its first onset, beginning with the physical signs they feel in their own body.

In the next step, the child and the therapist create a list of specific situations that create anxiety, ranking them by which creates the highest degree of anxiety. (Some therapists will use a "thermometer" as a scale.) This list is used during the behavioral exercises to follow.

The child is next taught how to relax. That process involves exercises such as focused breathing, progressive muscle relaxation, and guided visualization. So the child can practice relaxation at the first signs of anxiety, she is given a recording to keep with a description of the exercises (just as I did with Caroline).

After the child has made good progress through these steps, the focus changes. The child is now taught how to monitor her own thinking or self-talk—specifically the thoughts that seem to appear automatically when she begins to feel the physical symptoms of anxiety and that make the anxiety worse. For instance, when a socially anxious child sees another child and feels her heart rate increase, she might think, *So-and-so thinks I am a weirdo*. That thought then exacerbates her anxiety.

To break this cycle, the child is taught coping self-talk that might involve, for example, being more realistic in her own interior dialogue about what another child might be thinking. Because this exercise can be difficult for young children, Coping Cat uses a series of cartoons to help them understand. In the cartoons, a cat encounters potentially anxiety-provoking situations. The cartoons include blank thought bubbles, and the therapist coaches the child by asking what she thinks the cat might say or think in a given situation.

The rest of Coping Cat involves exposure exercises such as the ones I discussed in Caroline's case study. The child is carefully and gradually exposed to images or situations that induce fear, and remains exposed until the fear diminishes, recognizing and trying to change her anxious self-talk along the way. The process is very carefully managed. The first exposures are to situations that provoke a lesser anxiety, and the child repeats the exposure and the exercises until the situation no longer induces fear.

Exposure Therapy in General

As the description of Coping Cat indicates, at the heart of cognitive behavioral therapy for obsessions, compulsions, and related anxiety disorders is the process of exposure therapy, during which children, using previously learned coping skills, repeatedly do the very thing that has terrified them. For a client with OCD, this might mean purposely walking onto a crack that would make her anxious, and then standing still while taking three deep breaths or counting to ten as a way of controlling her fears and realizing that nothing bad will happen to her. For someone with obsessive thoughts, the therapy could mean purposely thinking about being in the uncomfortable situation or actually putting herself in the situation—for example, if she is afraid of heights, going to a mall and looking over the edge of a balcony rail while practicing positive thoughts or deep breathing exercises. Someone with panic attacks might be exposed to her trigger, such as a spider or public speaking, with a therapist guiding her through her new adaptive skills. Most often, the treatment involves working in the home, at school, or in the community where the therapist can address the uncomfortable thoughts or behaviors directly and in the setting in which they most often occur.

The basic principle of exposure therapy is that children will become less afraid of just about anything if they are exposed to it frequently and regularly. So if a child is afraid of heights, for example, the exposure would be to repeatedly but gradually spend time at greater heights—for example, on various floors in a shopping mall—until the fear is reduced to a minimal level. But this isn't something parents should try alone and without professional help. A good clinician *never* asks the child to confront something that will make her panic. One cannot just throw a child into a situation and ask her to swim without giving her new skills to deal with the situation first. Intervention as soon as possible is also important here, too. The earlier you intervene, the easier the fears are to treat, and they are *very* treatable.

Treatments for PTSD

Cognitive Behavioral Therapy (CBT)

Although PTSD symptoms may dissipate or disappear in the months following a trauma, that doesn't always happen. In fact, without treatment, PTSD symptoms can last for years. For children, the most effective treatment can be one form of CBT: trauma-focused CBT (TF-CBT). This therapy encourages the child to talk through her memories of the traumatic event, in the process learning techniques to lessen the stress and fear caused by the memories.

Although it may seem counterintuitive to encourage children to revisit traumatic events, under the guidance of a therapist that approach can be the best way of helping them to overcome their fears, and research shows that TF-CBT is safe as well as effective. Children can be taught at their own pace, without being pushed too soon.

Because parents should understand the effects of PTSD as well as how to help their children cope with those effects, CBT often provides additional training for parents and other caregivers.

Eye Movement Desensitization and Reprocessing (EMDR)

Although EMDR was once considered a fringe treatment, more and more evidence has found it effective in treating both children and adults with PTSD. EMDR combines cognitive therapy with eye movements that are guided by the therapist. The underlying theory is that controlling the trauma victims' involuntary eye movements as they recall the trauma helps to desensitize them to the memory. The exact mechanisms that make EMDR effective are somewhat controversial, however, and some studies indicate that the eye movements are not needed to make the therapy work. If that's the case, then it is not so different from the other types of exposure therapies described above.

Aside from its emphasis on eye movements, EMDR is based on the premise that disturbing experiences are stored in the brain with all the sights, sounds, thoughts, and feelings that accompanied the negative experience. The brain becomes unable to process experiences when a child is very upset in the same way as it would normally in a less stressful situation. As a result of this faulty processing, negative thoughts and feelings associated with the traumatic event are believed to be "trapped" in the nervous system. As a result, these negative experiences are often suppressed from consciousness since the brain cannot process them normally. However, the distress is still actively part of the nervous system, and causes disturbances in the child's emotional functioning.

The EMDR therapist works with the child, guiding her to revisit the trauma. This has two effects. First, it releases the negative memories and emotions stored in the nervous system. Second, it helps the brain process the experience in a more normal fashion, so that the feelings are reexperienced in a new way. As a result, the child can gain the perspective that helps her to choose how she responds to those memories, rather than feeling powerless over them.

Play Therapy

Finally, for children who are too young to deal with trauma more directly, play therapy can be a useful treatment. It uses games and drawings, for example, to help children express and come to terms with traumatic memories.

7

Sadness and Loss:
Is My Child Just Sad,
or Clinically Depressed?

Mike

Mike was nine years old and had been suspended from the third grade for the third time in several months. With the school's no-tolerance policy for bad behavior, he was on the verge of being expelled. Mike's teachers saw him as a disobedient and disruptive child who frequently got into fights on the playground and talked back to his teachers, often screaming at them. Screaming was the behavior that had produced his most recent suspension. To his parents, Mike seemed creative and bright. He loved to write stories and draw pictures. But he also seemed a little down. He was quiet and withdrawn and, lately he often stayed in his room. They attributed his mood at home to the fights he was having with other kids at school.

His parents brought him to me in part because of the suspensions but also because they thought I could help them persuade the teachers to give Mike more of a break and more support at school. In fact, Mike's parents were angry at the school and felt his teachers had it out for him. As a result, they were considering a new school for him, one that would provide more hands-on activities, such as making models and doing science projects, to engage Mike's desire to build things. But they also knew his current school was academically more rigorous, and they were concerned about his long-term educational future, especially getting into college. They believed this school, if he could stay with it and eventually graduate as a high school senior, would look better on his transcripts.

When Mike first came to my office, he seemed eager to help me figure out what was "wrong" with him. He asked me repeatedly if I could get him back into school, and he wanted to answer all of my questions as quickly as possible. Mike and I spent three or four sessions together talking about school, his life at home, and why he might yell at his teachers or get into fights. Then I had Mike and his parents fill out a number of checklists about his skills and abilities: for example, whether his parents had to tell him to do things three or four times and whether he completed his homework on his own. I also did some formal testing to rule out the presence of a learning issue such as dyslexia or ADHD.

In my office, Mike seemed a typical nine-year-old kid. I noticed, however, that his emotional affect seemed a little blunted or flat. He often talked in a low monotone and, on some days, didn't smile or appear animated at all.

His intelligence and ability tests all came back within normal ranges, so it was pretty clear he did not have a learning disability. But the checklists completed by his parents and teachers revealed that he was feeling sad more often than not during the day, and many times in the evening. When I asked Mike about these feelings, he found them hard to describe. After the second session, though, he came in with a very dark drawing about monsters who were lurking, ready to attack him. He used the drawing to explain more about sad feelings that at times seemed overwhelming. He said that it felt as if he were carrying a heavy backpack most days, and he wished at times that everyone would just leave him alone.

Mike's parents were shocked at this revelation. They were surprised by his feelings, somewhat skeptical, and uncertain how to respond. They didn't understand why he hadn't said anything to them before and wondered if he was saying these things now just to get a pass from them to go to a different, less academically rigorous school. I assured them that his feelings of depression seemed genuine. Indeed, children tend to under-report feelings, and it is rare that children at this age report much of what is bothering them, let alone these sorts of feelings. When they do, they will often, like Mike, use words such as heavy rather than saying they are sad.

The good news is that once Mike, his parents, and I figured out what the issue was, Mike quickly responded to treatment. In consultation with their family doctor, Mike's parents started him on a trial regime of medication for the depression; at the same time, Mike and I worked together with cognitive behavioral therapy. Choosing this combined approach was not an easy decision, but after reading the research that showed combined medication and talk therapy was the most effective treatment for depression, Mike's parents decided to try it.

Cognitive behavioral therapy involved my explaining to Mike that his negative thoughts—such as, *I know that kid is making fun of me*—were causing him to become upset at other people and to behave in ways that weren't very good for him. To understand his behavior, Mike, his parents, and I made charts of the events that prompted negative thoughts or led to bad behaviors such as pushing other kids. During the first week, Mike kept a chart of the times when he had negative thoughts or was tempted to scream at a teacher or get into a scuffle with a classmate. He wrote down for me what happened right before the incident, how he responded to the incident, and what happened after the incident.

Together, Mike and I identified a number of recurring situations that caused negative thoughts and behaviors. Next, we identified different kinds of thoughts he could have in these trigger situations and different ways in which he could respond. For example, if someone didn't want to play with him, instead of assuming the person thought he was stupid, he could realize that they just wanted to play with someone else, and that Mike could also approach someone else to play. We also did some role-playing, acting out how he might ask other kids to play with him or come over after school. As is often the case, Mike's issues seemed to result in part from poor social skills.

After about six months of treatment, everyone in Mike's life noticed a difference. His teacher reported that he was much less disruptive in class and his parents reported that he seemed to be enjoying school. Best of all, Mike reported that most days he didn't see things as so dark. The heavy burden he felt he had been carrying was gone.

How many children suffer from depression? Among teens, it may be as many as one in eight; among children in general, thankfully, estimates are under 3 percent. A diagnosis of depression involves more than occasional down moods or sadness. After all, feeling down or negative about life is normal in kids, especially during adolescence, just as they are in adults. But when a depressed mood continues for an unusually long time—weeks or months—and interferes with a child's life, a diagnosis of depression may be in order.

Symptoms of Depression

Some signs of possible depression in kids or teens can include the following, if they persist.

- sadness
- hopelessness
- guilt
- a feeling of worthlessness
- a lack of interest in or enjoyment of everyday pleasures
- difficulty concentrating or completing school work
- lack of energy
- sleep disturbance: sleeping too little or too much
- weight or appetite gain or loss
- irritability
- difficulty in interpersonal relationships, specifically in getting along with others
- cutting classes or skipping school
- dropping out of sports, hobbies, or other activities
- drinking or using drugs

Types of Depression

Types of depression include the following, all of which can affect children and teenagers:

- major depression
- dysthymia (Mike's diagnosis), or now called, persistent depressive disorder

- bipolar disorder
- disruptive mood dysregulation disorder (DMDD)

In this chapter I will also discuss schizophrenia. While it is not typically regarded as a form of depression, its symptoms can overlap with depression. When a child has schizophrenia, her thinking becomes disorganized or abnormal from what is typical for her age (for example, she may see or hear things that aren't there, not just have an imaginary friend). The child may also show less emotion, interest in social interaction, pleasure, or motivation.

I will describe each of these disorders briefly, then go into more detail about their causes, diagnoses, and treatments.

Major Depression

As the name implies, major depression is not to be taken lightly, even if a child doesn't talk about being sad or unhappy. Children with this condition typically feel depressed almost every day. They have trouble deriving pleasure from anything and they may be very down on themselves, feeling worthless or a failure. However, these feelings may well be hidden under the surface. The visible signs may be irritability or bad moods, rather than what an adult would take to be the more obvious signs of depression. Major depression typically interferes significantly with the child's day-to-day life—playing with other kids, completing homework assignments, and even eating and sleeping.

Dysthymia, or Persistent Depressive Disorder

In persistent depressive disorder, the depression is more chronic (lasting at least a year in children) than in major depression. Children with this diagnosis can have pervasive, continual feelings of low self-esteem and hopelessness. In addition, many kids with this condition have or develop poor social skills. The most recent DSM places dysthymia and chronic major depression under the diagnostic label of persistent depressive disorder, which may be diagnosed in children if sadness or irritability continues for at least a year.

Bipolar Disorder

Children with bipolar disorder, or manic depression, have episodes of low-energy depression and episodes of high-energy mania. In the most recent DSM, bipolar disorder was formally separated from the depressive disorders and placed between the chapters on them and the chapters on schizophrenia. That placement reflects the current belief that bipolar illnesses can be distinguished from depression and schizophrenia but share characteristics—symptoms, genetics, and history in families—with them.

Bipolar disorder frequently manifests in late adolescence and early adulthood, and it may affect as many as 1 to 2 percent of kids. (Over two million adults have been diagnosed with bipolar disorder.) Bipolar children experience intense mood changes that are far more severe than children's usual emotional swings. Sometimes they feel very sad and are much less active than usual, and sometimes they are very active—perhaps happy, perhaps irritable and having angry outbursts (called manic, or mania). And they may have mood episodes, as these periods are called, that are not purely manic or depressive but are mixed, displaying both manic and depressive symptoms. Children often have more mixed episodes than adults, although researchers aren't certain why this is the case.

During a mood episode, which can last a week or more, the symptoms continue every day for most of the day and are intense, with major swings in energy and behavior. If a parent tells me that their child has boundless energy one minute (cutting the grass, running several miles, and then staying up all night) followed by extreme bouts of sadness (crying for no reason for several days), I start to think about bipolar disorder as a diagnosis. However, many cases are not this severe or cut-and-dried.

The disorder can disrupt a child's relationships with family and friends, and it can also be dangerous, leading a child to hurt herself or even to attempt suicide. The research also suggests that kids and teens with bipolar disorder can also have other problems, such as attention deficit disorders (see chapter 5), oppositional behavior disorders (see chapter 9), and anxiety. One type of bipolar disorder involves psychosis, a condition marked by a disturbed or nonlinear thought pattern.

Following is a list of behaviors that a child or teen with bipolar disorder may exhibit.

During a manic episode children and teens may:

- feel elated or act inappropriately silly in a way that's unusual in the context
- be quick tempered
- talk rapidly about many things
- have difficulty sleeping but not feel sleepy
- have trouble focusing on schoolwork
- talk and think about sex more than same-aged peers
- do risky things

During a depressive episode, children and teens may:

- feel or act very sad
- complain often about pain, such as stomachaches and headaches
- sleep not enough or excessively
- feel guilty or worthless
- eat too little or too much
- have little drive and or interest in enjoyable activities
- think about death or suicide

The diagnosis of bipolar disorder in very young children is still controversial. Despite research conducted at Harvard and the National Institute of Mental Health, it is still very difficult for even well-trained health care professionals to identify behaviors that definitively distinguish this disorder in children under six. From my own experience in my practice, I believe it exists and can be diagnosed in young children, but I also believe it is being overused as an explanation for kids' behavioral problems. Many believe that the rapid increase in diagnoses of bipolar disorder in children resulted in part from a too-loose interpretation of the DSM-IV criteria. Many books were written for practitioners that suggested clinicians should deviate from DSM-IV criteria, and even before the DSM-5 had been released and some research groups began using different research criteria that then found their way into clinical practice before they had been well tested.

Disruptive Mood Dysregulation Disorder

Disruptive mood dysregulation disorder (DMDD) is a new diagnosis, included for the first time in the most recent DSM. It is designed to help children who may otherwise be diagnosed as having a bipolar disorder despite the fact that they do not show the more classic characteristics of individuals with the classic manic presentations of bipolar disorder. Children that tend to continue to display bipolar disorder behaviors into adulthood are those with the more classic manic presentations, whereas children with DMDD are more likely to have depression later in life.

The new diagnosis is applied to children whose symptoms appear between the ages of six and ten. (In fact, DSM-5 suggests that the diagnosis can be given up to the age of eighteen, as long as symptoms appeared before the age of ten.) DMDD's hallmark seems to be severe irritability and an angry mood. The irritability causes frequent and extreme temper outbursts or tantrums when kids get frustrated at home and school. Between outbursts, they remain angry most of the time. This disorder is thought to be more common than bipolar disorder in preadolescents.

Schizophrenia

Schizophrenia is a serious psychiatric condition that, fortunately, is uncommon in children. Additionally, it may be hard to identify when the symptoms first begin to appear, in part because a child's behavior may change only gradually. For example, a child may slowly seem to withdraw into her own world, appearing shyer or, in some cases, clinging to parents. Or she may talk about fears or thoughts that don't make sense. Sometimes teachers will notice these early signs before the parents do.

Here is a more specific list of some signs of schizophrenia:

- hearing and seeing things which are imagined (hallucinations)
- abnormal actions or speech
- unusual or bizarre thoughts
- clouding reality with images from dreams or television
- jumbled thinking
- intense moods

- thoughts that others are out to harm them or are speaking about them (paranoia)
- extreme fear or anxiety
- failure to interact with peers or maintain friendships
- increased periods of spending time alone
- loss of interest in personal hygiene

For this condition, as for many others, early diagnosis and treatment are critical. If you are worried your child may have seen some of the signs of schizophrenia, you should arrange an evaluation by a psychiatrist or psychologist who has specific training in diagnosing and helping children with schizophrenia. If a child is diagnosed with this disorder, she will need a treatment plan that covers all areas of life, often involving a combination of medication, individual therapy, family therapy, and other specialized programs designed to help children become independent adults. If medications are used, they should be carefully managed by a psychiatrist with specific training with children and adolescents.

Causes

Depression

Depression can have many causes, and often has more than one:

- *Physical*—or, more precisely, neurochemical—causes, such as lower levels of neurotransmitters, the chemicals that facilitate communication among cells throughout the nervous system in the brain (see appendix A). If these levels are too low, they interfere with our ability to feel pleasure. These physical causes can be inherited; a child is more likely to have the condition if others in the family also have or had it.

- *Disruptive or painful events*, such as the death of a family member or the loss of friends as the result of a move. Even losing a beloved family pet can be a trigger. Teens are particularly susceptible to these events because the increasing social demands and hormonal changes are difficult for the most resilient child to handle.

- *Chronic illness*, as well as the side effects of some medicines and infections.

Bipolar Disorder and Schizophrenia

The causes of bipolar disorder and schizophrenia are not entirely known. Genetic, neurochemical, and environmental factors may all be involved (see the discussion of the interaction between genetics and the environment in chapter 4). The current thinking is that these disorders are predominantly biological disorders, arising in localized parts of the brain and resulting from the faulty functioning of chemical messengers in the brain. Because the disorders are biological, they tend to be hereditary. The underlying biological condition may be triggered by stressors in life or may one day just start to "wake up" and affect a person's behavior.

Diagnosis

Depression

Although you as a parent may have a very good intuitive feel for your child's mood and know whether she is happy or sad, a formal diagnosis of major depression requires an evaluation by a professional that goes beyond impressions. A good clinician will use standardized checklists that compare your child's behavior with those of similar ages to guide the diagnosis.

For a diagnosis of major depressive disorder, five or more of the following types of symptoms must be present for at least two weeks, at least one of the symptoms must fall into the category of a depressed mood or a loss of interest or pleasure, and those symptoms must impair a child's functioning most of the time.

- being down or very sad, empty, or hopeless almost every day for no apparent reason
- lack of energy or ability to start simple activities
- failure to enjoy things, or to be with people, that used to bring happiness
- feelings of inordinate or inappropriate guilt or worthlessness
- inability to focus, think, or make decisions
- significant weight loss without dieting, significant weight gain, or significant change in appetite

- great difficulty falling asleep or, conversely, waking up frequently
- moving slowly or with great difficulty, or more than normal restlessness
- frequent thoughts of death or suicide

Additionally, because they look for ways to make themselves feel better at least for a while, depressed children are also more likely to use alcohol and drugs.

Dysthymia, or Persistent Depressive Disorder

For a diagnosis of persistent depressive disorder, a child must experience two or more of the following symptoms almost continually for one year:

- poor self-esteem
- sleeping too little or too much
- severe fatigue or very low energy
- difficulty making decisions or poor concentration
- decreased appetite or overeating
- feelings of hopelessness

To receive a diagnosis of dysthymia, a child or adolescent must show the symptoms continuously for a longer period than is necessary to diagnose major depressive disorder. In many children, the mood becomes so common that it may seem normal, and the child may not reveal negative feelings unless asked directly. Their mood may be irritable as opposed to sad. Then they might, as Mike did, speak in terms of being heavy or dark or just not feeling right. Persistent depressive disorder occurs evenly between girls and boys, and it is more common when parents or siblings have a diagnosis of major depressive disorder.

Before I describe bipolar disorder, disruptive mood dysregulation, and schizophrenia, along with the treatments for these disorders, I should address two topics that often come up in discussions of depression: the relationship between bereavement and depression, and the relationship among depressive symptoms, schizophrenia, and bipolar disorder.

Is Bereavement Different from Depression?

After a painful loss, it's perfectly normal to experience a period of profound sadness and mourning. This is known as grief or bereavement. Everyone, including very young children, goes through grief after a loss. It is an inevitable part of life, and grief can reemerge strongly even years after the loss if triggered by a later loss. However, when grief continues for too long to seriously affect a child's outlook and ability to function, then it may be something more than a normal response.

Here are a few things to keep in mind about grief in children:

- Children who are grieving will often act out in anger toward a parent or sibling. They may also experience feelings of guilt and self-blame that can be damaging to the entire family as well as the child if not addressed.

- Support groups can be one of the best forms of treatment. These groups allow children to share their experiences and worries with other children who are in similar situations.

- In some cases, grief can lead to PDD or major depression, requiring mental health treatment.

- Children or teens may be so severely affected by their grief that they have suicidal thoughts. Those thoughts should always be taken very seriously, and parents should seek immediate help.

One of the most controversial changes in DSM-5 was the removal of the so-called bereavement exclusion in the diagnosis of major depressive disorder—that is, the exclusion from the diagnosis of those who had recently suffered a loss that led to bereavement. This change occurred for two main reasons:

1. There have not been any adequately controlled clinical studies finding that symptoms of major depression following bereavement differ from depression in other contexts.

2. Major depression, the leading cause of suicide, is a very serious disorder with the potential for severe consequences if left untreated.

If a diagnosis of major depression is withheld only because the symptoms emerge after, for example, the death of a loved one, a serious problem may go untreated. The change in DSM-5 ensures that those children who meet full criteria for the diagnosis within the first few weeks after the death of a loved one will be able to get the help they need, including the insurance resources that a diagnosis brings.

The Latest Research: The Relationship Among Major Depression, Bipolar Disorder, and Schizophrenia

In 2013, scientists discovered that five major psychiatric disorders—autism, attention deficit hyperactivity disorder, bipolar disorder, major depressive disorder, and schizophrenia—share several genetic risk factors. In particular, several of these disorders seem to involve variations in two genes that help to regulate calcium in brain cells. Findings such as these may one day lead to reclassifying these disorders on the basis of causes rather than symptoms and may also lead to new treatments. To this end, the National Institute of Mental Health called in 2013 for a new effort to reclassify all of these disorders. Eventually, these disorders may be seen as parts of the same spectrum. For now, however, they still are diagnosed separately.

Let's now return to the diagnostic descriptions of the remaining disorders.

Bipolar Disorder

The DSM-5 lists seven types of bipolar disorder. Each type is distinguished from the others through either the nature of episodes your child may be experiencing or the cause (e.g., substance or medication use or a medical condition). In this section, though, I will focus on the disorder more generally.

The defining hallmark of bipolar disorder in children is the experience of intense periods of highs and lows, often in very rapid succession. Children with bipolar disorder experience extreme emotions, or highs and lows that bear no relation to the environment around them or the situations they may encounter with other children, or you. They may feel quite happy, on top of the world one moment, then shortly thereafter and without warning feel very sad, or worn out with no energy. These are the classic symptoms, but with children the picture is complicated.

Children with bipolar disorder can often have moods that are not readily categorizable as either high or low, and they experience such rapid shifts in their emotions from hour to hour that they can appear just plain ornery or irritable. (By contrast, adults with bipolar disorder tend to have more distinct periods of identifiable mood shifts over days and weeks.) In fact, children and adolescents with bipolar disorder may remain chronically irritable most of the time, or explosive with no recognizable pattern, and have few periods when they are more even tempered or well.

Because the symptoms of bipolar disorder can be so difficult to identify in children, it can be quite difficult to distinguish bipolar disorder from a depressive disorder. Clinicians distinguish depressive disorders from bipolar disorder by the former's absence of mania or manic episodes (periods of excessive energy or irritability). Kids with depression typically experience the more extreme lows without the periods of excessive energy or extreme irritability. However, mixed episodes can also occur during which mania and depression co-occur.

Because the symptoms of bipolar disorder in children often cycle from happy to sad so quickly, or may be dulled and present more as general irritability, the first episode of bipolar disorder can be very difficult to recognize in children, or mistaken for something else by even seasoned clinicians. With that understanding, here are some of the behaviors researchers and clinicians have identified in children in the depressive, manic, or mixed episodes of bipolar disorder:

- In a *depressive episode*, a child is primarily sad or tearful; irritable most of the time; or tired, listless, or lacking any interest in activities that have previously been favorites.

- As in a depressive episode, in a *manic episode*, she may be irritable or aggressive, but she is more likely to be restless, extremely active, and may talk rapidly about a lot of things; she may display risky behavior or hypersexuality beyond what you would expect from a child her age; she may also have extreme or grandiose thoughts, such as believing she has extraordinary powers; she may also hear voices. She may display explosive behavior outbursts with physical aggression or tantrums. (During periods of hypomania, a mild form of mania, adolescents can experience creativity and immense productivity.)

- In a *manic or mixed* state children may be silly, happy, or experience extreme elation but also be intensely irritable, aggressive, or inconsolable; their sleep patterns may also change from what is typical for them.

As you can see from these descriptions, the characteristics and behavioral signs of bipolar disorder are blurred and very difficult to apply in most instances to a child's daily behavior (especially in teens, who are normally quite moody by nature). Consequently, there has been a great deal of controversy surrounding the use of this diagnosis in children. In part because of the increase in such diagnoses, the new DSM-5 includes the new diagnostic category of disruptive mood disorder dysregulation to better categorize behaviors that are predominately marked by irritability.

Disruptive Mood Disorder Dysregulation

This new diagnosis includes children who experience chronic irritability and extreme behavioral outbursts three or more times a week for more than one year. To meet the criteria for disruptive mood disorder dysregulation, in between temper outbursts a child must be persistently negative (irritable, angry, or sad) and this irritability between outbursts must be distinct enough to be observable by others. Additionally, the irritability and outbursts must be present in at least two settings (for example, home and school). Symptoms must be describable in a child between chronological or developmental ages of six and ten. In addition to being misdiagnosed as bipolar disorder in children, DMDD symptoms can also result in a misdiagnosis of oppositional defiant disorder.

It is always very important to work closely as a partner with your mental health treatment providers. Especially when you are working with a clinician and thinking about bipolar disorder or disruptive mood disorder dysregulation as a diagnostic label to describe your child's symptoms, it is extremely important to chart your child's behavior very precisely, over time. Move slowly, and ask questions of your child's doctor before you arrive at a definitive diagnosis. Revisit (and chart) your categorizations of your child's behavior over time (was that really irritability for several weeks or something different?) to insure an accurate diagnostic picture that will inform the best treatment options.

Schizophrenia

Childhood onset schizophrenia—that is, the onset of psychosis before the age of thirteen—is very rare, according to treatment and research professionals. Typically, the onset of schizophrenia in children is preceded by behavioral symptoms and difficulties with thought processes, including significant delays in language and motor development, social isolation, or minor neurologic difficulties that are not associated with a specific neurologic disorder.

However, these early signs can overlap with symptoms of other disorders, such as ASD and speech and language disorders.

Schizophrenia symptoms fall into two broad categories: positive and negative. For a diagnosis of schizophrenia, two symptoms must be present for at least six months and there must be increased difficulty for the child in school, friendships, and or age-appropriate caring for oneself.

Positive symptoms include:

- delusions, which are beliefs not based on reality, such as that people are watching or conspiring against you

- hallucinations, during which you see or hear things that don't exist, especially voices

- incoherent speech, which often appears as an inability to maintain a conversation because the child is illogical or goes off-topic

- random or unnecessary motor behavior, which can range from silliness to agitation, or catatonic behavior

Negative symptoms include:

- reduced emotional expression
- lack of motivation
- social withdrawal
- diminished speech

Treatments: Evidence-Based Therapies and Medication

For each of these disorders, treatment will likely involve some combination of talk therapy and medicines—and bipolar disorders and schizophrenia will always require the use of medications. (See appendices B and C.)

Therapies

The most effective therapies for these disorders are forms of cognitive behavioral therapy, often in combination with family therapy or work with parents. (For example, two family therapy programs—Family Focused Therapy and the Rainbow Program—have been found effective in treating bipolar disorders.) These evidence-based therapy techniques work to remediate or compensate for cognitive deficits (such as memory or attention issues), teach behavioral or social skills, and educate the child and parents about the illness in general. More broadly, the therapies provide emotional support and build the skills the child needs to function effectively.

For depression and PDD, talking with a therapist is the most common intervention, in part because the therapy can assist the child to identify their negative feelings and the situations that provoke them. (Like in the case of Mike, who erroneously thought people were making fun of him or ignoring him.) Counseling can also help build self-esteem and teach emotional coping strategies and better social skills, all of which will help improve a child's friendships. Together, the therapist and the child will develop strategies to decrease negative thoughts and emotions, to keep them from interfering with academic and social life, and to improve learning and performance in school—which, in turn, helps to diminish the negativity.

Often teachers and guidance counselors can also participate in these positive strategies. In particular, they can help the child build more successful interactions with other children at school. Informed consent from the parents is required, however, before the therapist can communicate with anyone about a child's treatment, except in certain emergency situations.

Specific Forms of Therapy

Cognitive behavioral therapy (as I have described in treatments for other diagnoses) is a highly effective treatment that decreases many symptoms within three months and maintains gains. It works by changing cognitive distortions—that is, mistaken interpretations of an event or interaction—and teaching problem-solving and coping strategies. This is the type of therapy I used effectively with Mike, as I described at the beginning of this chapter.

Interpersonal psychotherapy (IPT), a form of cognitive behavioral therapy specifically developed for depression, teaches adolescents how to:

- self-monitor feelings: *I feel sad.*
- problem-solve: *What else could I do in this situation?*
- link feelings to events: *I feel sad because my friend didn't call me back.*
- foster communication skills: *I can approach other kids by calling or texting.*

As in all successful psychotherapy, in IPT the therapist empathically engages with the child, helps the child to feel understood and voice emotions, and provides a clear rationale and process for the treatment. IPT is built on two major principles:

- Depression is a medical illness, rather than the child's fault or a personal defect; moreover, it is a treatable condition. This definition helps children to avoid blaming themselves.

- Mood is related to what is going on in one's life. As a result, IPT focuses on the link between the patient's mood and disturbing life events that either trigger or follow the onset of the disorder.

Depression often follows a disturbing event or change, such as the death of a loved one, a disruptive move, or a physical illness. Once patients become depressed, the symptoms damage their relationships, and bad events can follow. Many depressed children turn inward, blaming themselves and losing sight of positive things in their life—and in spite of everything they seem outwardly fine to the adults in their lives. Whether the disturbing events follow or precede mood changes, the patient's task in therapy is to resolve the disturbance, rebuild social skills, and begin to reorganize her life. If the child can resolve the life problem, depressive symptoms will likely resolve as well.

For parents, dealing with depression, PDD, bipolar disorder, or schizophrenia can be frustrating since the symptoms are so persistent. Reacting negatively, however, can make things worse for everyone. So can simply accepting the situation and ignoring one's own negative mood or depression.

Family therapy often helps parents to understand their child's mood disorder and, more important, establish positive parenting routines and improve their communication and interaction with their child. Regaining hope and learning to be positive are important for all members of the family.

Finally, some children benefit from a social skills training group (see chapter 9) in addition to individual and family therapy.

Medication

In some cases, medication can be helpful for depression or PDD. It will always be recommended for bipolar disorder and schizophrenia. At times, a pediatrician may prescribe an antidepressant, but often a child psychiatrist is the professional to consult. Because there are many types of antidepressants, a doctor with the right qualifications should be involved in selecting the best option. Moreover, because antidepressants used with children and adolescents have been associated with increased reports of suicidal thoughts (although this is somewhat controversial), professional as well as parental supervision during the initial weeks of medication is important.

Here is a useful, commonsense approach to medication drawn from "Bipolar Disorder in Children and Teens," a publication of the NIMH.

Children respond to medications in different ways, so the type or combination of medications should be carefully chosen to meet your child's unique needs. It is also important to remember to be patient when beginning a trial of a medication; most antidepressants don't take effect for a while, often between ten days and three weeks, and the prescription may require adjustments.

Whatever the specifics of the medications, children should take the lowest doses of medications possible to treat their symptoms. A good way to remember this, as the NIMH suggests, is to "start low, go slow." Keep a list handy of any possible side effects and remember to chart your child's behavior. But don't ever stop medications without first consulting with your treatment provider. Stopping medication abruptly can make many symptoms worse and can be dangerous.

Sometimes a child's symptoms may change in length, duration, or intensity. Bad periods may lengthen, or sadness may give way to irritability. When symptoms change, treatment may need to change, too.

Treatment through medication can take time, but trying it long enough to give it a chance to work causes many children and teens to have fewer symptoms. Medicine can be worth it, despite the complications. Left untreated, depression or one of the other disorders described in this chapter can be much more devastating for a child—socially, physically, and academically—than any side effects of the medication.

8

Picky Eating and Eating Too Much: Does My Child Have an Eating Disorder?

Gina

Gina was sixteen and in tenth grade. Her parents called me because she was falling behind at the prestigious girls' school she attended. For a long time, her parents felt that she simply wasn't trying hard enough, but lately they were starting to believe that she might have dyslexia, a learning disorder.

Gina's history is pretty typical of what I see in my practice. Families tend to enter my practice when their child is in the third, seventh, or tenth grade—when the academic curriculum shifts—on the assumption that students have thoroughly mastered all the material in the grades below. For example, algebra assumes basic math abilities in addition and subtraction. As a result, a child who previously was able just to work harder or with a tutor to cover for a learning issue can no longer keep up.

When Gina arrived for her first appointment with me, she didn't seem concerned that she was falling behind in school. She thought that she was doing well enough with a C average and that her parents, and in particular her father, were just being too hard on her. She felt that she was not very smart and would never be a good student, and she didn't see the need to do testing for a learning disability. "My parents just don't understand that I won't be a lawyer or a doctor one day," she told me. Like many sixteen-year-old girls I see, she was more interested in boys—especially one boy who was much older—than in studying.

After I took a detailed history about her family, medical history, and school performance from Gina and her mother, Gina and I met in two additional sessions for testing to determine if she had a learning disability. The testing involved a number of pencil-and-paper tests, some like school tests and others more like puzzles. The tests revealed that she did have a learning disability, but it wasn't in reading.

Gina's ability in executive function was severely impaired, meaning she had difficulty in planning events; inhibiting an impulse, such as walking around when she should be sitting; not overeating; and switching from one task to another. In fact, on a scale of 1 to 10, with 10 being excellent, her ability in this area was a 1. What this meant for school was that she was extremely disorganized and that, when she read, she could rarely understand the bigger picture of what she was supposed to comprehend. Her essays were poorly organized, and her ability to follow complex instructions was almost nonexistent.

By the time I met with Gina to discuss her test results, she and I had spent about fourteen hours together over the course of three days. I started my feedback session with her by talking about her strengths, such as her social skills, ability in math, and vocabulary. She could likely do anything she wanted with the right help, such as a tutor.

I then moved the conversation to specific steps to help her: break her work into short segments, get a tutor to help organize and prioritize her work, and work with questions at the beginning of a book to help her extract the bigger picture from the assigned reading. During this feedback session, Gina seemed distant at times, and about three-quarters of the way through I stopped and asked her if she was all right. She burst into tears and began uncontrollably sobbing. We sat there for a good while and I just let her cry.

When she was finally ready to speak, I asked what the tears were for, since her crying seemed inconsistent with the young girl who declared that she cared very little about school. She explained that the previous night, her father had found out she was dating a twenty-four-year-old guy and had been sneaking out to meet him. As a result her father had tweeted her phone number, writing, "For a good time, call Gina: XXX-XXXX."

Gina went on to confide in me something that was even more concerning. For more than seven years she had been bingeing and purging, using laxatives to control her weight. More recently, she had been vomiting blood.

Her parents had no idea, and she did not wish to tell them. She had learned to disguise how thin she was with baggy clothes.

The immediate issue was to check her physical health, but that would require telling her parents about her condition. One of the hardest things you have to do as a therapist is breach confidentiality, but I explained, as I had at our first session, that if I considered Gina to be a danger to herself that I had to speak with her parents. She called her parents and asked them to come to the session. Her mother readily agreed to leave work, but her father said he was too busy. When her mother came to my office, Gina and I told her what Gina had relayed to me. It turned out that her mother had suspected this for some time and was somewhat relieved to get answers.

Her mother and I then walked Gina over to the emergency room just two blocks away and had her admitted for a workup to make certain her eating issues had not caused her medical harm. I also referred the family to the eating disorders clinic at the hospital.

A week later, when I called to check in with Gina and her mother, Gina told me that although her father had agreed to allow her to continue to see me, he had refused to allow her to be admitted as an inpatient in the hospital, which would have provided a protected environment in which she could stabilize both her weight and her behavior. I then conferred with the hospital. They believed that Gina was medically stable, although she had destroyed the enamel on her teeth with the stomach acid from so much vomiting, and her hair was falling out as a result of depriving her body of the nutrients it needed. However, the hospital believed the family was in need of family therapy.

Over the next two years, I worked with Gina and her parents. The first part of our work involved cognitive behavioral therapy, with the goal of understanding the thoughts that were causing Gina to binge and purge. Gina and I also worked to empower her mother to take more control of Gina's eating until Gina's weight was stabilized. For example, they ate all meals together in the morning and evening and agreed in advance what Gina would eat for lunch.

Her mother, Gina, and I concluded that Gina's episodes of eating and throwing up were often triggered by a fight with her father. Rather than deal with her feelings, she would eat, and often very large amounts: a bag of chips, a gallon of ice cream or two, and a liter of soda with five or six candy bars. This binge would be followed by a three- or four-hour session in the bathroom, sticking her fingers down her throat or drinking a mixture of a laxative, mustard, ketchup, and mayonnaise that would cause her to vomit.

Initially, Gina, her mother, and I were able to stabilize her weight and change her behavior so that she was purging much less, down from four or five times a week. Then slowly over time, her mother and I were able to transfer the control of her eating back to Gina. Her mother came to sessions to help improve communication between the two of them, but Gina's father appeared infrequently. When he did come, he was sullen and expressed doubts that it was worth his time.

After two years, at eighteen, Gina was able to move away from home and go to college. After about a year of being away at school, Gina made an appointment with me when she came home during spring break. When I asked how she was doing, she said fine, although her grades were mediocre in spite of the tutoring and special assistance I had helped arrange with the college. She seemed happy and said that her life was going OK. She admitted that because of the pressures of school she would sometimes still purge, perhaps once every other month, but that she had joined a support group at college. She was also seeing an individual therapist through the student health center.

At that point she stopped and asked me, "Do you feel that my father will ever love me?"

I answered that I thought her father did love her, but that he would never be able to show her that love in the way she wanted and needed. I also explained that grappling with facts like these was the work of all of us as adults. Seeing our parents as humans, with both good and bad traits, and choosing not to be ruled by trying to please them are difficult tasks for all of us. I explained that her father's inability to show his affection in the way she needed was *his* problem; it wasn't that she wasn't good enough.

She thanked me and said she understood. That was our last session, and she graduated from college and got married shortly afterward.

When people enter my practice with their child, they usually come because of a specific problem that is affecting their child's behavior and, sometimes, the family as a whole. Often, however, there is a larger, more serious issue influencing their lives. But they can focus only on the smaller issue because the larger issue is just too overwhelming or because, as big as it is, it is harder to grasp or more difficult to discern.

In my practice, perhaps the best examples of this phenomenon have been cases that involved teens with eating disorders. For example, families will come to me seeking testing for what they perceive to be a learning disorder or other difficulty their child is having in school, when in fact the teen has a much more serious issue to contend with: they are starving themselves.

According to a study conducted by the Agency for Healthcare Research and Quality, hospitalizations for eating disorders in children under the age of twelve rose by 119 percent between 1999 and 2006. More recent numbers aren't yet available, but experts say the problem isn't getting any better. With eating disorders on the rise, it is vital for parents to distinguish between their child's somewhat quirky adolescent eating preferences, such as living on junk food, and signs that indicate the start of an eating disorder. This chapter will help you make that distinction by understanding the symptoms of an eating disorder.

Types of Problematic Behaviors

Does your child:

- hoard or hide food?
- throw up after meals or spend long hours in the bathroom after eating?
- hate all healthy foods, such as vegetables, protein, or fruits?
- eat too much, especially unhealthy foods such as chips, soda, and candy?

Possible Diagnoses

Eating disorders in children and teens can lead to major, life-threatening health problems as a result of a persistent and severe disturbance in a child's eating patterns. Three types of eating disorders are most commonly identified in children.

- *anorexia nervosa*: eating far too little because of an irrational fear of gaining weight or becoming fat, and a distorted perception of one's shape or weight

- *bulimia nervosa*: recurrent bingeing followed by vomiting or using laxatives to avoid gaining weight, usually accompanied by worries about one's weight or shape, such as a conviction that one is too fat
- *binge eating*: eating that is out of control, such as eating large quantities of food, sometimes quite rapidly, without purging

Children may exhibit the symptoms of more than one of these disorders simultaneously. For example, Gina alternated between periods of anorexia and bulimia.

Eating disorders can start in childhood, and I have seen the disorders in girls as young as eight or nine. The disorders are much more common among females, according to studies sponsored by the National Institute of Mental Health. That said, boys are vulnerable too: an estimated 5 to 15 percent of people with anorexia or bulimia are male and, according to the NIMH, that percentage is rising. Approximately 35 percent of binge eaters are male.

What Causes Eating Disorders?

Mental health professionals and researchers aren't certain what causes eating disorders. As with many other issues I discuss in this book, researchers suspect a combination of genetic, behavioral, environmental, physiological, and social-cultural factors. For example, and perhaps most pressing today, on a social level young girls may be influenced by images projected in movies, TV, and magazines that depict unhealthily underweight female bodies as desirable. Women are praised for their beauty more often than for their brains, and this pattern begins in early childhood. Think about it: how many times have you commented on how smart a girl is, rather than how pretty or cute? In males, these disorders are often tied to athletic performance and the need for a lean and muscular physique.

If a child has an eating disorder, it may be accompanied, as it was in Gina, by other problems, such as low self-esteem, feelings of helplessness, or lack of control at school or with life in general. Eating disorders often occur in the context of other mental health problems, some of which you have already read about in these pages, such as anxiety disorders, depression, and substance abuse. For example, to cope with a problem such as low self-esteem, children may adopt harmful eating habits as a comfort or as a means of controlling at least one thing when they can't control most of their lives. While Gina's case was certainly influenced by her family dynamic, there is still uncertainty about the role of the family in causing an eating disorder.

The Consequences of Eating Disorders

Eating disorders in children and teens can result in serious medical problems including damage to major organs. In extreme cases, they can even lead to death. If you spot symptoms that lead you to suspect an eating disorder, call your child's pediatrician right away. Eating disorders are not overcome by simply telling children to try harder not to overeat or vomit. A doctor will stabilize them medically, and treatment by a mental health professional can then help them change their eating habits and address the underlying psychological issues. As is the case with other childhood mental health issues, the best results occur when eating disorders are treated by a qualified professional at the earliest stages.

Anorexia

Children with anorexia are convinced they are overweight even when they are thin, perhaps even dangerously thin. Because they want so badly to be skinny, they can fall dangerously below a normal weight. According to the National Institute of Mental Health's data, about one out of every twenty-five females will have anorexia during her life. Because sufferers have a distorted body image, however, most will deny that they are anorexic and may even be unaware that they have a problem.

The symptoms may include:

- extreme dieting, or an intense fear of becoming fat, despite being thin
- compulsive exercising
- infrequent or no menstruation
- rapid weight loss, sometimes concealed by loose clothing
- avoiding meals, eating in secret, or other unusual eating habits
- unusual interest in how food is prepared or its texture or colors
- unrealistic perception of weight itself or importance of weight to self-image

Treating Anorexia

In treating anorexia, the first goal is to restore a child to her normal weight and reestablish healthy eating habits. If there is severe malnutrition, the child may need to be fed intravenously or through a tube. Even if that is not the case, she may require hospitalization to monitor physical problems such as internal bleeding.

Long-term treatment tackles the psychological roots of anorexia. It may include some combination of behavioral therapy, psychotherapy, support groups, and antidepressant medication.

Bulimia

Bulimia is roughly as prevalent among women as anorexia. Children with bulimia, like those with anorexia, dislike their bodies and fear becoming fat. In contrast, they will repeatedly binge on food. Afterward they will make themselves vomit or use laxatives, diet pills, diuretics, or enemas to avoid gaining weight. As a result, they usually maintain a relatively normal weight, although some are overweight.

For a formal diagnosis of bulimia, there must be a persistent pattern: two or more episodes of overeating, followed by compensating behaviors such as purging, per week for at least three months.

Symptoms may include:

- a lack of control over eating
- consuming excessive quantities of food quickly
- unusual eating habits such as eating secretly or only at specific times, or taking an unusual length of time to eat
- vomiting or using laxatives or other medications after eating to prevent weight gain
- regularly occupying the bathroom after eating
- overemphasis on physical appearance, perhaps accompanied by excessive exercising
- scarred knuckles from inducing vomiting with one's fingers

Bulimia can lead to severe health consequences. For example, stomach acids from chronic vomiting can damage tooth enamel and inflame the esophagus, and purging can reduce potassium levels, leading to abnormal heart rhythms.

Treating Bulimia

The goal is always to end the binge-and-purge cycle. Treatment will likely include some combination of medication, behavioral therapy with the child and family or with a group, and nutritional counseling.

Binge Eating

Like children who are bulimic, those who binge eat engage in chronic binge-ing on food, but they do not then purge afterward. Not surprisingly, they often—although not always—become overweight or obese. To qualify for the diagnosis, binge episodes must occur at least once a week, on average, for three months.

Binge eaters may be having trouble handling their emotions, and the typical angst of adolescence, which is often replete with anger, stress, or sadness—even boredom—may trigger a binge. For example, I once treated a college student who was preparing for the exams required to apply to graduate school. She had no previous history of an eating disorder but lately had started to eat a gallon of ice cream, a bag of potato chips, and several candy bars at night before going to bed. She had a binge-eating disorder.

Often, binge eaters may become depressed because of their overeating. In addition, if they become overweight they may suffer some of the typical problems related to obesity, such as high blood pressure, elevated cholesterol, heart disease, and type 2 diabetes.

Treating Binge Eating

Similarly to other eating disorder treatments, treatments for binge eating will include some combination of medications and therapy.

Obesity

These days, it seems as if more and more children in the United States are becoming obese. According to the American Academy of Child and

Adolescent psychiatry, between 16 and 33 percent of children and adolescents are now classified as obese. And studies cited by the academy show that a child who is obese between the ages of ten and thirteen has an 80 percent chance of remaining obese as an adult. Both medically and economically, it is a large—no pun intended—problem. Obesity not only damages individuals' health, contributing to more than three hundred thousand deaths in the United States each year, but it also costs the country nearly $100 billion in medical bills and other health costs.

The line between being overweight and obese may be somewhat fuzzy, but the World Health Organization defines obesity as abnormal or excessive fat accumulation that presents a risk to an individual's health. Under the guidelines of the American Academy of Child and Adolescent Psychiatry, children are not considered obese until their weight is at least 10 percent greater than what is recommended for their height and body type.

Obesity is not currently considered to be a mental health disorder, but its treatment often involves addressing an underlying mental health issue, such as anxiety or depression, which can cause a child or teen to overeat as a form of coping. Obesity's causes include genetic and biological as well as behavioral and cultural factors. Medications, such as steroids and some psychiatric medications, can also be a cause, as can certain medical disorders such as endocrine and neurological problems—although less than 1 percent of all obesity is caused by physical problems. The condition tends to run in families: if one parent is obese, for example, there is a 50 percent chance that their children will also be obese; when both parents are obese, the odds increase to 80 percent.

Most often, obesity in childhood arises from:

- behaviors such as poor eating habits or lack of exercise
- stressful life events or changes
- family and peer problems
- psychological or emotional issues, such as low self-esteem or depression

Whatever the causes, obesity can lead to emotional and physical problems even if they were not the cause. Teens with weight problems tend to have much lower self-esteem and be less popular with their peers, putting them at a greater risk for bullying. Physical consequences of obesity include increased risk of heart disease, high blood pressure, diabetes, breathing problems, and trouble sleeping.

If your child is obese, you should first have her evaluated by a pediatrician to rule out a physical cause. If there is no physical cause, she will be able to lose weight only by reducing her intake of calories and increasing her physical activity. (The math of this is simple, and there are no shortcuts or quick fixes in spite of what the diet industry tries to sell us. Quite simply, 3,500 calories equals one pound, and you must eat less or burn more calories than that to lose one pound.) Weight loss will occur only if she is motivated, and the family can help by establishing healthy eating and regular exercise as family routines. On the other hand, if an obese child does not change her eating and exercising habits, obesity frequently becomes a lifelong issue.

Ways to Treat Obesity

- participate in a formal weight-management program
- plan meals and select healthier foods
- change eating habits (for example, eating only at certain times, eating slowly or eating smaller portions, and eating meals as a family at a table)
- increase exercise or other physical activity

In addition, parents of an obese child should emphasize her strengths rather than focusing just on her weight problem—especially because the problem is often a symptom of a larger issue that needs to be addressed. When a child with obesity also has emotional problems, a children's mental health worker can work with the family to develop a treatment plan for managing diet and physical activity, with the goal of changing the behaviors that are causing or maintaining the problem.

Start slowly, make it fun, and get moving.

Other Possible Treatments

A range of treatments, including individual cognitive behavioral therapy and family therapy, has been used to tackle eating disorders in children. Although the studies are few, most show that effective treatments of eating disorders in adolescents involve some sort of family therapy. In fact, approximately two-thirds of patients in such studies were helped the most by family therapy. I provided this therapy for Gina and her family, and it clearly helped—even though one of the parents was not frequently involved.

Successful family therapy involves the following components:

- removing the blame from the child or the parents for the eating disorder
- having parents and the child attend sessions with the therapist together
- coaching the parents to support the child in healthy eating habits
- restoring the parents' authority to take control over the child's eating
- returning control of eating to the child once she has reached a healthy weight
- focusing on developmental milestones, such as an appropriate amount of independence for a certain age once the child has reached a target weight

The two most common types of family therapy for eating disorders, among those supported by good research, are behavioral-systems therapy and Maudsley (named after its founder) family-based treatment. These two types of therapy in essence use the methods described previously.

9

Bullying and Aggression: Could My Child Have Oppositional Defiant or Conduct Disorder?

I OFTEN MEET with groups of parents to talk about their concerns about their kids' behavior and their parenting. At almost every event, I hear such sad stories of kids being mean to other kids. Teens tell me that these behaviors are worst in the middle-school years. At that stage, when the need to be accepted by peers is at its peak, bullying becomes a means of deflecting their insecurities about their own acceptance in a group, which is so often predicated on excluding others. Teens also report that they often don't talk with adults about these problems because it can make the problems worse. It's true that parents shouldn't intervene in every disagreement or overreact by pulling their child out of school. It's important to give your child some tools for negotiation and to teach "turning the other cheek" problem-solving skills. However, sometimes it is important to intervene. The key is to listen carefully and to look for the duration, intensity, and impact issues described in chapter 1.

Rebekah

One recent story from Rebekah, who was fourteen, involved relational aggression—that is, using relationships to harm another's relationships with their peers. While used by both sexes, relational aggression is primarily employed by girls and, in some cases, has been found to be more harmful than physical aggression.

Rebekah told me that she brought her lunch to school. Her mother packed her a special treat, dark chocolate almonds. Rebekah didn't want to disappoint her mother, but she didn't want the almonds and gave them to her friend Joan every day. Then one day, Rebekah decided she wanted to keep the almonds for herself. When she did, Joan spread nasty rumors about Rebekah to the other girls and told them they shouldn't speak to her. The other girls complied, leaving Rebekah feeling terribly alone and very isolated.

This sort of relational aggression is considered a form of bullying, and it happens on a daily basis among groups of teenage girls. Moreover, some researchers believe that this sort of behavior among young girls carries over into adulthood, leading women to feel competition, envy, and jealousy toward other women in the workplace and to behave in ways that are unsupportive and even undercutting of each other.

Bullying is on the rise. As you see in the news almost every day, social media outlets provide even greater opportunities for kids to bully other kids. But what if your child isn't mean to other kids but seems to be mean to you: disobedient, hostile, or constantly defiant? I have put these issues in the same chapter because they both involve a child who is acting out—either by hurting other kids or by defying your rules—and these sorts of behaviors often stem from the same sorts of diagnoses. Whether your child breaks the rules with other kids or with you, you should know how to identify when your child is more than just strong-willed in his refusal to comply with your directions, learn about effective bullying prevention programs, and know how to stop your child from falling victim to or victimizing other kids.

Types of Problematic Behaviors

Does your child:

- often lose his temper?
- often get into arguments with you or other adults?
- refuse to follow the rules set by you or other adults?
- often seem angry and resentful?
- cause or seem likely to cause damage to property?
- act aggressively or in a very controlling way toward his friends?

Bullying

Bullying can take a variety of forms, either physical or, as you read about with Rebekah, verbal. Boys most often bully in physical ways, while bullying by girls is more often verbal, usually focused on another girl as the victim. Whatever the form, bullying can damage a child's relationships and self-confidence in ways that can have long-lasting effects. Some victims of bullying have been so humiliated that they have committed suicide to escape harassment and ridicule. Although bullying and relational aggression are not included as diagnoses in the DSM, I discuss them here because they have become so pervasive and problematic for kids.

Unfortunately, bullying is a huge problem in our schools, and it also seems to be occurring more frequently online, especially through social networking sites. Studies show that many schoolchildren, perhaps as many as half, are bullied at some point, and at least 10 percent are bullied on a regular basis.

At its core, bullying is about power. Children who bully thrive on controlling others. However, bullies have often been the victims of physical abuse or bullying themselves. They may also be depressed, angry, or upset about their lives. Additionally, bullying can damage the one doing the bullying, emotionally and academically. In this chapter's "Possible Treatments" section, I provide some guidance about what to do if your child is bullying or being bullied.

Relational Aggression

Girls frequently use their relationships with peers to bully other girls, such as by spreading rumors, persuading a group to shun someone, or simply refusing to talk to the target. This form of bullying can be harder to detect than physical bullying, but the psychological effects on the victim can be devastating.

Relational aggression stems from the fact that girls have a more difficult time than boys expressing their frustrations because they are taught that "good girls" shouldn't show anger. In addition, because children in our culture are predominantly raised by women, girls learn to be girls in the context of a same-sex relationship. Psychologically, this sets girls up to value sameness. By contrast, boys learn to be boys by being different from their mothers, so it is much easier for them to learn to deal early on with conflict and expressing difference.

As a consequence, girls are less likely to disagree openly with friends or playmates. Instead, they will often just take their dolls and go home, expressing that disagreement passively rather than through the use of words. As girls grow older, rather than directly address the behavior of a friend, they will lash out by asking other girls to shun the target or spreading rumors about her. Similarly, if girls feel jealousy toward someone, they will frequently act out these feelings by the same methods. That can then set off an entire cascade of similar events in a group.

The best way to combat relational aggression is to teach girls how to express their emotions, including anger and frustration, honestly and openly. This can be as simple as leading by example. Showing your daughter how to deal with uncomfortable emotions as they arise will help her avoid acting them out on others.

While bullying, whatever form it takes, is not a formal diagnostic category, the following two behaviors, oppositional defiant disorder and conduct disorder, are defined by the DSM as disorders in self-control of emotions and behaviors.

Oppositional Defiant Disorder (ODD)

Betty

A few years ago, I was running a program for young children with emotional and behavioral problems. A mother and father came to see me with their four-year-old daughter, Betty, who was having difficulty getting along with others in preschool and following her teacher's directions. When Betty played outside during breaks, she would frequently throw a tantrum when her teacher tried to get her to come back into the classroom. At home, Betty would frequently play the same song over and over, and she would get "stuck" playing with the same toy until it was worn and dirty beyond repair. Her father called me to say that Betty had recently been diagnosed with oppositional defiant disorder (ODD) on the basis of a checklist used by another provider at their local hospital. They wanted to know if I could help.

When Betty arrived at my office, I was astounded to see that she was missing large chunks of hair on her head. When I asked her mother and father about it, they said that no one had ever asked them about it before! I then proceeded to take a full history, during which I discovered that Betty's mother had been diagnosed with obsessive-compulsive disorder when she was a child. After spending an hour talking with the parents, I proceeded to play with Betty and to observe her with other children in our play area. After a time, I told the parents what I thought.

Betty had trichotillomania, which researchers think is a type of OCD. Basically, it is compulsive hair pulling. That coupled with the family history of OCD and some other behaviors that fit the current profile of OCD led me to believe that Betty was not defiant or oppositional; she just couldn't stop playing. For example, I observed her with a small cricket outdoors. Even when I tried to redirect her or take the cricket away she refused to play with anything else and broke down crying. If I were willing to play with the cricket, however, she could interact with me (or another child) quite normally. I told her parents that I knew of effective behavioral treatments for this kind of obsessive behavior that would allow us to teach her new coping mechanisms. I would have her practice those new skills while we gradually exposed Betty to situations that caused her to start obsessing.

I started treatment right away and, within a few months, her parents and I were able to see Betty's compulsive behaviors lessen. She also did much better in preschool.

All kids are contentious or argumentative at times. They talk back, disobey, or set out to do what they know their parents don't want them to do. Especially for two- to three-year-olds and early adolescents, this kind of oppositional behavior is not only normal, it is an important developmental step as they learn to assert themselves and become more independent. However, there's a difference between a normal pattern and openly hostile behavior that is so frequent that it clearly differs from the behavior of other children the same age. If there are repeated instances of uncooperative, defiant, and hostile behavior toward adult authority figures in the child's life that continue over time and seriously interfere with his ability to be in school or to be part of regular family activities, ODD is a possible diagnosis.

Symptoms of ODD include:

- a pattern of defiance of adult requests and rules, or of excessive arguing about them

- deliberate attempts to upset or annoy people

- blaming mistakes or misbehavior on others

- frequently being touchy or easily annoyed by others

- frequent anger, resentment, or temper tantrums

- seeking revenge or spitefulness

As many as 16 percent of school-aged children and adolescents have ODD. Although the root causes of ODD are not well understood, biological, psychological, and social factors can all play a role. Some research suggests that children with the disorder may have subtle abnormalities in the parts of their brains responsible for judgment and impulse control. They may also have more trouble reading social cues correctly, thus increasing the chances they will respond inappropriately. Many parents of children with ODD report that from an early age their child was more rigid and demanding than his siblings.

Conduct Disorder

Although ODD and conduct disorder have overlapping symptoms, conduct disorder typically involves more serious behaviors that may be more difficult to address. ODD can develop into conduct disorder, and the research indicates that about 30 percent of ODD children eventually develop the more serious disorder.

Children with conduct disorder have great difficulty following rules and behaving in socially acceptable ways. They are often viewed by peers, adults, and social agencies as bad or delinquent. They may exhibit some of the following behaviors and, for a diagnosis to be given, they must have exhibited three of these behaviors in the past twelve months, with at least one in the last six months.

Aggression to People or Animals

- frequently bullies, threatens, or intimidates others

- often initiates physical fights

- uses a weapon against others that could cause serious physical harm, such as a broken bottle
- has been physically cruel to people or animals
- has stolen while confronting a victim
- has forced someone into sexual activity

Destruction of Property

- has deliberately set a fire with the intention of causing damage or deliberately destroyed property

Deceitfulness or Theft

- steals or breaks into buildings or cars
- lies to obtain items or favors to avoid obligations
- steals items of nontrivial value without confronting the victim, such as shoplifting

Serious Violations of Rules

- often stays out at night despite parental limit setting
- has run away from parent's home overnight at least twice without returning for a lengthy time
- often truant from school (before the age of thirteen)

Many factors may contribute to a child's developing conduct disorder, including genetic vulnerability, child abuse or neglect, and other traumas.

Possible Treatments

Dealing with Bullying and Being Bullied

If you suspect your child is consistently bullying others, ask for professional help. A mental health professional can help you understand what is causing the bullying and develop a plan to stop the destructive behavior. The treatment will vary according to the underlying reasons for the child's behavior (e.g., depression or conduct disorder).

On the flip side, if your child is being bullied, talk to him about it openly and straightforwardly, emphasizing that it's not his fault. Children are often reluctant to talk about being bullied because they feel embarrassed or humiliated, so it is important to do everything you can to restore their self-esteem. Other specific suggestions include the following:

- Help your child practice what to say to the bully, in a way that is assertive but does not escalate the confrontation. Simply insisting that the bully leave him alone may have a surprising effect.

- Ask your child what he thinks should be done and what he has already tried.

- Ask your child's teacher or school guidance counselor for help.

- Encourage your child to be with friends whenever possible, especially when traveling back and forth from school. Bullies are less likely to pick on a child who is in a group.

In addition to individual treatments, some approaches have consistently been proven effective when addressing bullying school-wide. The US Department of Health and Human Services has proposed best practices that you may want to make certain are implemented, at least in some form, at your child's school. The aim of most of those interventions is to change the social norms at the school so that bullying is no longer considered an acceptable activity.

Zero-Tolerance Policies

Zero-tolerance policies punish any infraction of a rule, regardless of accidental mistakes, ignorance, or extenuating circumstances. They have proven to be ineffective and in most cases do more harm than good. They don't offer school personnel enough flexibility to deal with situations that are complex, and most bullying situations are indeed complex.

Zero tolerance began as weapons prevention. In 1994, Congress required states to adopt laws that guaranteed one-year expulsions for any student who brought a firearm to school. All fifty states adopted such laws as a condition for receiving federal funding. Many legislatures went further, expanding the definition of a weapon and broadening the zero-tolerance policies to include other behaviors. Now, zero tolerance has been overlaid on the issues of bullying, drugs, alcohol, and any act of violence, be it physical, verbal, or attitudinal. Often, zero tolerance interferes with a teacher's ability to make fair and appropriate disciplinary decisions.

A zero-tolerance policy can often end up targeting the victim it should protect. For example, if a child who has previously been the victim of an attack decides one day to defend himself, he can often find himself suspended right along with the bully who had previously been the instigator of the aggression. It may be that school personnel didn't witness the prior incidents or that the child who was getting bullied finally "upped" the bullying to a level that got the administration's attention. Under most zero-tolerance policies there is no latitude for the school in fitting the level of punishment to the level of involvement.

Zero-tolerance policies can also take away a thoughtful teacher's ability to settle minor incidents of misconduct or poor behavior, or to use incidents as teachable moments and prevent future bullying. Recently, in a kindergarten class in New York City during free play, a number of children exposed themselves. Let's assume the teacher wanted to use the incident as a teaching moment, by talking to the students about what they had done. Tough luck: under the zero-tolerance policy, she was required to report the incident to the administrator. The administrator then dealt with the situation by expelling half of the kindergarten class.

Treating Oppositional Defiant Disorder

For children with ODD, treatment usually includes a type of psychotherapy and parent training. The treatment often lasts for months, if not longer, and involves the parents as well as the child. Medications aren't generally prescribed for ODD alone, but they can be helpful if another disorder, such as ADHD, is also present in the child, as is sometimes the case.

Types of ODD therapy may include:

- *Individual and family therapy*: individual therapy helps your child to manage anger and express feelings in more constructive ways. Family counseling may help the family communicate and interact more effectively.

- *Cognitive problem-solving training*: this therapy helps your child identify and change the inaccurate or negative thought patterns that lead to his problem behavior. Through a method called collaborative problem solving, you and your child may also find ways of changing his behaviors together.

- *Social skills training*: this form of therapy teaches your child how to interact with peers more effectively and less aggressively.

- *Parent training*: the goal of this training is to help you find ways to interact with your child that are less frustrating for both of you and that address problems more effectively. Parent training teaches you to avoid power struggles and remain calm in the face of push-back or testing from your child, recognize and praise your child's positive characteristics and good behaviors (I call this "catching your child being good"), give your child some age-appropriate control by offering him choices that are acceptable to you, schedule family meals that will be eaten at home together and activities for the child with one or both parents, and give effective time-outs, limiting other consequences to ones that can be applied consistently and are relatively brief.

As simple as some of these techniques may sound, using them with a child who has ODD is difficult. They require persistence, practice, and patience. Despite the stresses and your own emotions, it's critical to continue to consistently express that you love and accept your child, even when his behavior is at its most difficult. But don't expect perfection from yourself. No matter how patient you try to be, living with ODD will be tough.

Although traditional behavior therapies work with most children, as many as 20 percent of children don't respond to them, as research shows and as I have found in my own practice. In those cases—although it is based on less evidence than many of the treatments described previously—a system called collaborative problem solving (CPS) can sometimes be quite effective.

As described by the REACH Institute, CPS views the child's behavior as an ineffective attempt to solve a problem in his life. The chosen solution may seem entirely unacceptable, even outrageous, to others, but the child has no other way of dealing with the problem. CPS asks parents to figure out what the problem is from the child's perspective, such as trying to control an unpredictable environment or being unable to understand adults' requests. Once the parents understand the child's problem, the next step is to help him find a different solution by using different skills and behaviors, ones that the child may have to learn and practice. This is usually a slow, step-by-step process, and it requires skilled, empathetic coaching to ensure the child is not overwhelmed by being asked to change too much too quickly.

Treating Conduct Disorder

Treatment for conduct disorder must involve both the child and parents. The most-researched treatment, parent management training, involves training parents in new techniques to handle their child's destructive behavior. Parents learn to use positive reinforcement techniques, negative consequences, active ignoring of negative behaviors, and other behavior-shaping skills to change a child's behavior.

There is very little research to support any success for the wilderness programs or boot camps that have become quite popular in recent years as a means for parents to deal with children with extreme behavioral issues. In contrast, the research suggests that treating children at home or in school, where the problematic behaviors most often occur, is most effective. Parental involvement is almost always essential to successful treatment.

A Note About Sexting, Texting, and the Internet

A large number of questions I receive from parents these days are about the use of the Internet and other new communication outlets. Unfortunately, the relative anonymity of various social media sites can increase the incidence of bullying. It is a lot easier to be mean if you aren't physically face-to-face with someone. What I tell parents generally is this: they should be limiting and supervising the use of social media sites used by their children. That includes the amount of time children spend on various sites and how they use those sites. I liken it to getting a learner's permit for driving. Start out by first monitoring all of their communications. During this time, it is important to talk openly about what they should do when they see someone else bullied or someone says something inappropriate (use examples that you see online together). As they show that they can handle the sites responsibly, you can to cut back your supervision gradually, eventually allowing them to go it alone. But always keep the door open for nonjudgmental and frank discussions about what they are seeing online.

10

Problems with Homework:
Does My Child Have
a Learning Disability?

LEARNING ISSUES ARE extremely varied, so I do not to describe a specific case here. If you suspect your child has a learning disability, the single most important piece of advice I can give you is to believe that your child *can* succeed. However, even with your support and the support of teachers, and with modifications made to how he is taught, he will have to work harder than other children. The children I have seen who have done the best at overcoming their challenges had parents who understood early on what was required, helped their children learn to advocate for themselves in school, and were determined that their children succeed in spite of their learning differences.

Types of Problematic Behaviors

Identifying learning disabilities can be difficult, but following are some typical signs. Does your child:

- do poorly on tests (when you know he has studied)?
- have difficulty doing math?
- have difficulty reading?
- have difficulty speaking?
- consistently fall behind in school?
- have difficulty relating to schoolmates because of how he communicates with them?

Most children have difficulties at school occasionally. If your child is consistently struggling with a particular subject or with school or homework in general, however, it's probably time to see if a learning disorder is at the root of those problems.

Contrary to the beliefs of many, a learning disability is not the same as a lack of intelligence. In fact, most children with these disorders are just as smart as other children, and sometimes much smarter. Children with learning difficulties simply process information differently than most of us do. Consequently, they learn differently—sometimes very differently. These learning differences affect how they absorb the information a teacher is trying to convey, which means that they often need modifications to the typical *way* the curriculum is delivered (not necessarily *what* is delivered) in the classroom so they can learn effectively.

How common are these disorders? They affect an estimated 10 to 20 percent of children and adolescents. Reading disorders are probably the most common problem, but an estimated 6 to 7 percent of elementary school children have been recognized as having a math disorder. Oftentimes children have more than one disorder. For instance, 56 percent of children with a reading disorder also show poor math achievement, and 43 percent of those with a math disorder show poor reading skills.

In this chapter are the most common learning disabilities and the most common problems that appear in children with learning issues. But first, a warning: the multisyllabic terms that professionals use to describe specific learning difficulties can be intimidating, and the differences between apparently similar disabilities can be baffling to anyone except an expert. For example, the DSM-5 devotes separate chapters to communication disorders and learning disorders, but some of the latter also involve difficulties with communication. To simplify matters, I use "learning disabilities" as the overall label for all of these disorders.

It's also worth noting that a child who is having problems in school doesn't always have a learning disability. All kinds of issues—anxiety, depression, stress, just to name a few—can make it very difficult for a child to concentrate on or care about schoolwork. In addition, ADHD sometimes occurs along with or is confused with learning disabilities. Although ADHD is not considered a learning disability diagnosis, it can certainly disrupt learning because an ADHD child will find it hard to stay focused and organized and, in some cases, even sit still throughout a class.

Types of Disorders

Difficulties with Reading

While there are a number of types of learning difficulties that involve reading, the three recognized specifically in the DSM-5 involve reading words accurately, reading rate or fluency, and reading comprehension.

The first two types create basic problems with reading. They may show up, for example, in the form of reading single words aloud incorrectly or slowly and hesitantly, frequently guessing words, or having difficulty sounding out words. These basic problems occur when a child has difficulty understanding the relationship between the sounds associated with individual letters and words. For example, a child may struggle with the sounds required to produce the word *cat*, or confuse sounds, or omit or slur their words so that "the cat chased the bird up the tree" becomes "the tac said over the frees."

Dyslexia is a well-known term for these problems. If children are dyslexic, when they read aloud they may reverse words or parts of words—for example, reading the word *cat* as if it were *tac*. They may also reverse letters and words in written language, although some children who do this do not have dyslexia. And they may also have difficulty with receptive language—the understanding of language—because they frequently have difficulties perceiving sounds or words. As a result, whether reading aloud, reading silently, or listening to spoken language, they often cannot recall important details. Often they cannot repeat phrases that are spoken to them, and they may also have difficulty following instructions. The most prominent theory about the cause of dyslexia is that it is a genetic condition, passed on through families, that changes how the brain processes information.

The third type of reading disability recognized by the DSM-5 involves poor comprehension. Reading comprehension problems include difficulty understanding broader meanings, such as the relationships among pieces of information, how information or ideas fit into a sequence, and the inferences that can be drawn from a passage. Children who have this problem may be able to recognize the words on the page, but they have trouble extracting concepts or themes from paragraphs, books, and other documents. This problem is relatively common, although it often goes unrecognized in the classroom. Its origins, including the degree to which it stems from more basic reading problems, are not yet clear. However, researchers do know that children who have comprehension difficulties may also have executive-function difficulties (such as organization or conceptualization) or attention issues (such as skipping words on a page) that interfere with their ability to extract the larger meaning from what they read.

Difficulties with Spelling and Written Expression

Although it may seem artificial to separate these difficulties from the ones just described, the DSM-5 treats them as a separate diagnostic category because they show up specifically when children write. These include problems with accuracy in spelling, grammar, and punctuation, as well as with the clarity or organization of the writing. As with all of these disorders, the problem has to be measurably worse than would be expected for the child's age and to be causing significant problems in school or life in general in order for a formal diagnosis to be given.

Difficulties with Math

The DSM-5 lists four categories of math difficulties:

- "number sense," or the ability to see the relationship among numbers and to use them for calculations or measurements
- memorizing arithmetic facts
- calculating with numbers accurately and easily
- accurate math reasoning

The first three difficulties include a poor understanding of number basics, such as their relationship and magnitude; difficulty recalling math facts as easily as the child should at their age (for example, having to use fingers to add single-digit numbers); and getting lost in math computations. Mathematical reasoning difficulties include severe difficulties applying math concepts or performing the procedures necessary to solve quantitative problems.

Learning disabilities in math are often mistaken for a lack of motivation to do math—or, in girls, to a lack of ability they or others wrongly attribute to their gender. Math disabilities can be especially difficult to diagnose because they vary greatly depending on the child's other strengths and weaknesses. A language learning disability, a visual-spatial disorder, difficulty with working memory, or a difficulty with organization will affect different areas of math, or make math in general difficult. Determining the exact nature of the difficulty is crucial for effective intervention. For example, one of my own studies found that if children have difficulties with the visual-spatial aspects of math, such as lining up numbers in columns, they can still learn math if the information is conveyed verbally.

The terms used to describe specific math difficulties can be particularly intimidating. The first three difficulties listed by the DSM are often referred to as dyscalculia, but there are other terms are used for specific forms of dyscalculia. For example, children who have difficulty performing numerical operations are often said to have anarithmetria.

Math-learning disability affects about 5 to 8 percent of school-aged children nationwide, about as many as affected by dyslexia. However, research on reading disabilities has outpaced studies of math disabilities by a margin of twenty to one.

Difficulties with Communication

In the DSM, communication disorders are placed in a different category from learning disorders, although the distinctions may be hard for a layperson to discern. The DSM lists four main types of communication disorders:

- language disorders, which result in a broad range of problems with acquiring or using language. They may show up as a limited vocabulary, difficulties in constructing sentences, or difficulties in putting sentences together to explain something or carry on a conversation.

- speech sound disorder, or difficulties pronouncing words and phonemes, which are the building blocks of words

- stuttering

- social or pragmatic communication disorder: children with this disorder typically have problems using language for social purposes, a very important skill for getting along with other kids. They may find it difficult to follow the unspoken rules of social communication, such as taking turns in conversation, or to change how they communicate to suit different situations. (See chapter 4.)

Other Learning Disorders: Auditory, Visual, and Sensory Processing Difficulties

Reading, writing, spelling, math, and communication aren't the only abilities affected by learning disorders. In addition to the learning disabilities already described, practitioners recognize others—for example, difficulties with interpreting visual information. Unfortunately, these disorders are much less likely to be identified by school personnel because many of their definitions, and even their existence, have become controversial. Many haven't yet received recognition in the DSM because there hasn't been sufficient research to validate their existence. I mention them, however, because many practitioners will diagnose them—only to leave parents unpleasantly surprised when the school will not recognize the disorders.

The disorders described below involve the eyes and the ears, the main channels by which the brain receives information.

- *auditory processing disorder*: children with this problem may be unable to distinguish subtle differences between sounds or may hear sounds at the wrong speed. Those difficulties then create problems sounding out words and, more generally, in reading and writing.

- *visual processing disorder*: just as auditory processing disorder involves difficulties with sounds, visual processing disorder involves difficulties in seeing subtle differences in shapes or seeing distances accurately. As a result, the child may, for example, confuse or reverse letters or numbers or have difficulties with hand-eye coordination. All of these difficulties, like auditory difficulties, can cause real problems at school.

- *sensory integration or processing disorder*: this is still a very controversial diagnosis, but I see a lot of children who receive it. Although it is not included in the DSM (other than as a part of another diagnosis like autism), it is included as a diagnosis for younger children in the DC-0-3R. (As you may remember, that abbreviation stands for the

Diagnostic Classification of Mental Health and Developmental Disorders of Infancy and Early Childhood, the manual written specifically for diagnosing young children.) Children with this disorder have difficulty processing information from the five major senses and responding appropriately to that information. These children typically have one or more senses that either over- or underreact to stimulation. Many professionals believe this disorder is a component of other disorders, such as autism spectrum disorders.

Difficulties with Motor Skills

These difficulties, which are referred to as dyspraxia, result in problems with coordination and movement. The problems can show up in small-scale activities such as using scissors or a ruler or in the larger-scale activities involved in sports or a gym class. In effect, the brain does not send the right signals to the limbs to control them. If your child has hand-eye coordination problems or has trouble with activities that require good hand-eye coordination abilities, such as holding a pencil or buttoning a shirt, or with activities such as running or jumping, you should explore their causes.

Children who have these difficulties may qualify for a formal diagnosis of developmental coordination disorder, the DSM-5's label for dyspraxia. The DSM places this disorder in a different category ("Motor Disorders") than learning or communication disorders, but I include it in this summary because it can also affect a child's performance at school.

Diagnosing and Treating Learning Disorders

Diagnosing a learning disability can be particularly tricky. Even experts sometimes mix up ADHD with learning disabilities or other behavioral struggles. As a result, it's important to ask for recommendations, do your research about providers, and take your time to make sure you find the right professional who will conduct an evaluation. Because diagnosis in this area requires specialized knowledge and expertise, don't hesitate to explore the professional's experience and ask about the assessments and methods he will use. You should also not hesitate to consult a second opinion if you're not comfortable with the first one.

There has been an increasing amount of good news about treating learning disorders in recent years. The progress results from an understanding of a fact I discuss in appendix A, "Brain Development 101": the brain has an inherent capacity to change in response to experience, and especially to repeated and sustained patterns of experience. This understanding about brain function has led to new treatments that strengthen weak areas of the brain through a series of exercises. In addition to exploring these treatments, however, you will probably need to collaborate with your child's school to arrange specialized help or accommodations for classroom work or testing. For some children, a public school may never be as effective as a school that specializes in educating children with learning disabilities.

The specific treatments for learning disabilities vary widely, and little research has been done on their effectiveness for problems other than reading issues. Because there are so many types of disorders, and so many possible treatments for them, it would be more confusing than helpful for me to try to summarize them all here. You will be better off researching specific treatments recommended to you by a professional. When that happens, make sure to ask for data about how effective the treatment is.

With these qualifications in mind, here is a description of the most popular evidence-based interventions for reading disorders.

Lindamood-Bell

This collection of programs, which are named for their original developers, target the fact that some children with reading disabilities don't hear the sounds of the phonemes (the smallest units of speech) that make up words in the same way everyone else does. The goal is to teach them different ways to perceive these sounds. Before instruction begins, children are given a series of tests to determine their reading strengths and weaknesses. After that assessment, an individualized education plan is designed, focusing on the skills each child needs to develop.

According to several studies, the Lindamood-Bell individualized programs can help dyslexic and severely disabled readers at all ages. The approach has also been adapted for groups and entire classrooms. There have been some promising results regarding this development, but so far there has not been enough research to be definitive about the approach's effectiveness for groups.

Inspiration.com

Kidspiration! and Inspiration! are widely used software programs that employ graphic organizers such as concept maps, idea maps, and webs. Independent research seems to show that these organizational methods can improve students' performance in reading comprehension, thinking skills such as organizing ideas and seeing relationships, and remembering information.

Final Thoughts

I have seen many students succeed despite a range of learning issues and degrees of severity. Two ingredients have been most important in their success.

The first is the student's willingness to work harder. Yes, you can get accommodations such as more time on tests or modified instructions, but ultimately these students must master the same material as other children. To do this, they will have to work differently from their peers and take more time.

Second, as with the other problems discussed in this book, your role as a parent is critical to your child's emotional well-being and academic progress. Your support may be particularly important because children with learning disabilities—especially if they are bright—can easily become frustrated and lose confidence. In turn, those feelings can lead to behavior problems—especially if their parents and teachers are not providing the right kinds of emotional and educational support.

To conclude, I can do no better than to paraphrase the excellent advice provided in the article "Learning Disabilities and Disorders" by Gina Kemp, Melinda Smith, and Jeanne Segal, which I have drawn on elsewhere in this chapter. Proactively explore all of your options, learning about new treatments and services, and overseeing your child's education. The availability of the Internet and new technology in most classrooms makes learning about new interventions and support more readily available to children than in years past. Learn the specifics of your child's learning disability and research treatments and services. Above all, nurture his strengths.

11

Self-Injury, Suicidal Feelings, and Substance Abuse: When Things Get More Difficult

Maria

Maria's mom first noticed cuts on her arms when Maria, age thirteen, was sitting at the dinner table and leaned over to pet the family dog. Maria explained that the dog had scratched her when he got tangled up in his leash during his daily walk. Her mother was surprised that their normally easygoing dog had been so rough, but she didn't think much more about it.

Her mother had also noticed that although Maria was typically outgoing and fun, lately she hadn't been hanging out much with her friends, had spent a lot of time alone at home, and was often angry or defensive. But she wrote it all off to typical teenager moodiness.

Finally, late one night when Maria's mother heard a noise in the bathroom, she opened the door to find Maria scraping her arms with a razor blade. Maria was cutting, intentionally injuring herself by using razors to dig long marks into her arms. Thinking back, her mother realized that Maria had taken to wearing long-sleeved tops.

When Maria's mother called me to discuss her daughter's behavior she expressed a range of emotions: anger for not knowing about Maria's behavior until now, sadness, and helplessness. Fortunately, I got Maria started immediately with some dialectical behavior therapy (described in chapter 12) that taught her skills to cope with her anger toward herself and others, skills such as learning just to sit with uncomfortable feelings instead of acting on them through self-mutilation. It was a long road, but after a year

> Maria stopped cutting herself altogether. She was able to speak about her feelings to her parents and friends rather than taking them out on her body.

Self-injury, suicidal feelings, and substance abuse are the behaviors that are most likely to catch parents off-guard; they often go undetected until there is a crisis. The positive news is that there are effective treatments for each of them. Again, the key is intervention *as early as possible*.

Cutting and Other Forms of Self-Injury

The most common form of self-injury is believed to be skin cutting or scratching: making scratches or cuts on your own body with sharp objects. However, most children and adolescents who self-injure have also used other methods, such as burning their skin with a cigarette or lighted match. Although cuts or burns often leave scars, children who injure themselves usually conceal the marks and are sometimes successful in hiding these injuries from others, including their parents, for a long time.

Parents are often horrified and perplexed by this behavior. Why would their child intentionally mutilate himself when most people try to avoid pain and injury? Unfortunately, the research on cutting and other forms of self-injury is pretty sparse, but it does yield some facts. Typically, cutting begins around the age of thirteen or fourteen. Although data about its prevalence is mixed, most research seems to indicate that about 14 or 15 percent of adolescents have reported at least one incident of self-injury. Historically, it was thought that most people who cut—the behavior most parents and clinicians think about first when we think about self-injury—are girls. But boys self-injure, too, and more recent studies have found that the rates of self-injury in girls and boys are about equal. Girls appear to be more likely to cut themselves, while boys appear to be more likely to burn themselves. Teens are most at risk for self-injury, but some people continue to cut into adulthood. Self-injury appears to be more prevalent among Caucasians.

Why would a child self-injure? One theory arises from research showing that teens who self-injure experience more frequent and intense negative emotions than other teens. They may hurt themselves to alleviate these intense, painful feelings by shifting their focus to the physical pain. The research also shows that children who self-injure have difficulty expressing emotions, especially negative emotions such as anger. Some describe often feeling numb, or feeling nothing at all unless they are cutting. In addition, they often have difficulty with the social skills, such as making and maintaining friendships, that are so important in the teen years. Not surprisingly, they tend to be very self-critical, and many children cut as a way of expressing anger toward themselves.

Although children who self-injure share some risk factors with children who attempt suicide, the link is not straightforward. Suicide risk must always be considered in a comprehensive evaluation of children who self-injure, but it is also important to remember that self-injury is not equivalent to suicidal behavior.

Treatments for Self-Injury

Many of the treatments described in other chapters, including cognitive behavioral and psychodynamic therapies, have been adapted to treat self-injury. More specifically, dialectical behavior therapy, which teaches the child how to cope with difficult emotions in ways other than acting on them by injuring themselves, has been found to be particularly effective.

Suicidal Feelings

Suicide is the third leading cause of death in the United States for fifteen- to twenty-four-year-olds, and the sixth leading cause of death for five- to fourteen-year-olds. It is a serious problem, and it is not getting better.

Many of the symptoms of depression are similar to suicidal feelings. In particular, parents should be aware of the following signs:

- distinct and recognizable changes in eating or sleeping habits
- withdrawal or isolation from regular activities, family, or friends
- violence toward others
- consistent use of drugs or alcohol
- sudden neglect of his appearance
- noticeable personality changes

- frequent physical complaints such as headaches, fatigue, or stomachaches
- loss of interest in activities that were once enjoyed

A teenager who is thinking about suicide may also:

- complain of feeling rotten or being a bad person
- share verbal signals such as, "I won't be a problem for you much longer," "Nothing matters," "It's no use," or "I won't see you again."
- put his life in order in anticipation of death; for example, give away treasured possessions, tidy his room, or discard important personal effects
- become suddenly happy after a period of depression
- experience sights or sounds that aren't real, or bizarre thoughts

However difficult the conversation may be to broach, if you have reasons to worry, it's critical to ask your child if he is very sad or thinking about suicide. Asking the question gives him assurance that somebody cares and the opportunity to discuss his problems. Asking is particularly important because research tells us that few teens seek help for their suicidal thoughts or suicide attempts. While 15 percent of high school students have suicidal thoughts, fewer than one in five communicate them to parents. Similarly, up to 60 percent of teens who attempt suicide did not tell anyone. Only 10 percent of suicide attempts are known to parents.

It should go without saying that if your child says anything that indicates he is thinking about suicide, you must take it seriously and seek help right away.

Not surprisingly, most adolescents who commit suicide—more than 60 percent—had depression or other mental health symptoms for more than a year before their deaths. For teens with major depression, the risk of suicide is about twenty times greater than in the general population, and the risk is especially high for those who have had multiple episodes of serious depression or who have a dependence on alcohol or drugs. In some cases, the depression that leads to suicide may be genetic, but it can also be triggered by extremely painful experiences, such as being bullied or sexually assaulted. (As chapter 7 discusses, the risk of suicide is not the only reason for treating teen depression promptly. Even if it does not lead to suicidal feelings, it can result in strained relations with the rest of the family, problems at school, isolation, and increased chances of using drugs and alcohol.)

Most suicide attempts do not result in death, and many are arranged in a way that makes rescue possible. Often they are a cry for help. However, about one-third of people who try to commit suicide will try again within a year, and about 10 percent of people who threaten or try to commit suicide will eventually kill themselves.

While some of this information may understandably alarm you, my goal is to underscore the importance of recognizing the signs and acting to help your child as soon as possible.

Treatments for Suicidal Feelings and Suicide Attempts

Children who attempt suicide may need to be hospitalized and, while in the hospital, should be evaluated for other mental health problems such as bipolar disorder or major depression. Going forward, therapy—often involving the family as well as the child—is one of the most important parts of treatment to prevent future attempts.

Of course, it is far better to get treatment *before* a child attempts suicide. At that stage, many of the treatments for depression discussed in chapter 7 are relevant. You can also help prevent suicides by taking some precautions:

- Keep all prescription medicines out of reach and locked up.
- Do not keep alcohol in the home, or keep it locked up as well.
- Do not keep guns in the home. If you do keep firearms in the home, lock them in a gun safe and keep the ammunition in a separate, secure place.

Substance Abuse

Some experimentation with alcohol and drugs during adolescence is common and normal, because teenagers have to explore, test limits, and take risks in the process of becoming an independent adult. But teenagers frequently don't see the link between today's actions and tomorrow's consequences. It's not their fault: the part of their brain that makes this connection isn't fully developed yet. They also have a tendency to feel that problems that happen to others won't happen to them and that they are immune to risk. As a result, normal experimentation can slide easily into something much more dangerous. While some teens will stop after brief periods of experimentation, or use drugs or alcohol only occasionally and without significant problems, others will develop a dependency or will move on to substances that are more dangerous.

The warning signs of alcohol and drug abuse can include:

- repeated physical ailments, red and glazed eyes, a persistent cough, or general fatigue

- abrupt mood changes, extreme irritability, or sustained personality changes

- poor decision-making, depression, lack of interest, or overall low self-esteem

- frequent arguing, rule breaking, or more general withdrawal from the family

- decreased interest in school activities or a negative attitude toward academics; multiple absences, attendance, or disciplinary problems that may result in a drop in grades

- new friends who have problems with the law or are known to have used drugs

While any teenager can end up abusing alcohol or drugs, those at particular risk include those who:

- have a history of substance abuse in the family

- are depressed

- suffer from poor self-esteem

- feel that they are nonconventional or don't fit in

How Many Teenagers Use Drugs?

Although the use of alcohol and tobacco is down in teens, the use of marijuana and other drugs is up and at dangerous levels. Although marijuana use by adolescents declined from the late 1990s until the mid- to late 2000s, it has been on the rise since then. According to the National Institute on Drug Abuse (NIDA), in 2012, 6.5 percent of eighth graders, 17.0 percent of tenth graders, and 22.9 percent of twelfth graders reported using marijuana in the past month. Six and a half percent used using marijuana every day, compared with 5.1 percent in 2007. Even before the most recent trends, there was cause for concern. A statewide survey in Minnesota conducted in 1996 provided researchers the first methodologically rigorous look at the rate of substance-use disorders in a large student population. It found that 11 percent of ninth-grade students and 23 percent of twelfth graders met the formal diagnostic criteria as established in the DSM for drug abuse or drug dependence disorders.

One reason for rising marijuana use may be changing perceptions about its risks. Many young people don't think that marijuana is dangerous, a perception that may reflect recent public discussions about medical marijuana and marijuana legalization. However, the significance of nicotine and marijuana as possible gateway drugs—a first step toward using more dangerous drugs—has been repeatedly linked, so the concern over its increasing use is not just hype. In addition, marijuana today is much stronger than it used to be, with twice the content of THC (tetrahydrocannabinol, the chemical responsible for most of marijuana's effects). This matters because the effects of marijuana on the developing brain have been found to include irreparable impairment of intelligence, decision-making, and reasoning capacities.

Teenagers can abuse an assortment of drugs and substances, both legal and illegal. In addition to alcohol, legally available drugs include prescription medications, inhalants, and over-the-counter diet, sleep, and cold and cough medications. Household products are also frequently abused: the percentage of youths from twelve to seventeen years old who tried readily available glues, aerosols, and solvents (otherwise known as inhalants) has risen steadily. Alcohol remains a problem and drinking can begin even before the age of twelve. Sadly, one of the major sources of alcohol for underage drinkers has become parents who host parties for teens—they mistakenly think it is better to have them drink under their supervision rather than outside the home. In addition, the "heroin chic" look as glorified by super-skinny rock stars and fashion models has boosted the popularity of that drug among teens. In some areas, NIDA reports that the use of heroin mixed with water and then inhaled has increased among adolescents.

The Parents' Role

A recent study found that, unfortunately, most parents think that talking to their kids about drugs doesn't help. That's wrong. Parents can help prevent drug use in their children by talking to them about the issue directly. Open communication and recognizing any problems as they may develop are crucial. Many parents are hesitant to have these conversations because they themselves experimented with drugs in their youth, but they should be open and honest anyway. Have a discussion about how the effects of drugs and alcohol can be different for someone whose brain is still developing.

Fortunately, studies also show that children who know their parents disapprove of their using drugs are less likely to abuse them. Moreover, and more generally, clarity about their family's values can help children begin to think independently and to develop a personal value system that affects how they behave outside their home.

Parents need to be *parents first*, not buddies.

Treatment for Alcohol and Drug Abuse

A study conducted by the Substance Abuse and Mental Health Service Administration (SAMHSA) shows that treatment can significantly reduce substance use (and the criminal activity that may come along with it). What type of treatment works best? Intensive outpatient treatment is the most cost-effective type of program to help kids with drug and alcohol problems, according to the US Department of Health and Human Services and the Duke University Medical Center, Center for Adolescent Substance Abuse Treatment Intensive Outpatient Program. Unfortunately, intensive outpatient programs for substance abuse in children or teens are rare. Most programs place young people in a hospital or residential treatment facility rather than keeping them in their own communities. Achieving sobriety at home or in college requires extraordinary effort from everyone involved but ultimately, I believe, results in greater long-term success.

Whatever the approach, treatment that approaches young people as "little adults" is bound to fail. An effective treatment must be based on an understanding of adolescent development, including the nuances of cognitive, emotional, moral, and social development. During adolescence, new cognitive abilities emerge. In particular, the abilities to think abstractly, generate hypotheses and consider alternative solutions, and reflect about thinking in and of itself are still developing. These emerging cognitive skills are crucial to understanding the consequences of substance abuse as well as forming strategies for changing destructive behavior.

In addition, adolescents are forming an individual sense of self for the first time in their lives. They are moving beyond attachment to their families to increased identification with their peers. To further complicate matters, they may also be undergoing the significant physiological changes of puberty. For treatment to be effective, and for parents and professionals to understand why a child fell prey to substance abuse, all these contexts have to be taken into account.

The spectrum of possible treatments ranges from occasional outpatient therapy to intensive residential programs. There are several points to keep in mind and discuss with the professionals with whom you are working:

- Programs must be careful not to label adolescents prematurely or otherwise persuade them that they have a disease. That classification may do more harm than good in the long run if they mislabel an occasional user as a child who has become dependent.

- Many adolescents are pressured or even coerced by parents into treatment. However, that coercion doesn't help them change their behavior and may even be an obstacle. As treatment begins, the providers must understand and know how to deal with motivational obstacles.

- Adolescents differ from adults because of their developmental issues, differences in their values, and environmental considerations such as strong peer influences. As a result of these differences they must be approached differently than adults—indeed, adult treatment programs rarely work for teens. Although there may be no choice in some places because treatment programs developed for children aren't available, an adult program should be used only with great caution and with an alertness to the complications that may result.

- Programs should also evaluate the impacts of the child's age, gender, ethnicity, and culture. Adolescents who have abused alcohol or drugs for an extended period of time may have already negatively affected their cognitive and social-emotional development. As a result, treatment should identify these delays and deal with their effects on school performance, self-esteem, and relationships with family and peers.

- Family involvement in the program is essential, because of the family's possible role in the problem and because it will be essential to bringing about changes.

Final Thoughts

I have walked you through some of the most difficult issues that parents may have to tackle with kids. If you are facing one of these issues, know that you can get through it. Giving kids clear values and limits while allowing them some flexibility to question authority and experiment is important. Most of all, reassuring your child that they can always come to you, without fear of reprisal, is essential. The message should be clear that the door is open and they always have an ally in their family.

Part III

Supporting Your Child

12

The Medical Professionals:
Who to Turn to, What to Know,
and What to Ask

ARMED WITH ALL the information you've absorbed from this book so far, a Project SKIP screening, and preliminary talks with teachers or your pediatrician, perhaps you feel reassured that your child's behavior is not particularly unusual or extreme and your worries have been alleviated. Or perhaps these chapters have convinced you that you should take another step and consult with a specialist, but you're unsure what to do next. I talk to many parents and teachers asking for advice about how to navigate the mental health care system. While each child's situation is different, a few consistent themes emerge.

First, parents are confused about when to seek help and whom to see.

Second, parents often feel intimidated when they see professionals and don't ask the questions they need to in order to feel empowered to make better choices for their child's care.

Finally, the system has become fragmented, and most of the time the professionals in different parts of the system don't communicate with each other. That leaves the parents trying to navigate the system without all the information they need—not to mention the uncertainty that results from not knowing what is going on.

Here is a recent example from my own practice.

Jonathan
Jonathan was a fifteen-year-old who had a fairly extensive history of difficulties over the last two years in school. Small things can understandably

cause teachers to be overly concerned these days, and it was my feeling that this was true for Jonathan. For example, he was seen as being "difficult and oppositional" by his teachers because he once brought a small knife to school and because he frequently stared out the window instead of doing his schoolwork. These difficulties started around the same time he was diagnosed with a seizure disorder for which he was receiving treatment with three medications. The neurologist who diagnosed the seizure disorder had written a letter to the school explaining that the medications might not control the seizures and that Jonathan could continue to have symptoms. However, the letter did not describe what the symptoms might look like in the classroom, such as not appearing to listen when called upon or frequently staring out the window.

The school had done some pencil-and-paper tests as part of an Individual Education Plan (IEP) (see chapter 13). The tests had found that Jonathan's intelligence was above average, but his working memory—the ability to hold facts in his head for a short period of time so that he could use them for tasks such as solving math problems—was below average compared to other children his age. Jonathan's grades were mostly Ds and Fs.

Initially, Jonathan was classified by the school as having emotional difficulties, for which he received support. Later, the school changed this classification to "Other Health Impaired" because of his seizure disorder diagnosis. Under this new classification he was granted extended time on tests and extra support in the classroom for learning. Then Jonathan was seen again in his classroom staring off into space and was overheard talking to other kids about how he was very depressed and wanted to hurt himself. The school expelled him. This reaction, unfortunately, is not uncommon in zero-tolerance school environments these days.

Jonathan had been seeing a therapist for a few weeks and seemed to like the therapist, but his parents were uncertain what his therapy sessions consisted of and didn't want to pry. Additionally, Jonathan was seeing a psychiatrist who felt that he had symptoms of ADHD and that more medication should be added to the three already being used to control his seizures. The psychiatrist didn't believe in tests or checklists; instead, he favored just talking with his patients for a short time to determine how they were doing on medications before making adjustments to prescriptions.

Jonathan's parents were frustrated and felt disempowered. They found me through one of their friends and called me out of desperation because they didn't see their son improving and wanted to know what else they could do.

I first spent several hours reading all of the records in Jonathan's case. In my review, two themes stood out: the parents didn't feel Jonathan was better, and his school performance wasn't consistent with his intelligence level. The central question was why he was having difficulties in school, both academically and emotionally. I looked for a medical cause first. Seizures can look like ADHD and can cause kids to have emotional symptoms. Before anything else, his parents and I needed to understand the effect that Jonathan's seizures were having on his daily functioning.

As a first step, I sent the family for a neuropsychological evaluation at the hospital where their neurologist practiced. A neuropsychologist (that is what I am) studies the relationships between the brain and behavior and helps patients understand how biological factors such as seizures affect their actions. Jonathan's mom called right away for an appointment. At the same time, I provided her with a list of questions to ask the therapist. These wouldn't violate Jonathan's privacy with his therapist. Instead, they were designed to see if the therapy would be effective in getting at the core issues with which Jonathan was struggling. Primarily, they were intended to help the parents understand the therapist's plan for treating their son's issues and whether she was using evidence-based therapies. Evidence-based therapies are those therapies such as family therapy, cognitive behavioral therapy, and certain other treatments that have been found by sound research studies to be most effective, as I have described throughout this book.

Once his parents and I got the neuropsychological report, it was clear that part of Jonathan's difficulties could be explained by the number of seizures he was having and the fact that his medicines were not controlling his seizures well. His medications needed to be increased so that he would have fewer seizures during school. This would help him pay more attention, but a side effect would be that his working memory would get worse. His school would have to give him more support to bolster his working memory, such as by writing things down for him to refer to later, so he wouldn't have to keep the facts in his head.

The big issue still left was Jonathan's depression. Certainly, some of the depressive symptoms could be explained by the seizures, but others seemed to indicate deeper issues with his overall engagement in life. For example, he was spending a lot more time alone in his room and increasingly less time with friends. Was this issue best dealt with through medications or through therapy?

I suggested to Jonathan's parents that they first work with the neurologist to get the seizure medications right. Some of these medications would also help alleviate depression. I also suggested that the therapist treat the depression head-on by using interpersonal psychotherapy, a form of talk therapy that has been found to be particularly helpful for adolescents with depression. (See chapter 7.)

Next, I suggested that Jonathan's parents take this information to their psychiatrist and explain that they didn't want to add more medications for ADHD until these two steps had been taken, since the adjustment in seizure medications might fix the attention problems in school and because they didn't see how adding ADHD medications would help the depression or seizures. They now understood, supported by a neurologist and the neuropsychological report, that the attention issues might be at least partly a result of the seizures, and they were very concerned about all the medication Jonathan was already taking.

They were somewhat apprehensive about taking this approach with the psychiatrist. They wondered if he "didn't know best"—after all, he was the medical doctor and they were just the parents. So I suggested they ask the neurologist for his thoughts. He agreed immediately that they should wait to see what the medication adjustments for the seizures would do. But he didn't have time to call the psychiatrist to explain the situation.

I again prompted Jonathan's parents to be firm with the psychiatrist. When they called to speak with him, however, he explained that he didn't have time to discuss the issues on the phone. Anticipating this, I suggested to Jonathan's parents that they schedule a session with him to discuss all of this information, and they did. At the appointment, the psychiatrist backpedaled pretty quickly when faced with the overwhelming information that the new neuropsychological evaluation provided, the neurologist's recent findings, and the questions that the parents now knew to ask about treatment.

After the adjustment in seizure medications, Jonathan's behavior at school noticeably improved. He also seemed less depressed and liked the sessions with his therapist. Armed with their questions and their better understanding about all the pieces, his parents went back to the school to request different services to support Jonathan's working memory issues in class.

Jonathan is doing better socially and academically, his parents feel he is much happier, and they feel empowered to ask questions and orchestrate a team approach to his treatment in concert with all the professionals.

The Professionals: Where to Start?

Often parents don't take action when they think something may not be normal or they are worried because they don't know where to start. The easiest and quickest first step is to call the medical professional you see most regularly with your child. That is likely your pediatrician, family doctor, nurse practitioner, or physician's assistant. Make an appointment to check that everything is medically OK with your child and to discuss the specific issue you are concerned about.

If you did the online SKIP screening, you can share the results with your doctor. Likewise, if you have charted the behavior you are concerned about, you should take that information with you so you can discuss the behaviors that concern you in detail.

Next, ask your doctor for a referral to someone who specializes in mental health. This could be a psychologist, psychiatrist, a marriage and family therapist (MFT), licensed clinical social worker (LCSW), or licensed clinical professional counselor (LCPC).

Let me give you my thoughts on the services that each of these professionals offers.

If you want someone who specializes in psychological testing, start with a psychologist. A good, thorough assessment of the problems using objective data helps you decide the best treatments to pursue, and only a psychologist is trained extensively in these sorts of assessments. And, although psychologists cannot prescribe medicines in most states, they often work closely with psychiatrists, who can prescribe, and they can help you navigate the entire system.

While a psychologist will have a doctorate (or a master's degree in some settings, such as the government), a psychiatrist will have a medical degree. Psychiatry has recently gotten a bad rap because psychiatrists, especially those who work with children, are in short supply, and many have gone to shorter sessions (sometimes less than an hour) designed to deal solely with medication management. There are still good psychiatrists who want to spend time collaborating. However, as Jonathan's story demonstrated, it is important that you ask informed and specific questions and bring relevant data to help them with their jobs.

If you already have a diagnosis and know you want a certain type of therapy, then you can start with a master's-degree-level professional such as an LCSW, LCPC, or MFT who specializes in treatment. What is an LCSW, LPC, or MFT? Each state has its own definition and requirements for these master's-level practitioners. This chart provides some general guidelines to better understand how they may be able to help you.

LCSW	These practitioners have a two-year degree that focuses on counseling and therapy with individuals, families, or groups, or referral services. An LCSW can provide you with a diagnosis.
LCPC	Professional clinical counselors also have a two-year degree that teaches counseling interventions and psychotherapeutic techniques (including assessment) for mental health issues. In most states, LCPCs do not assess or treat couples or families unless the professional has completed additional training and education.
LMFT	The practice of marriage and family therapy, which is also supported by a two-year degree, involves therapy performed with individuals, couples, or groups, focusing on improving relationships. This practice also includes premarriage counseling.

No matter which professional you choose to deal with, your preparation and involvement are essential. Come to appointments organized with questions and with material to support your concerns. And don't expect someone to answer numerous questions on the phone or by e-mail. Make a separate appointment to discuss the issues that concern you. If any mental health professional won't answer your questions, or you feel dismissed, *you should find someone else*. There is no harm in saying that the relationship isn't a good fit, and you should ask for a referral to another specialist.

The following chart shows the main types of assessments and examinations performed by doctoral-level professionals.

Professional	Exam	Purpose
Psychologist	Psychological	Psychologists provide information about cognitive, emotional, and social functioning. They use multiple sources of data in forming their opinions, including pencil-and-paper tests; teacher and parent reports; behavioral observations; social, academic and family history; and any medical findings.
Neuropsychologist	Neuropsychological	Neuropsychologists examine relationships between brain functioning and behavior. They clarify the impact of neurological injury or disease (for example, head trauma or seizures) on an individual's behavior and test a number of areas of functioning, including attention, motor skills, visual-spatial abilities, memory, language, executive function, academic skills, intelligence, and social-emotional functioning.
School psychologist	Psychoeducational	School psychologists focus on cognitive and academic or achievement testing or emotional issues that interfere with progress in the classroom. This assessment is often used to develop an Individualized Education Program (IEP), if a child meets the criteria for an IEP under federal law.
Psychiatrist	Psychiatric	Psychiatrists assess mental status, level of functioning, appropriateness of medication, and recommended courses of treatment. This assessment will likely be shorter than that provided by a psychologist and it will generally not involve formal computer or pencil-and-paper tests.

Questions to Ask Professionals *Before* You Begin Working with Them

No matter what types of professionals you choose to start your journey with, you should ask them or their staff a number of questions up front that will help you understand their point of view and whether you will be a good fit with their practice.

Licensure and Training

First, determine whether the person is a licensed mental health professional. Whether they are psychologists, psychiatrists, doctors who are general practitioners, pediatricians, LCSWs, or MFTs, these folks have to be licensed. Being licensed means that they are authorized by the state, based on their education, training, and experience, to provide a certain clinical service to the public in that state. Each state has its own specific requirements for licensing and certification. You would be surprised by how many organizations—including hospitals—use unlicensed staff to provide mental health services and how many people will call themselves a mental health professional or doctor without being licensed. If someone isn't licensed, they should not be practicing, and they most certainly should not be giving you a diagnosis or assessment. You can check with your local licensing board for the specialty of the person you are seeing. In addition, many professional organizations now allow you to check a person's license status online.

Experience with Patients

Choose someone who has specialty training with children and who makes treating children the mainstay of what they do every day for a living. To become a neuropsychologist for children, I did two additional years of training in diagnosing and treating kids and completed an extra fellowship in brain imaging and research methods. In my practice, I see mostly children (or adults who have had a developmental disability since childhood), and I read every day to keep current about the latest research into kids' development.

Each professional has a specific area of expertise. I would not be the psychologist to consult about your grandmother who is forgetting things. She deserves someone who has the same passion and expertise for treating elders that I have for kids.

Views on Medication

Ask the professional how they feel about the use of medication versus talk therapy. Most mental health professionals will tell you that the best choice depends on the case, and that they have seen great success with the use of either or both. In many cases, they will tell you the best approach is both: using medication to help get the chemical changes in your child's brain under control (see the section on medications later in the chapter and also appendix C), but also talking through the problem and setting goals to control unwanted behaviors.

Cultural Competence

A culturally competent professional:

- respects a family's values and beliefs
- understands the impact upon the family of factors such as culture, socioeconomic status, religion, gender, and sexual orientation
- considers the needs and abilities of the entire family, such as child care or transportation issues
- understands the impact of the professional's culture and ethnicity on the therapeutic relationship
- encourages the family to be actively involved in the treatment process
- is comfortable discussing alternative treatments (e.g., religious healing, acupuncture, massage)

Types of Therapy Professionals Can Provide

Most simply, talk therapy is talking about yourself with someone who is a trained listener, can help you spot thoughts or behaviors that are creating difficulties in your life, and can then help you to tackle those problems and more effectively cope with things you can't fix. Talk therapy can be practiced with a trusted friend or impartial family member, but it is best with someone who is a trained therapist. That person knows how to use therapeutic methods that have been proven effective and can also be objective, setting aside his needs to focus solely on yours.

When you are consulting a professional who provides talk therapy, it is important to understand what type he provides. Here are three common types. All of these can help children to feel better and live more fully, but some are better than others for addressing certain types of problems in kids. In chapters 3 through 11, I also discussed additional types of therapy that are specific to the mental health problem the chapter describes. See appendix B for a list of the evidence-based therapies that have been found most useful for specific diagnoses.

Cognitive Therapy

Cognitive therapy helps children change harmful or negative ways of thinking by modifying their thoughts about events, people, and their own lives.

For example, your daughter texts a friend, but the friend says she doesn't have time to chat. Your daughter's first thought is that her friend is mad at her. That belief makes her feel worried and anxious. Soon she is thinking even more negatively: she doesn't have any friends or no one likes her. Cognitive therapy helps your daughter focus on her negative thoughts about her friend's behavior so she can change them. Maybe the friend was really busy or having a bad day. Perhaps she was upset about something else and didn't feel like hanging out online. Helping your daughter think of other reasons for her actions will help her see the event in a more positive—and, usually, more accurate—way, rather than interpreting what happened in the worst possible way.

Behavioral Therapy and Cognitive Behavioral Therapy (CBT)

Behavioral therapy helps your child change harmful behaviors by gaining control over the actions that are causing problems. Unlike cognitive therapy, which focuses on how people think about a problem, this therapy focuses on how they behave.

Cognitive behavioral therapy focuses on how people think *and* act. In CBT, therapists first work with patients to identify thoughts and images that precede and co-occur with negative actions. They can then help patients detach themselves from the beliefs that are indirectly related to, or rooted in, those thoughts and images. By helping patients gain distance from these thoughts the patients can gain control over their unwanted feelings, images, or behaviors. Next, patients are asked to question the validity of their thoughts. For example, they might ask, "What facts or concrete proof are there for this belief? Are there any alternative explanations for what happened?" They are then asked to identify common themes in their beliefs across a variety of situations.

Finally, the therapy addresses the child's behavior. For example, your son was with you in a store when it was about to close. The lights were turned off, and he couldn't find you. As a result of that experience, he is now terrified of going into a store with you. You can't take him with you even to do the weekly grocery shopping. Behavioral therapy can help your son face and deal with his fears. A therapist would work with him to employ coping mechanisms, such as being accompanied into a store that was closing while practicing behaviors such as taking deep breaths or closing his eyes and quietly singing a song to calm himself. In time, this process allows him first to reduce and eventually overcome his fears.

Interpersonal Therapy

Interpersonal therapy helps your child learn to relate better to others. It focuses on how to express feelings and how to develop better people skills so that a child can feel more confident in a variety of situations.

For example, your daughter and her best friend are not getting along. She doesn't like her friend's new boyfriend or group of friends. Your daughter feels that her longtime friend is hanging out with the wrong crowd, and she feels that her friend has abandoned their relationship in favor of more popular kids. To make matters worse, your daughter doesn't find it easy to make friends and doesn't have anyone else she regards as a close friend.

Interpersonal therapy can help improve your daughter's relationship with her friend and also help her make new friends. If she finds it difficult to make friends, the therapy can show her ways of talking with other children that will make her more comfortable and successful in forming new relationships. It will also allow her to practice talking through the issues with her current friend and, more generally, to learn how to conduct a difficult social conversation in the future through role-playing with the therapist.

Talk therapy doesn't have to be difficult, expensive, or long-term, and the new interpersonal strategies that result can be quickly helpful.

These three types of therapies are the most common and considered the most effective. But there are other types too.

Psychoanalytic Therapy

Although many critics of psychoanalytic therapy claim it takes too much time and is expensive and generally ineffective, it has benefits if you are able to sustain it. Your child can reveal feelings or actions that have been the cause of stress in the context of a supportive and safe, more neutral relationship with a therapist. Simply having someone to share these feelings with who is a well-trained and an empathic nonjudgmental listener can have a positive result. In addition, your child can gain insight into why they behave as they do, and that insight frequently leads to changes in behavior and thoughts. During the sessions, the child is encouraged to examine how relationships and experiences in the past can subconsciously affect their behavior and thinking in the present.

Family Therapy

Family therapy was developed with families whose members were experiencing drug or alcohol addictions, gambling problems, eating disorders, or other self-destructive behavior. More recently, family therapy has been modified to deal with families caring for a wide variety of other issues. Family therapy has been found to be effective at delaying, if not preventing, relapses of a number of serious mental health issues; in the case of eating disorders, it is crucial to recovery. Family therapy requires that everyone go to the therapist to discuss a family dynamic and engage in talk therapy with each other to support the person with the mental health issue. The premise is that the family dynamic often contributes to the difficulties the afflicted family member may be having—sometimes it can reinforce the problem or keep the child from getting better.

Creative Therapies

Creative therapies use disciplines such as art, dance, or drama to increase self-awareness, reduce anxiety, and increase self-esteem. These therapies encourage children to express emotion and explore their problems using a wide range of artistic materials. They can be especially helpful for people who may have difficulty expressing themselves verbally.

Dialectical Behavior Therapy

Dialectical behavior therapy (DBT), a form of cognitive behavioral therapy, was originally created for people with a personality disorder, a specific kind of mental health disorder typically found in adults that results in an unhelpful and intractable way of viewing the world. Now, however, DBT is used more widely to treat a number of other difficulties.

DBT is based on the fact that, for a variety of reasons, some people often have more extreme emotional reactions to people or to events. For example, if your child overreacts to another child at school and becomes enraged or out of control, the anger becomes part of the problem for the child and compounds the initial problem to which they reacted. In the therapy's most basic form, the child is taught to sit with those uncomfortable emotions and to not react in a way that would make the situation even more difficult. Typically, the child attends both individual and group sessions. With children, this therapy is used most frequently for disorders such as depression.

Motivational Interviewing

Being in therapy can be scary at first. When a child is scared, he often perceives that he is under attack, and he uses defense mechanisms to protect himself. Motivational interviewing is designed to avoid confronting your child, thus increasing the defensiveness. Instead, it strengthens his own motivation for and commitment to changing. It involves a collaborative conversation in an accepting and compassionate atmosphere, during which the therapist asks questions that will harness the child's internal motivation and show that change is within his power.

Parent-Child Interaction (or Attunement) Therapy

Parent-child interaction therapy (PCIT) (or, for younger toddlers, parent-child attunement therapy) is a treatment for children aged two to twelve who have behavior or conduct problems. It focuses on the parent-child relationship and on changing the pattern of their interaction. In PCIT, parents are taught specific skills for creating a supportive and effective relationship while helping their child to behave in more positive ways. This treatment focuses on two basic interactions. During child-directed interaction (CDI), parents play with their children with the goal of strengthening their relationship. During parent-directed interaction (PDI), parents learn to incorporate specific behavior management techniques as they play with their child.

Medication

Medication often yields faster results than talk therapy. On the other hand, therapy allows a child to develop the skills to create healthy relationships, deal effectively with difficult emotions, and manage negative thoughts. Medication won't. For some issues such as schizophrenia, however, medication is essential. For other issues, such as ADHD, medication may enable your child to catch up on a subject in which they are behind and make academic progress. For some issues, talk therapy alone can be at least as or even more beneficial, but it requires a substantial commitment of time and resources.

For example, some research has shown that cognitive behavioral therapy and antidepressants are equally effective when treating depression. Other research has shown that CBT helps to prevent relapses, probably because it helps to develop skills for coping with depressive symptoms. (See Appendix C.)

None of those studies suggests that you should necessarily disfavor medications. In fact, a study of teenagers showed the benefits of using both antidepressants and CBT. One of the study's authors, John Walkup, a child and adolescent psychiatrist at New York Presbyterian/Weill Cornell, wrote, "Not only do the results support the use of antidepressants for depressed teens, but when used in conjunction with talk therapy, these medications actually provide teens with the best chance to alleviate their depression."

Despite the value of medications when they are used appropriately—and, when treating depression, in combination with CBT—there are legitimate concerns about both their overuse as well as their potential side effects. Some psychiatrists are quick to prescribe medications, often without considering how the medication fits into a more comprehensive plan for treating a problem. To compound the difficulties, medications—especially antidepressants—are sometimes prescribed by people who don't have the appropriate training.

The most obvious medical side effects are physical or behavioral, such as agitation, insomnia, panic attacks, or irritability. For more detailed information about potential side effects, a useful resource is the website of Dr. Peter Breggin, a psychiatrist: www.breggin.com. However, there are other, less obvious, side effects, such as encouraging patients to rely too much on drugs and not enough on their own work, in combination with therapy, to get better. In addition, Dr. Breggin speculates that antidepressants can increase the risk of suicide and violence, although those links have not been shown to my satisfaction, and I think they have been exaggerated.

The debate over side effects is impossible to resolve in general terms because so much depends on the specific medication. To complicate the issue further, for many medications there are no long-term studies of their effects in children. The bottom line: educate yourself about any medication that is being proposed for your child and ensure that those prescribing it have considered all the alternatives before prescribing. With children under the age of six, behavioral interventions should be tried first for most issues I have described (see chapter 3). And again, once medication has been tried, careful and repeated monitoring is essential.

See appendix C for a list of commonly prescribed medications for mental health problems.

Questions to Ask Your Professional About Diagnoses and Treatments

What diagnoses and treatments have you ruled out and why?
It is important that your treatment provider explain how he reached his diagnoses and recommendations. If you think he should consider another diagnosis or treatment, ask directly if he did. If you are thinking anxiety and he says ADHD, ask why. If parents ask me these questions during a scheduled appointment, I never mind—in fact, I always encourage parents to understand my thought process. But please don't ask your provider as you are going out the door after the session has ended or, unless it's an emergency, in an e-mail or voice mail just because you prefer not to wait for the next appointment.

What research supports the treatment you are suggesting?
Before I suggest a treatment, I do a literature search to obtain the latest data about the treatment's efficacy. I also explain to parents the pros and cons of the treatment I am suggesting, and I will often give articles to parents to read for themselves. I don't expect them to become the experts, but I do want to give them all the facts. If your clinician isn't doing this, I suggest finding someone who can help you understand the latest advances in treatment. The research into childhood disorders is growing daily, given new research techniques such as neuroimaging, and clinicians need to draw on that work when making decisions for your child. They should tell you what research supports the approach they are suggesting.

How many patients have you worked with who chose not to use medications?
It is important to assess whether the professional you are working with has a bias toward medications over behavioral treatments. In some cases, medications are very important or absolutely necessary, but in other cases behavioral treatments should be tried first or in combination with medications. Your providers should be able to describe all your options and provide support for their recommendations in the form of research or experience with other patients. In my case, I work with an equal number of parents who use and do not use medication for their children.

How soon will we start to see symptoms improve?

Change rarely occurs overnight, but you should be able to measure it. Make certain your treatment provider gives you a realistic time line of when to expect improvement in symptoms, how much those symptoms will improve, and what benchmarks you can use to measure your child's progress. If I am working with a patient, I expect to see gains in most instances quite soon, even if those gains are small. At times, however—especially when behaviors or symptoms are long-standing—they will get worse before they get better. In the short run, a child may throw more tantrums or get more frustrated. (In depressed children, you sometimes see a burst of energy before they level out in terms of mood.) At times, this behavior is a necessary part of change. Hang in there and stick to the plan. Ask your provider when you might expect things to change for the better and use checklists to quantify those changes.

Alternative Treatments and What You Should Ask About Them

It is difficult to define an alternative therapy precisely, but I will use the term to mean an approach to mental health care that emphasizes the interrelationship between mind, body, and spirit, and that may not yet have a body of scientific literature to back it up. I certainly understand the desire to try every possible method of helping your child, especially if the method seems less invasive or difficult than more conventional methods. However, the decision to pursue alternative treatments for your child is not one to be made lightly. Following are some questions to help guide you in making that decision so that you can consider issues such as costs, time, burdens on the child, the invasiveness of the treatment, and its effectiveness.

Although some people claim that they recover from mental health problems using alternative methods alone, most people combine alternative therapies with other, more traditional treatments. If you are considering alternative treatments, including any "natural" or "herbal" supplements, it is crucial that you inform your health care providers. If you are open with them, you are less likely to have unpleasant surprises about unexpected consequences. For example, a friend recently told me that she found out after the fact that a very common over-the-counter medication, which she never would have thought to disclose to her doctor, had a negative reaction with grapefruit.

Although some alternative treatments such as acupuncture have historical roots, many others do not. For more information about specific treatments, visit nccam.nih.gov, the website of the National Center for Complementary & Alternative Medicine at the National Institutes of Health. The center was created in 1992 to help individuals and health care providers assess alternative methods of treatment and to integrate effective alternative treatments with more mainstream traditional methods of health care.

Questions to Ask

This is what I have learned as a practicing professional in this field: if a therapy and its healing effects seem too good to be true, they probably are. I have worked with families who have spent thousands of dollars on barometric chambers (see chapter 4), brushing techniques (used for sensory integration disorder), and other programs in a desperate but ultimately unsuccessful attempt to help their child.

My bottom line is this: if you can afford the alternative treatment and it doesn't interfere with established practices that researchers and clinicians have proven to work, then go ahead and try it—*after* you have asked plenty of questions, such as those I provide here. Personally, I use acupuncture, meditation, and massage to relieve stress, increase my focus, and find pain relief from an old knee injury, and I wouldn't do without these treatments. But do your homework, research the provider on the Internet, get a recommendation, and proceed with caution.

Here are questions to ask before you adopt an alternative health treatment or technique:

- Does the provider have clinical experience using the treatment effectively with similar patients? Are there any clinical studies to back up the provider's belief?

- What does the treatment entail or involve?

- What is the recommended frequency of treatment and what is the expected course of therapy?

- How will we determine if the therapy is effective?

- What is the average cost per treatment, with or without any additional recommended or required products that supplement the treatment, such as special vitamins and materials for home use? What is the total cost for a specified time period?

- Is the treatment eligible for third-party reimbursement?

- Are there any potential side effects?

- Is the provider willing to communicate diagnostic findings and treatment plans? Will he coordinate with other mental health professionals as part of a team that may include traditional treatment providers?

- Most important: is the provider accredited according to the current standards of approved practices for his profession?

Below is a chart that may help you with your consideration of an alternative treatment.

Is this treatment safe for children?
Is it invasive?
Have there been studies with children?
What are the costs?
Emotional
Out-of-pocket cost
Time
What's the evidence that it's effective?
Is the evidence from a source independent of the treatment's provider?
How many children have been enrolled in studies of the alternative treatment?
Can it be used with established effective treatments?
Can we afford the additional time and cost?
Is it too much for the child to tolerate?
What are the risks?
Physical
Emotional

Who Pays?

Mental health services can be costly. If your child, or someone else in your family, needs mental health treatment, you will inevitably be thinking about how to pay for it. Some families pay out of their own pockets, which provides them with complete freedom in choosing their providers and avoids paper-work and bureaucracy. For most of us, though, this approach isn't feasible, and it's therefore imperative to find the right kind of insurance or a government or nonprofit program that will cover some or all of the cost.

Although most families use health insurance, other valuable resources exist. However, trying to understand the system of available benefits can be confusing and frustrating. Fortunately, there are a number of good online publications that present the range of resources available to pay for services: federal and state government programs, community nonprofit programs, and employer-based and other private insurance and public insurance programs. Many of these publications also describe common difficulties encountered in using those resources, offer tips for navigating the insurance labyrinth, and summarize the most important federal laws that govern insurance coverage for mental health issues. For more information see http://ectacenter.org/contact/ptccoord.asp to search by state.

For children over three go to http://msppinterface.org/guides/insurance-guide.

Working in Partnership with Your Provider

Getting the best care for your child usually depends on your ability to work effectively with a number of treatment professionals. Here is a checklist of some of the hallmarks of the most successful partnerships:

- Be clear. Let the professionals know what your expectations are and how they can help you to get your needs met. Ask them about their policies and about how they will communicate with you. Tell them if you have beliefs or values that will affect your child's treatment as the treatment plan is formulated.

- Seek out professionals who are willing to work effectively with you, within your style of communication, and satisfy your reasonable need to stay informed about your child's treatment. If you don't feel you are working well with a professional, or if there is tension, let them know. If you can't solve the issues between you, find another provider.

- Share the whole picture. If your child has complex medical issues, it may be useful to call a meeting, or schedule a conference call, with all the treatment professionals involved in your child's care in order to discuss the complete picture together.

- Commit to creating a team effort. Tell providers how important their support and cooperation are to your child's care. Let them know what you like about what they are doing. Celebrate even small gains, and recognize that sometimes, through no one's fault, solutions may not come easily or quickly.

How Do You Know If Your Child Is Making Progress?

This is one of the most important questions for a treatment provider, but it can also be the hardest to answer. Sometimes change can happen quickly. At other times, a child may get worse before getting better. First, make sure you understand the overall treatment plan. Ask your provider to share the plan with you and to work with you in understanding its specific goals, including all the methods and actions that will lead to the goals. Once you know the goals and the plan, you will be better prepared to watch your child for improvements in behavior, an ability to cope with emotions more effectively, improvements in relationships, or improvement in academic performance.

Final Thoughts

None of the information in this chapter is intended to replace your relationship with a good mental health professional. It is simply to educate you to become a better consumer.

That said, many positive outcomes for children with mental health issues result from some combination of therapy and medications. If you have strong concerns about using medications or embarking on a specific course of treatment with your child, ask your provider not only about the medication or therapy that is being considered, but also about the latest research regarding the problem for which your child is being treated. (You can also consider taking "vacation" breaks from medicines, such as on weekends or school holidays, and you should ask your provider if this approach makes sense for your child.) Be honest and realistic with your provider about what you can reasonably be expected to follow through on as a family (for example, be up front about your time or financial constraints).

And remember, there isn't a stupid question. You should take control of your child's care, and that requires asking as many questions as you need to.

13

Getting Services for Your Child from Your School or State

In addition to working with the professionals discussed in the previous chapter, you will likely also be working to obtain services for your child from your school or state. This process should be easier than it used to be because the education of children with disabilities has been made a national priority through the Individuals with Disabilities Education Act (IDEA), which applies to people with special needs from birth through twenty-one. It sets standards for evaluating their needs and creating plans to meet those needs. Unfortunately, in a time fraught with state budget cuts, it is important to know what to ask for and how the process works so you can ensure that you are getting all that you are entitled to from the various entities tasked with providing services to children with special education needs.

Children can get the help they need at different stages of their development and through a variety of channels. Sometimes, it is clear soon after a child is born that he will need support, and the hospital itself may refer the parents to an early intervention program. Preschool children are often identified because a pediatrician or nurse suggests referring them to the system known as Child Find or to another early intervention program, or because they have participated in a screening session conducted by a community agency. School-aged children may be identified by teachers or other school personnel who suggest that a child be evaluated by the school system or, sometimes, by another agency.

Of course, you don't have to wait for a referral. If you're concerned about your child's development, you may contact your local early intervention program or your school directly and ask to have your child evaluated. While working with your own pediatrician may be preferable, if you work within the state-mandated system, the evaluation may be paid for by the state program responsible for supporting young children. These laws vary by state and it is important to know the resources available for your state before you start the evaluation process. A state-by-state resource guide for early intervention services, which provide evaluations free of charge, may be found at the links provided in the resources section under "Early Childhood." Child Find, which operates in each state, has the obligation to screen and identify children who need help, and it requires schools to identify and evaluate all children with disabilities under age twenty-one.

A tip: if you make a request, it's best to put it in writing even if you begin with a phone call. This will help if there are any questions later about whether you made the request or followed the appropriate procedures.

Once you or someone else believes your child may need extra support or services, there are two key steps in the process that follow: an evaluation or assessment and, if that shows that your child in fact needs special support, the creation of a plan. I'll describe each step briefly here, and then in more detail later in this chapter.

Whether your route is through Child Find or a school, the process must begin by conducting a thorough, formal evaluation of your child's developmental strengths and weaknesses. Before that takes place, you must consent to the evaluation. Then, under federal IDEA regulations, an evaluation must be completed within sixty days, unless a state's IDEA regulations give a different time line, in which case the state's time line applies. For children under three, the schedule is shortened: IDEA allows only forty-five days for the entire assessment and recommendation process.

If the evaluation shows that your child is eligible for special support or services, the next step is to create a formal plan.

If a child is under three (or older in some states), the formal plan will be an Individualized Family Service Plan (IFSP). This plan guides the early intervention process so that it provides the most effective support for the child's development. The plan also takes into account the family's goals and resources, and the family should be closely involved in creating it.

If your child is older, the plan may be either an Individual Educational Plan (IEP) or a 504 Plan. ("504" refers to Section 504 of the US Rehabilitation Act.) The IEP is for children who have a disability that interferes with their education and performance in school and who need accommodations and special education services in order to be successful. The 504 Plan is for children who have physical or emotional disabilities, are recovering from chemical dependency, or have an impairment that restricts one or more major life activities, such as caring for themselves or performing manual tasks, but do not need specialized instruction.

There are several similarities between the two plans. Both include accommodations and modifications for delivering the school curriculum in the child's classroom. They can also provide a number of services, such as speech, occupational, or physical therapy. They allow the student to receive services in the classroom or the least restrictive environment—that is, an environment that looks most like the classroom provided for all kids who don't need accommodations or special instruction. They also provide for reviews by various administrators and for hearings by an administrative law judge or hearing officer in the event of a disagreement between the parents and the school.

As these paragraphs have implied, creating an individualized program is a systematic process that involves a number of steps:

- defining the problem
- referral for an evaluation
- identification of the issues causing the problem (not just the symptoms)
- determining your child's eligibility for support from the school or elsewhere
- developing the IFSP, IEP, or 504 Plan
- implementing the plan
- evaluating the plan and revising it as needed

Following is more information about this process, first for little children and then for school-aged children.

Little Kids

For infants and toddlers, most of the process can take place within the framework of your state's early intervention services. Because these services are available only to children with eligible conditions, the early intervention system can also be your first step in assessing your child's development and identifying any issues that would qualify your child for services.

As you begin the process, it's important to understand how the professionals involved may be defining the term *developmental delay*. Under Part C of IDEA, the term includes delays in five basic areas:

- cognitive development

- physical development, including vision and hearing

- communication

- social or emotional development

- the ability of the child to care for him or herself in an age-appropriate way (adaptive development or behavior)

In addition to this very broad definition of developmental delay, each state provides its own, more specific definition. That definition will specify the criteria by which the state decides what constitutes a developmental delay in each of the five areas, as well as the evaluation and assessment procedures for measuring the criteria. Aside from your state's formal definition of a developmental delay, appendix A outlines some of the typical skills that babies and toddlers learn by certain ages. This outline may be helpful, but it is no substitute for a formal evaluation.

Next Steps

When you contact your local early intervention agency or Child Find, you should ask that your child be evaluated under part C of IDEA because you are worried about his development. Early in the process, you'll be assigned a service coordinator as your liaison and your guide through the next steps.

After you connect with the early intervention system, it has forty-five days to complete an initial evaluation of your child and, with your approval, an assessment of the family. If the child is found to be eligible for services, the agency must also create your IFSP (remember, that's jargon for Individual Family Services Plan) within that period.

The evaluation is typically conducted by a group of professionals with different expertise, and it can take place only with your written consent. In some states, a full evaluation may be preceded by a preliminary screening (typically, the same sort of screening provided at www.ProjectSKIP.com, except that it will be conducted in person by a professional). Some children are automatically eligible for services, without the need for a screening or evaluation, because they have a condition—such as Down syndrome or some other genetic abnormality—that almost always results in developmental delays.

A tip: As you move through what will be a long and often stressful process, create a written system for keeping track of all the information, including everyone you speak with or contact as well as the dates of the conversation or communication.

Creating a Plan

After the initial evaluation and further assessment of your child's needs, the next step will be for you and the professionals involved to create a written plan—the IFSP—that describes the specific services your child will receive, the specialists who may be involved in providing those services, and when and where they will be provided. Each state has specific guidelines for an IFSP. The family will always be heavily involved in creating the plan and following through with it, however, and your written consent must be provided for each service the plan proposes. Once it has been created, the IFSP should be reviewed twice a year and updated at least once annually.

School-Aged Kids

For older kids, in many school districts the teacher will first try a number of informal interventions to help your child in the classroom. If those don't provide enough support, you will need to pursue a more formal plan to help your child. For school-aged children, that planning takes place within the framework of the special education system.

As it is defined by IDEA, special education is instruction designed specifically to meet the needs of a child with a disability. Public school systems provide special education and related services for free. (Related services can include, for example, physical therapy, speech therapy, and psychological services.) Special education can be provided not just in the classroom but also at home or in institutional settings. Although these services are free, they may be less than what you want for your child. So, if you can afford to do so, I often advise parents to work in conjunction with their own pediatrician or other treatment professional.

Children with disabilities are eligible for special education and related services if they meet IDEA's definition of a "child with a disability," as that definition is applied through state and local policies. IDEA's definition lists fourteen categories of disability:

- visual impairment

- deafness

- hearing impairment

- speech or language impairment

- developmental delays (which may include some of the other genetic disorders listed in chapter 4)

- emotional disturbance, which includes much of what has been discussed in this book

- intellectual disability

- a specific learning disability (including disorders listed in chapter 10)

- autism

- multiple disabilities

- orthopedic impairment

- other health impairments, such as ADHD or seizures

- traumatic brain injury

- deaf-blindness

For children to be eligible for special education and related services, their educational performance must be adversely affected by one or more of these disabilities.

First Steps

If teachers and family have concluded that a child's difficulties cannot be effectively addressed by the teacher in the classroom and the child has been referred for special-education services, the first step is an assessment or evaluation, just as it is for younger children.

How do you arrange for an evaluation? In practice, you have two options:

1. You can tell the school you plan to have an initial evaluation conducted by an independent professional of your choosing. You will have to pay for that evaluation yourself, and it may cost up to several thousand dollars. The school does not have to accept the evaluation's conclusions, but if the evaluator meets certain criteria—more about those following—it must at least consider them. The advantage of this option is that, if you choose the right professional, you can be sure of a thorough evaluation conducted by someone who is on your child's side.

2. You can ask the school to undertake the evaluation, in which case it will be free. You will still have the option of requesting an independent evaluation later if you disagree with the school's conclusions. In some situations, the school will even pay for that additional evaluation.

If the school undertakes the evaluation, it will involve professionals who have different types of expertise, and the team will be coordinated by a person who may be a school psychologist, teacher, or expert in assessing learning problems. The team will use several assessment instruments and methods and will collect information from a broad range of sources, including parents and other family members. IDEA gives clear instructions about how schools must conduct these evaluations. For example, tests and interviews must be given in the language or communication mode, such as sign language, that is most likely to yield accurate information about what your child knows or can do. IDEA also says that schools may not decide a child's eligibility for special education based on the results of a single test or an observation.

In some cases, schools will be able to conduct a child's entire assessment within the school. In other cases, a school won't have the staff to conduct all of the evaluations needed, and will have to hire others to help. If your child is evaluated outside of the school, the school must make the arrangements and tell you in writing exactly what type of testing is to be done. Again, all of these evaluation procedures are conducted at no cost to parents.

In some cases, however, once the evaluation has begun, the outside specialist may ask to do more testing. Make sure you tell the specialist to contact the school. If the testing will go beyond what the school originally asked for, the school needs to agree in advance to pay for the extra testing.

If the school has completed an evaluation, that doesn't prevent you from arranging an independent educational evaluation (IEE) from a person who typically is not employed by the school district as a staff member. If you need more or different information about your child's learning difficulties, or a different perspective about your child's needs and how to accommodate those needs, an independent evaluation can be extremely helpful to the IEP process. It is absolutely critical if you want to dispute the school's assessment or believe it isn't adequate in some way. An IEE can be invaluable in the following situations:

- You believe the school's assessment doesn't accurately reflect your child's abilities or the tests chosen by the school's evaluator don't reveal the nature of your child's learning difficulties.

- The assessment report does not provide you with enough data to help you determine if your child has a learning disability or to discuss with an IEP team how to best accommodate your child's specific educational needs.

If you want the results of the assessment considered by the IEP team, the professional you hire must have credentials equivalent to or greater than those of the person the school would use to assess your child. If you're unsure what those credentials might be, ask the school what their assessor's credentials are. For example, school psychologists typically test students for eligibility for special education services. If you hire someone who is also a psychologist, the IEP team must consider the independent evaluation as it makes decisions.

Under IDEA, your child has the right to a "free appropriate public education." That doesn't mean the IEP team has to adopt all of the recommendations in the IEE evaluation. The IEP team only must take the IEE under consideration when reaching its decisions and creating the IEP. In addition, however, if you decide to challenge the school's recommendations, the IEE may be used in a hearing as evidence of your child's needs.

You can pay for an IEE out of pocket at any point during this process. But if you disagree with the school's most recent evaluation or reevaluation you can also ask the school district to pay for an IEE. You have the right to ask for a free IEE each time the school evaluates your child.

The school has two choices if you ask it to pay for an IEE. It may request a hearing to allow a hearing officer to determine whether the evaluation is necessary, or it may agree to pay for the IEE outright. If the school requests a hearing, it will have to prove to a hearing officer that its own evaluation was suitable. The hearing officer will decide either that the school's evaluation was inadequate and that it must pay for an IEE or that the school's evaluation was appropriate, in which case the school will not have to pay. The school has a right to assess your child's learning needs, and it is only when that evaluation is not adequate that it will have to pay for an IEE.

When you start the process of requesting an IEE, ask your school what criteria it uses to conduct its evaluations. You can also ask where you can get an independent evaluation, including asking for a list of qualified evaluators who have worked with the school in the past. You can choose anyone you want as long as they have the credentials identified by the school. It can be advantageous to work with someone with whom the school has worked collaboratively in the past; however, I personally have been brought into IEE evaluations as a fresh set of eyes and that perspective can also be advantageous. It is frequently helpful to ask other parents who they used to have their child evaluated.

Finally, you should be aware that the IEP process includes several formal safeguards for children and parents:

- prior written notice of all evaluations and changes to the IEP or a placement

- a right to independent evaluations

- arbitration or mediation about disagreements or an administrative complaint process

Next Steps

The evaluation process can lead to one of three results:

1. Your child is found not to have a disability. In that case, the IEP process ends, and your child's education remains the responsibility of the school's regular teachers and staff.

2. An evaluation finds that although your child has a disability, he does not require special instruction, but he does need other forms of support or accommodation. In that case, a 504 Plan—described earlier in this chapter—is created. The plan outlines your child's specific accessibility requirements, and it is—or should be—updated annually to ensure that he continues to receive the most effective accommodations.

3. Your child is found to have a disability and qualify for special education services. In that case, an IEP is developed, and IDEA continues to govern the process. The IDEA process requires documentation of measurable growth so it is more involved than the 504 process. A 504 accommodation plan is created for those students with disabilities who do not require specialized instruction as specified in the IDEA but do require the assurance that they will receive equal access to public education and services.

Creating and Implementing an IEP

For those children who meet the requirements for special education services, the next step is for the parents and the IEP team to decide what services and type of education will best benefit the child. Those decisions involve defining goals for the child, such as doing better in the normal educational setting or developing the skills to be independent as an adult. The goals will guide the choice of services and supports that will aid teachers in delivering the curriculum, as well as decisions about the extent to which he participates in general education courses and the accommodations he will receive for instruction and testing. For example, some children will receive what are known as direct services: a special education teacher will work directly with an individual or a small group of students to build skills that will enable them to compensate for their disabilities. Others may receive indirect services: consultations between the special education teacher and the general education teacher to adapt teaching methods and the general classroom environment to better meet the student's needs.

Once it has been created, the IEP will probably not be a static document. Some changes may be minor; others may be serious enough to require the IEP team to reassemble. For example, if there are serious disciplinary issues—such as drugs or violence—a behavioral intervention plan must be created and included in the IEP.

Accountability

IDEA requires states to review each student's IEP once a year, and the student must be reevaluated every three years. These reviews are designed to measure a child's progress toward the goals outlaid in his IEP. In addition, all students are required to participate in annual state or district testing under the mandates of the No Child Left Behind Act and IDEA. That testing is usually adapted to meet the child's needs through accommodations similar to those they typically receive in the classroom. Other forms of assessments can also be provided if, for example, a child's IEP goals focus more on secondary skills related to independence or interacting with others and less on skills that are part of the general academic curriculum.

Some Practical Advice

Over the years, I have participated as a psychologist and advocate in many Independent Educational Evaluations and in IEP meetings. My experience has taught me a number of important things for parents to consider. First, when schools and states become more burdened financially, school services under IDEA and state programs like Child Find suffer from cutbacks the most. The demand for thorough evaluations far exceeds the number of people adequately trained to conduct them. If at all possible, I recommend that you get a comprehensive evaluation of your child from a mental health professional of your own choosing who meets the school's criteria and present it to the school. If you can't afford an independent evaluation, allow the school or state agency to conduct one, but educate yourself about the evaluation process and ask questions at every step.

Next, stay involved in every step of the planning process and get your evaluator to help you understand how the steps proposed in the IEP or 504 Plan—or, for younger children, the IFSP—will meet your child's needs. Be persistent throughout the process (the squeaky wheel will indeed get the grease), and ask for everything to be explained.

The parent who demands the most for their child gets the most. Advocating for your child is one of the most important things you can do. Kids with developmental or mental health issues can succeed, but they will have to work harder than and differently from other kids and they will need extra support. So be sure they get it.

14

FAQ: Answers to the Most Commonly Asked Questions in My Practice

HERE ARE THE answers I give to some of the most common questions that my clients ask about their children's behavior, working with a mental health professional, and the mental health system. For answers to other questions not found here, please go to my websites www.ProjectSKIP .com or www.AskDrForrest.com to submit a question to other parents or to me.

Will my child grow out of this?
Probably not—and, in any case, it's a risk not worth taking. Although it is true that with age some children lose some of their symptoms without intervention, most will need some sort of intervention in order to see significant and lasting improvement. And as I've repeated many times in this book, the sooner you intervene, the more effective treatment is likely to be.

Can my child be cured?
Only sometimes in mental health do researchers and clinicians speak of a "cure." In most cases, a mental health issue will probably continue to be part of who the child is, but the way it presents itself will change over time. At times, it may be totally unnoticeable, and at others it may flare up and need attention. Again, with good support and effective treatment, it will rarely be an obstacle to your child's progress in life.

Can my child still be successful?

In my years of experience as a clinician, I have seen many kids grow into successful adults when they have a mental health intervention and the right support from family and professionals. They may need to work harder and differently—for example, not cramming for an exam as their friends do—but they can succeed.

Is this my fault?

Most likely not. Many mental health issues have biological or genetic causes, or result from an interaction of nature and nurture. Only severe forms of neglect or abuse are likely, by themselves, to give rise to significant psychological problems. And, in any case, assigning blame to yourself or others won't help you or your child. That said, good parenting pays dividends, and bad or indifferent parenting can have consequences for a child's behavior and mental health. It is important to form a positive bond with your child early in life and to continue to nurture your child. The good news is that even if you need to improve your parenting skills, there are parenting classes and other resources that will help. Check your local place of worship, a community parenting magazine, or my website AskDrForrest.com for more details.

At what age can children start to get depressed or suffer from other mental health issues?

See chapter 3 on infant and preschool mental health. Researchers now know that even infants can be depressed, and autism spectrum disorders can now be reliably diagnosed in children as young as two. If you see behaviors that give you good reason to be concerned at any age, don't wait to see if your child will grow out of them. Seek help from someone who works with small children and get a good assessment.

What is the difference between the blues and depression?

If the child's sadness is outside the typical range in duration, intensity, or behavior (see chapter 1), it may be a sign of depression. If you have concerns that persist, it is always better to seek help than to wait and see.

How do I know whether or not to trust my doctor?

Only you can answer that question, but first and foremost make certain that he or she is a credentialed professional and has the specialized expertise you are seeking. Second, ask yourself if you feel comfortable asking questions and if the doctor would be open to your asking anything you want to ask. If there doesn't seem to be a good fit, it's OK. Ask for referrals and find someone else with whom you do feel comfortable. In my practice, there have been patients and families who needed more than I could give them and who chose, with my encouragement, to work with other providers.

Don't doctors disagree?

Yes, sometimes doctors will disagree about diagnoses and treatments. That is why it is important to know what they are basing their opinion on and how they made their decisions. It's your responsibility to ask the right questions and be prepared to make your own decisions based on the answers that they give you, the facts of your individual case, and your knowledge about what is best for your child. Providing the tools for you to do that is the reason I wrote this book.

Is it really OK to medicate young kids?

Drugs should not always be the first-line treatment for younger children for every mental health issue. For example, the first step in treating ADHD in young children is behavioral treatment, not medication. Yet, sadly, a recent study found that pediatricians prescribed medications in 90 percent of ADHD cases of children younger than six. That is why it is crucial for you to understand the evidence on which doctors base their decisions and the process they used to reach their conclusions. Ask what the latest research says on the issue, because they must be able to back up their opinion with science. Also ask how many children with this issue the doctor has treated. As I have written throughout this book, however, in the right circumstances and with the right supervision, medications can be an important part of a treatment plan.

My parents spanked me. Isn't that OK for my kids?

The single hardest job is being a parent and not a friend or boss. Effective parenting involves setting firm limits and being authoritative, not authoritarian or permissive. The research on spanking is clear: it leads to increased aggression in kids. There are effective ways to set limits without resorting to corporal punishment, which rarely leads to the behavior you want in the long term.

After Newtown

I HAVE THOUGHT a great deal about what to say in conclusion. In this book I have tried to demystify mental health issues and the mental health system so you can navigate your way more easily and less anxiously. Yet it is impossible to think about mental health issues now without thinking about the massacre at Sandy Hook Elementary School and similar tragedies in recent years. So, in this chapter, I have decided to talk about why our mental health system seemingly fails those who commit these kinds of outrages, and to advocate for changes, including changes in funding at the state and federal levels. By the end of this chapter, I hope you will be ready to support those changes as well.

On December 14, 2012, Adam Lanza, age twenty, entered the Sandy Hook Elementary School and shot dead twenty children and six adults. As first responders arrived, he committed suicide by shooting himself in the head in one of the classrooms. Before driving to the school, Lanza had shot and killed his mother, Nancy, at their home.

The incident was the second-deadliest mass shooting by a single person in American history, after the shooting at Virginia Tech in 2007. But the year prior to Sandy Hook also saw a fatal shooting at an Aurora, Colorado, movie theater, and another horrible shooting in Tucson, Arizona, of Congressperson Gabrielle "Gabby" Giffords and several bystanders. It has been widely reported that the people who committed these acts of violence had mental health problems, in spite of the fact that people with mental health difficulties are more often victims rather than the perpetrators of violence. Although the horror of the events did spark some debate about changes to the mental health system, that discussion was overshadowed by the gun control debate and, as of this writing, attempts to shore up the gaps in the US mental health system have stalled.

In my years working with children who have behavioral and mental health issues—sometimes very serious ones and sometimes ones that have led them into violence—I have found that kids typically don't get the help they need for one of three reasons: the parents don't understand how much the child needs help, they can't force an older child to get help, or they can't access services because they can't afford to or because the services don't exist in their community. It isn't entirely clear what happened in Newtown or Aurora (although we now know that Adam Lanza was seen by some very competent mental health professionals at the Yale Child Study Center where I once trained), but in those and other violent outbursts it seems that the help a child or adolescent needed wasn't provided.

The rest of this book has been about the importance of seeking and getting help as early as possible. But what happens when a family lacks access to professional help, a problem that has been exacerbated by funding cuts?

Larry

When I represented Larry as an attorney, I quickly learned his earliest years were filled with violence. His father threw him against the wall and sexually abused him from at least the age of two. His mother frequently beat him, at times with a hammer to the head. The family was often homeless, living a nomadic existence, and he often went hungry. He was diagnosed with childhood schizophrenia and suffered from epilepsy, which was not diagnosed until later in life. His repeated, untreated seizures, coupled with the trauma to his brain as a result of the beatings, caused severe and irreversible brain damage. At ten, Larry was sent away to a state child psychiatric facility where he lived until he was almost twenty-one, when he was forced out because its funding was cut. Ultimately, Larry ended up in prison on death row for killing someone during a robbery.

Larry's story is far from unique. Too often, I have seen children with histories similar to Larry's in programs in which I have been involved. Nothing excuses Larry's crime. But his life could have been different, and the costs he imposed on society and his victims much less, if clinicians had intervened early enough. The programs that could have helped are in place in many counties and states, but they did not reach Larry. What if society had protected him from his abusive parents and then provided adequate medical and psychological treatment before the damage became irreparable? How might his life and his victim's life have been different, and the financial costs to society been smaller, had we intervened in his early years? In Larry's case, the price of failing to provide that intervention has been tremendous: two lives (his victim's and his own) and millions of dollars spent on trying and appealing his murder case, not to speak of the cost of his imprisonment.

Individual stories are important, but for those who aren't persuaded by such anecdotes that society needs to do more, several studies by the RAND Institute, economists, and other think tanks provide the solid data. These studies have found not only that targeted early interventions benefit children and their families, but also that investing early in the lives of some children saves money that our society would spend later on services such as special education, welfare, and imprisonment. (As one small example of the costs of failing to address children's problems early enough, in my city of San Diego the cost of housing an adolescent in a juvenile detention facility has been estimated at $60 per day, or $22,000 per year.) In fact, according to the RAND study, well-designed programs for children four and younger can produce economic benefits ranging from $1.26 to $17 for each dollar spent on the programs. In the last few years, the Federal Reserve Bank has endorsed similar figures, and a noted economist, James Heckman, has written on this topic extensively.

In the 1980s, there was a renewed interest in the influence of early childhood, especially the first three years of life, on health and development. New scientific studies revolutionized our understanding of the complex ways in which those years shape the developing brain and the emotional, social, self-regulatory, moral, and intellectual capacities that emerge from early childhood. As a result, there was a new understanding of the importance of intervening effectively and quickly to address childhood problems, including mental health issues. At the same time, budgets were flush, and governors and legislators directed budgetary surpluses toward interventions for young children.

Now that budgets are tight, however, cuts to local mental health services have become commonplace. In fact, they are often among the first programs to be cut, along with cuts to preschools and other services for children. These cuts are devastating to many children and families, and they will cost everyone more in the long term. Aside from the cuts' effects on mental health care, they have an effect on the development especially of the approximately 22 percent of children who live in poverty. Researchers, clinicians, and economists know that not having a rich, stimulating environment as a child grows—put aside being hungry or unable to afford a doctor when he is sick—impedes learning and other forms of development.

There are difficult choices to be made with our budgets on both state and national levels in this time of huge deficits and fiscal belt tightening. But short-term thinking got us into this financial mess to begin with. As we focus on the long-term health of our country, voters must make choices that focus on longer-term, lasting results for our most pressing societal problems—and, therefore, we must make funding mental health programs, especially early prevention and intervention programs for children, a priority. A society cannot sacrifice the well-being of its children to short-term considerations, as pressing as they may appear.

I urge you to get involved in these discussions locally and nationally in whatever way you can. Volunteer with your local chapter of the National Alliance on Mental Illness (NAMI), or find a mental health organization near you at VolunteerMatch.org. Donate money to any one of the organizations listed in the resources, such as the Child Mind Institute or the National Federation of Families for Children's Mental Health. Share the contents of this book with friends and other parents. Whatever you find appropriate for you, do *something*. Just, please, join the discussion!

Acknowledgments

THIS BOOK OWES more than I can ever express in words to the many children and families with whom I have had the great privilege to work over the years, first as an attorney, and then as a neuropsychologist. Their courage has renewed my commitment to this work when it has flagged, and they have been an unfailing source of inspiration and hope.

I also owe a great deal to those who have taught me about how to work with children and families, neuropsychological assessment, and mental health issues in general, at Columbia and Yale Universities and the National Institute of Mental Health—in particular, Michael Westerveld and Ken Perrine for their constant support and guidance throughout my career. My students have consistently asked me questions and made me better at explaining things in ways that everyone can understand, and their influence on me is readily apparent in many of the descriptions in this book. Finally, my heartfelt gratitude to my colleagues in a number of neuropsychological and psychological organizations, including the American Psychological Association and the National Academy of Neuropsychology. Your willingness to discuss ideas and innovations inspires me to be better at what I do on a daily basis.

This book has benefited greatly from the people who touched it during the process, from idea to tangible product. It has been a pleasure collaborating with Lisa Reardon and the entire team at Chicago Review Press. Thank you for your wise, helpful, and spot-on editorial advice. To my literary agent, Jill Marsal of the Marsal Lyon Literary Agency, I cannot thank you enough for believing in this project from the very beginning and helping me make this book available as a resource for parents. Leslie Sharpe was supportive from the initial stages of my proposal and through the many drafts. You are a kind and wonderful friend and incredible writer.

Most especially, I am grateful to my husband, Stephen Armstrong, who helped me heavily edit the original manuscript and provided constant support and love throughout this process (and survived it!). It has been an inspiration to watch my husband's grandchildren thrive under the guidance of their parents and uncles. To my family of origin—Mom and Dad, Terry,

Debbie, and Sarah—thank you for being there when I needed you most and giving me the love and support (and challenges) I needed to grow, which shaped the kind of professional I would become so many years later.

Finally, thank you to those who continue to provide me with wide venues to help children and families and to speak about mental health more broadly, including CNN, Fox News, Clear Channel Networks, and *The O'Reilly Factor*.

Brain Development 101

WHY IS IT worth taking the time to understand how the brain develops? For two reasons. First, before you can understand if your child's behavior is developing as it should, you need to understand the range of what is typical for your child's age—and that hinges on how the brain develops during a child's first years. Second, understanding how the brain develops will help you to ask better questions of the mental health professionals with whom you deal.

The Roles of Nature and Nurture

Researchers and clinicians used to believe that children came into this world as blank slates or canvases upon which we painted values. Researchers now know that social and emotional growth results from a complex interaction between nature and nurture: a child's genetic inheritance on the one hand and, on the other, his environment, especially the relationship between parent and child.

Your child is born with a certain makeup derived from your genes, and that inheritance results in a basic brain structure and, yes, temperament. But a child's early environment and experiences powerfully affect the development of his brain and influence the specific way in which the circuits of the brain are wired. During the early years, the brain develops rapidly, and this early development holds the key to a child's future. All the research highlights the importance of early childhood experiences in building and nurturing the skills children will need to succeed as adolescents and adults.

Among those experiences, none is more powerful than your child's interaction with you or a loving caregiver. Your most important job as a parent is to support your child's development, especially in the first years, by providing a stimulating set of everyday experiences and consistent support. Touch, talk, read, smile, sing, count, and play with your child. These are the basic building blocks of parenting in the early years. Later, you can begin to teach and demonstrate more complex skills, such as bouncing back after a failure, giving to others, being hopeful, and maintaining social connections. These sorts of lessons come only through spending quality time with our children. That time instills a sense of confidence and direction that helps them to navigate their lives successfully.

The simple message: whatever nature has given your child, good or bad, you can profoundly affect your child's development through your parenting practices. That is true whatever stresses or obstacles you or your child may encounter. I have worked with single parents with very few financial resources who instill a sense of belonging and confidence in their children that far exceeds any bank-account balance. Often, that confidence arises from simple, consistent acts of play and ritual that a parent develops with a child. For example, does the morning routine of getting ready for school become a dreaded race out the door, or does it provide an opportunity for you and your child to prepare for the uncertainty of the day ahead through a bit of laughter and planning?

Before you begin to parent, however, your child comes into this world with his or her own unique biological canvas upon which you will both begin to sketch out their existence. The purpose of this appendix is to help you understand how biology and early experiences interact during your child's early development. And the place to start is with the basic structure of the brain.

Understanding Brain Development

Let's begin with an understanding of some of the simple structures that comprise the brain. I spent a large portion of my graduate education learning this stuff, and I know that you will find it as fascinating as I do if you just hang in there with me.

The brain and spinal cord together make up the central nervous system, which is in charge of all activities of the body and, in coordination with the rest of the body's nervous system—the peripheral nervous system—controls behavior.

The brain's building blocks are neurons, cells that process and transmit information through electrical and chemical signaling. As unromantic as it sounds, we are all basically governed by these signals, and a neuron is the brain's messenger. The core of a neuron—its cell body, or soma—is tiny, about one-hundredth the size of the period at the end of this sentence. From that cell body emerge branches, which are called dendrites. These dendrites pick up chemical signals and transmit them to other neurons across synapses, the connection between neurons.

The signals travel along an axon, a long, slender projection from the neuron's cell body, like an arm that links with arms of other cells. Each axon has a sac containing neurotransmitters, or chemical messengers, at its tip. An electrical impulse causes the release of the neurotransmitters, which in turn either excite the neighboring cells, making them more active, or inhibit their activity.

In this way, neurons connect to each other to form networks. A single neuron can connect with many thousands of other neurons, and the human brain has a huge number of these connections or synapses. Each of the hundred billion neurons has an average of seven thousand synaptic connections to other neurons, and it has been estimated that the brain of a three-year-old has about one quadrillion of these connections.

These connections are no less than miraculous in their functioning.

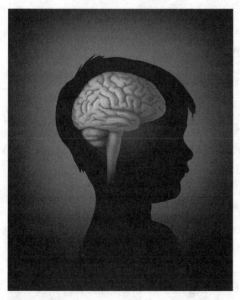

The brain

The incredibly complex networks of connections that result from cells communicating with each other become the brain's wiring, as you can see in figure 2. It is in the formation and refinement of this wiring that experience, or nurture, can shape the way circuits are laid down or connected in your child's brain.

In the early years, the shaping takes place in two related ways.

First, the brain reduces the number of connections, getting rid of connections that aren't being used or won't be needed. Neurons must have a purpose in order to survive.

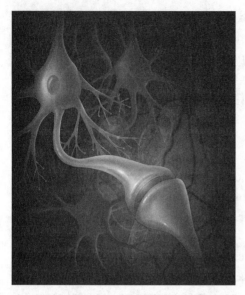

Neurons and connections

In the brain's development, there is a golden rule: *use it or lose it*. If a neuron isn't being used, it is eliminated through a process called apoptosis, in which neurons that do not receive or transmit information become damaged and ultimately die. Synaptic pruning eliminates these weaker synaptic connections, while other connections are kept and are subsequently strengthened—in much the same way a gardener would prune a tree, giving the plant a new shape.

Strengthening is the second and most important way in which the brain is shaped. This shaping is possible because the brain—and especially the infant brain—has a quality called neuroplasticity, which enables it to reorganize the connections between neurons based on experiences. Put simply, repeated experiences will strengthen the relevant synapses in your child's brain. Connections that are activated most frequently, such as those necessary for talking or seeing, grow stronger. Those new or strengthened connections represent new knowledge and skills, and they in turn structure the way your child perceives and remembers the world.

Children learn through their interactions with their parents or other adults in all kinds of ways that will affect the growth and pattern of the connections in their brains. You can affect the number of these strengthened connections in your child's brain through the experiences or instruction you provide for him. Those experiences directly determine which connections will be strengthened and which will be pruned.

For example, if you repeatedly play with your child by pointing to the alphabet, then connections will form that allow your child to recognize the names of the letters, and these connections will form the foundation for the later, more complex skill of reading. If the early connections are not made, or

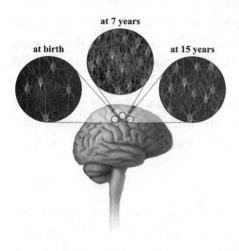

at birth

at 7 years

at 15 years

Pruning and synaptic connections

made poorly because they have not been used often enough, then the corresponding, more complex skill will be more difficult or impossible for the child to learn later on.

Here is another example: if your child becomes frustrated and cries, you can tell him, "You are upset because the dog walked away and you wanted to pet him." In this way, your child learns that this horrible feeling inside of them is frustration and that it won't eat them up, as scary as it is. Furthermore, you will teach your child to cope by verbalizing the feeling, as opposed to hitting or throwing something to deal with the uncomfortable sensations in his body. In this process, the neural pathway and chemical pathways that signal to the brain, "Hey, I am frustrated," begin to be established as emotional road maps within the brain. You are helping your child create that road map. On the other hand, if you respond by asking, "What's wrong with you? Stop crying!" you are creating a pathway for fear and anger.

As the synapses in your child's brain are strengthened through repeated experiences, connections and pathways are formed that structure the way your child perceives and remembers the world. If a pathway is not used consistently, it's eliminated. As a result, things you do as a parent a single time, either good or bad, are thus less likely to have an effect on brain development. It is children's repeated exposure to language and play—or stress or trauma—that affects how their brain develops and, ultimately, how they perceive the world around them. For example, if a child is repeatedly exposed to danger or stress, such as the emotional turmoil of parents who constantly argue, then the brain will become wired to perceive danger and stress more frequently, and this will become your child's most likely response to new situations.

Imagine you are startled by a loud noise in the morning and then another, softer sound in the afternoon. Do you flinch at the soft noise or sound because you are still reacting to the noise you heard earlier? This is exactly what happens in our brain when we are young. If you are exposed to repeated anxiety or fear, those neural pathways become stronger in order to assist with our survival, so we can remain alert and try to avoid a new threat. Because those pathways are so strong and sensitive, children who have experienced stress and trauma in the past may automatically perceive a person who is somewhat ambiguous in their approach as angry or threatening.

Building the Brain

We have reviewed neurons, the basic building blocks of the brain, and how neurons develop connections as your child learns to take in the world surrounding him. The earliest connections created within the brain provide the foundation for more elaborate systems of communication that allow more sophisticated forms of behavior. First, these systems give rise to networks that allow you to breathe, control the temperature of your body, run away, or fight. Eventually, more elaborate systems enable what is called executive function, which allows you to plan actions and coordinate multiple activities simultaneously. For example, at first children can only catch a ball, but ultimately they learn to play an entire game with a strategy to win as the systems grow that allow them to learn the more complex act of strategizing.

We will now look at the different parts of the brain and how they function together to coordinate more complex activities as we get older.

If you draw a line from the forehead to the chin and open the head for a side view, you would see the brain as it is shown in Figure 4.

The basic elements of the human brain include the following:

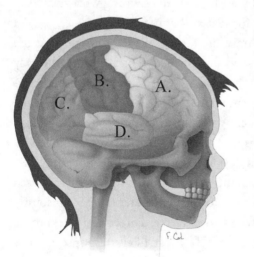

Structure of the brain

- temporal lobe (D): concerned with taking in things from our environment, speech, recognizing sounds, and memory.

- parietal lobe (B): contains the areas for perception of things related to touch, pressure, temperature, and pain. It also controls the perception of objects in space.

- occipital lobe (C): behind the parietal lobe and temporal lobe, it contains the neurons responsible for the many aspects of vision or seeing.

- frontal lobe (A): concerned with reasoning, planning, understanding parts of speech, movement, emotions, and problem-solving. It regulates decision-making and our most complex actions.

- brain stem: At the base of the skull, it protrudes downward, between the cerebellum and the temporal lobe (D), and connects with the spinal cord. The brain stem controls your most basic biological activities, including blood pressure and body temperature. It is believed to be one of the oldest parts of the brain from an evolutionary standpoint. It has been with us for a very long time.

- cerebellum: at the top of the brainstem, below the temporal and occipital lobes, it looks sort of like a small cabbage. The cerebellum coordinates movement and balance, and therefore physical activities such as walking.

Together, these structures form the outermost tissue, or the cerebral cortex, of the human brain. The cerebral cortex continues to develop into late adolescence and early adulthood.

Critical Periods of Brain Development

All parts of the brain do not develop at equal rates during every stage of development. Specific parts develop more rapidly at different times, when they can absorb new information most readily. During these periods, a part of the brain can take a dramatic leap forward. For example, young children come into the world primed with a sense of smell, and it is the first sense to mature after birth because it enables them to recognize their parents from their earliest days. Think about what is needed for a young lion cub to seek out comfort and warmth from a parent in the wild.

While these developmental sprints continue throughout early childhood and adolescence, for basic skills they are especially important in the first three years of life. After age six or seven, it is usually more difficult for your child to improve dramatically in skills related to vision, hearing, or speech. This does not mean that it is impossible to improve some basic skills throughout life, just more difficult. For example, you can learn a foreign language in adulthood. It's just that a young child will master the language more quickly because the critical period for language development is before age six.

In contrast, executive functions, or the abilities to plan, change direction, think creatively, or reason about the risks associated with an action, are more complex functions that don't fully develop until much later. Although the ability to self-regulate, or control our emotions, begins to develop in the early years, in the areas of higher reasoning the brain doesn't fully mature until at least age twenty-five.

You should provide your child with the best opportunity for learning and growth during the periods when their minds are most ready to absorb new information. See figure 5 for an overall schematic of these critical periods for development.

Human Brain Development

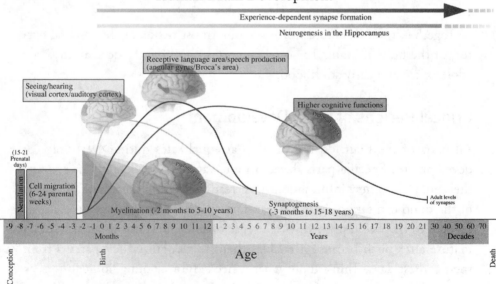

Critical periods for brain development

Vision and Hearing

For seeing and hearing, the crucial period is from birth to four or five years old. During the first few months especially, babies need to see shapes, colors, and objects at varying distances so their brains can learn how to see. Babies also need exposure to a variety of sounds during this time so their brains can learn to process and respond to that information. Most important, babies need to be able to identify through their seeing and hearing the people on whom they depend for survival. This is why it is crucially important for children to get regular eye and hearing exams as they grow. You can't learn to respond to your mother's voice, for example, if you can't hear it.

Language

The most important window for language development is from birth to age six, especially the earliest years. During those early years, children need to hear caregivers talk, sing, and read to them constantly. Respond to their early efforts at language, even if it's only babbling, by talking to them in a back-and-forth manner: "Oh, you like that when Mom gives you a bottle. That is good." Help them verbalize feelings and emotions that they don't yet understand: "Oh, you seem so upset. You are tired. Should we go to sleep to feel better?" Encourage them to ask for what they want instead of just giving them an object or toy, because that will help them use language to communicate for a purpose.

Here are some milestones to look for:

- babbling, pointing, or using other gestures by twelve months

- using single words by sixteen months

- using two-word phrases by twenty-four months

In their first years, children develop language at different speeds, and parents should have some patience with their development. However, if you have persistent concerns that your child isn't meeting these language milestones, you should ask for an evaluation by a qualified professional. Language intervention is one of the things trained professionals do well and, at this critical period for development, it can make all the difference in fostering successful reading and writing skills later in life.

Motor Skills

The critical period for developing motor skills is from birth to twelve years. Children will master gross motor skills, such as walking, before they master fine skills, such as using a pencil. Developing the coordination to play games or sports takes even longer. Again, although you should keep an eye on your child's development in this area, you should expect variation in how he develops compared to other children.

Emotional and Social Development

The critical period for emotional and social development is also from birth to twelve years, but different emotional and social abilities develop at different times. From birth to eighteen months, when a young child forms attachments with parents or other caregivers, is the most important stage for developing emotional attachment, the feelings that bond children to the most important people in their lives. This early attachment provides the foundation for other aspects of emotional development and for relationships later in life. More complex aspects of emotional and social abilities, such as empathy and trust, mature later during these first twelve years.

This emotional development is critical to success in life. The parts of the brain that regulate emotion, the amygdala and the limbic system found deep inside the brain, are shaped early on by experience and come to form the brain's emotional wiring. As a result, early nurturing is vital to learning the emotional skills of empathy, hopefulness, and resilience.

Social development, which involves both self-awareness and your child's ability to make friends, also occurs in stages and continues throughout adolescence. For example, a two-year-old's brain is not yet prepared to share toys spontaneously, so this is something you as a parent must teach your child through the use of verbal prompts, such as "I like that you are sharing your toy and giving it to your sister." Think of it as you would teaching a foreign language to a child; he must be presented with the information in order to absorb it.

In the context of all we now know about how the brain develops, let's look at some developmental milestones.

THE FIRST YEAR

TWO MONTHS OLD

Social and Emotional
- begins to smile at people
- can briefly calm himself (may bring hands to mouth and suck on hand)
- tries to look at parent

Language / Communication
- coos, makes gurgling sounds
- turns head toward sounds

Cognitive (Learning, Thinking, Problem-Solving)
- pays attention to faces
- begins to follow things with eyes and recognize people at a distance
- begins to act bored (cries, is fussy) if activity doesn't change

Movement / Physical Development
- can hold head up and begins to push up when lying on tummy
- makes smoother movements with arms and legs

FOUR MONTHS OLD

Social and Emotional
- smiles spontaneously, especially at people
- likes to play with people and might cry when playing stops
- copies some movements and facial expressions, such as smiling or frowning

Language / Communication
- begins to babble
- babbles with expression and copies sounds he hears
- cries in different ways to show hunger, pain, or being tired

Cognitive (Learning, Thinking, Problem-Solving)
- lets you know if she is happy or sad
- responds to affection

- reaches for toy with one hand
- uses hands and eyes together, such as seeing a toy and reaching for it
- follows moving things with eyes in a side to side motion
- watches faces closely
- recognizes familiar people and things at a distance

Movement / Physical Development
- holds head steady when unsupported
- pushes down on legs when feet are on a hard surface
- may be able to roll over from tummy to back
- can hold a toy and shake it and swing at dangling toys
- brings hands to mouth
- when lying on stomach, pushes up to elbows

SIX MONTHS OLD

Social and Emotional
- knows familiar faces and begins to recognize if someone is a stranger
- likes to play with others, especially parents
- responds to other people's emotions and often seems happy
- likes to look at self in a mirror

Language / Communication
- responds to sounds by making sounds
- strings vowels together when babbling ("ah," "eh," "oh") and likes taking turns with parent while making sounds
- responds to own name
- makes sounds to show joy and displeasure
- begins to say consonant sounds (jabbering with m, b)

Cognitive (Learning, Thinking, Problem-Solving)
- looks around at things nearby
- brings things to mouth
- shows curiosity about things and tries to

get things that are out of reach
- begins to pass things from one hand to the other

Movement / Physical Development
- rolls over in both directions (front to back, back to front)
- begins to sit without support
- when standing, supports weight on legs and might bounce
- rocks back and forth, sometimes crawling backward before moving forward

NINE MONTHS OLD

Social and Emotional
- may be afraid of strangers
- may be clingy with familiar adults
- has favorite toys

Language / Communication
- understands "no"
- makes a lot of different sounds like "mamamama" and "babababababa"
- copies sounds and gestures of others
- uses fingers to point at things

Cognitive (Learning, Thinking, Problem-Solving)
- watches the path of something as it falls
- looks for things he sees you hide
- plays peekaboo
- puts things in his mouth
- moves things smoothly from one hand to the other
- picks up things like cereal Os between thumb and index finger

Movement / Physical Development
- stands, holding on
- can get into sitting position
- sits without support
- pulls up to stand
- crawls

THE SECOND YEAR

TWELVE MONTHS OLD

Social and Emotional
- is shy or nervous with strangers
- cries when parent leaves
- has favorite things and people
- shows fear in some situations
- hands you a book when he wants to hear a story
- repeats sounds or actions to get attention
- puts out arm or leg to help with dressing
- plays games such as peekaboo and patty-cake

Language / Communication
- responds to simple spoken requests
- uses simple gestures, like shaking head no or waving good-bye
- makes sounds with changes in tone (sounding more like speech)
- says "mama" and "dada" and exclamations such as "uh-oh!"
- tries to repeat words you say

Cognitive (Learning, Thinking, Problem-Solving)
- explores things in different ways, through shaking, banging, throwing
- finds hidden things easily
- looks at the right picture or thing when it's named
- copies gestures
- starts to use things correctly; for example, drinks from a cup, brushes hair
- bangs two things together
- puts things in a container, takes things out of a container
- lets things go without help
- pokes with index (pointer) finger
- follows simple directions such as "pick up the toy"

Movement / Physical Development
- gets to a sitting position without help
- pulls up to stand, walks by holding on to furniture (cruising)

- may take a few steps without holding on
- may stand alone

EIGHTEEN MONTHS OLD

Social and Emotional
- likes to hand things to others as play
- may have temper tantrums
- may be afraid of strangers
- shows affection to familiar people
- plays simple pretend games, such as feeding a doll
- may cling to caregivers in new situations
- points to show others something interesting
- explores alone but with parent close by

Language / Communication
- says several single words
- says and shakes head no
- points to show someone what he wants

Cognitive (Learning, Thinking, Problem-Solving)
- knows what ordinary things are for; for example, a telephone, brush, or spoon
- points to get the attention of others
- shows interest in a doll or stuffed animal by pretending to feed it
- points to one body part
- scribbles on his own
- can follow one-step verbal commands without any gestures; for example, sits when you say "sit down"

Movement / Physical Development
- walks alone
- may walk up steps and run
- pulls toys while walking
- can help undress himself
- drinks from a cup
- eats with a spoon

THE THIRD YEAR

TWENTY-FOUR MONTHS OLD

Social and Emotional
- copies others, especially adults and older children
- gets excited when with other children
- shows more and more independence
- shows defiant behavior (doing what he has been told not to do)
- plays mainly beside other children, but is beginning to include other children, such as in chase games

Language / Communication
- points to things or pictures when they are named
- knows names of familiar people and body parts
- says sentences with two to four words
- follows simple instructions
- repeats words overheard in conversation
- points to things in a book

Cognitive (Learning, Thinking, Problem-Solving)
- finds things even when hidden under two or three covers
- begins to sort shapes and colors
- completes sentences and rhymes in familiar books
- plays simple make-believe games
- builds towers of four or more blocks
- might use one hand more than the other
- follows two-step instructions such as "Pick up your shoes and put them in the closet."
- names items in a picture book such as a cat, bird, or dog

Movement / Physical Development
- stands on tiptoe
- kicks a ball
- begins to run
- climbs onto and down from furniture without help
- walks up and down stairs holding on

- throws ball overhand
- makes or copies straight lines and circles

THE FOURTH YEAR

THIRTY-SIX MONTHS OLD

Social and Emotional
- copies adults and friends
- shows affection for friends without prompting
- takes turns in games
- shows concern for crying friend
- understands the idea of mine and his or hers
- shows a wide range of emotions
- separates easily from caregivers
- may get upset with major changes in routine
- dresses and undresses self

Language/Communication
- follows instructions with two or three steps
- can name most familiar things
- understands words like in, on, and under
- says first name, age, and gender
- names a friend
- says words like I, me, we, and you and some plurals (cars, dogs, cats)
- talks well enough for strangers to understand most of the time
- carries on a conversation using two to three sentences

Cognitive (Learning, Thinking, Problem-Solving)
- can work toys with buttons, levers, and moving parts
- plays make-believe games with dolls, animals, and people
- does puzzles with three or four pieces
- understands what "two" means
- copies a circle with pencil or crayon
- turns book pages one at a time
- builds towers of more than six blocks

- screws and unscrews jar lids or turns door handles

Movement / Physical Development
- climbs well
- runs easily
- pedals a tricycle
- walks up and down stairs, one foot on each step

THE FIFTH YEAR

FORTY-EIGHT MONTHS OLD

Social and Emotional
- enjoys doing new things
- plays "house"
- is more and more creative with make-believe play
- would rather play with other children than by himself
- cooperates with other children
- often can't tell what's real and what's make-believe
- talks about what he likes and what he is interested in

Language/Communication
- knows some basic rules of grammar, such as correctly using he and she
- sings a song or says a poem from memory such as "Itsy Bitsy Spider" or "The Wheels on the Bus"
- tells stories
- can say first and last name

Cognitive (Learning, Thinking, Problem-Solving)
- names some colors and some numbers
- understands the idea of counting
- starts to understand time
- remembers parts of a story
- understands the idea of same and different
- draws a person with two to four body parts
- uses scissors

- starts to copy some capital letters
- plays board or card games
- tells you what he thinks is going to happen next in a book

Movement / Physical Development
- hops and stands on one foot for up to two seconds
- catches a bounced ball most of the time
- pours, cuts with supervision, and mashes own food

THE SIXTH YEAR

SIXTY MONTHS OLD

Social and Emotional
- wants to please friends
- wants to be like friends
- is more likely to agree with rules
- likes to sing, dance, and act
- shows concern and sympathy for others
- is aware of gender
- can tell what's real and what's make-believe
- shows more independence (for example, may visit a next-door neighbor by himself [adult supervision is still needed])
- is sometimes demanding and sometimes very cooperative

Language/Communication
- speaks very clearly
- tells a simple story using full sentences
- uses future tense; for example, "Grandma will be here tomorrow."
- can say his full name and address

Cognitive (Learning, Thinking, Problem-Solving)
- counts ten or more things
- can draw a person with at least six body parts
- can print some letters or numbers
- can copy a triangle and other geometric shapes
- knows about things used every day, such as money and food

Movement/Physical Development
- stands on one foot for ten seconds or longer
- hops; may be able to skip
- can do a somersault
- uses a fork and spoon and sometimes a table knife
- can use the toilet on his own
- swings and climbs

These are typical developmental milestones that you can use to monitor your child's early development. Again, these are averages, and every child develops at different rates. However, if you have concerns, you should speak with your pediatrician or a developmental psychologist. For children at least two years of age, you can take a first step by logging in to www.ProjectSKIP .com to fill out questionnaires about your child's development. (For children younger than two you can contact me at www.AskDrForrest.com.) The questionnaires are gold-standard screening instruments for cognitive, social-emotional, and mental health delays in children.

If the results show that your child is not within the typical ranges displayed, tell your professional that these questionnaires, which you should cite by name, resulted in atypical ratings. The questionnaires cannot diagnose issues in and of themselves; they simply indicate whether the issues about which you are concerned warrant further exploration. In particular, you can look at the results of your responses to the Social Communication Questionnaire to see how your child compares in social communication skills compared to others their age. A score in the green range means that your child compares favorably or is within the typical range of development. A score in the yellow or red range means that your child may have issues that should be explored.

Although I have focused on early brain development because this sets the stage for later growth and maturation, growth during adolescence should also be monitored for typical progression. However, later childhood and adolescence are more focused on social and emotional development, areas in which it is more difficult to quantify progress and therefore create lists of milestones. Still, the questionnaires provided at www.ProjectSKIP.com can be helpful. They are relevant for children through the last year of high school.

I can't stress enough the importance of early intervention. Early intervention positively changes the outcomes associated with mental health and developmental issues and drastically increases the odds of success for your child. Doing nothing is not a realistic option, and getting this book to help you find answers to your questions is a great first step in supporting your child's development.

Therapies Found to Be Most Effective for Various Diagnoses

IN THE CHART below, "ages" refers to the ages of the children included in the studies on which the findings are based, and "length" refers to the duration of the treatments for those children. The numbers in those columns shouldn't be taken as a guide to what will work best for your child, as each child's treatment is unique.

Diagnosis	Therapies with the Greatest Evidence of Effectiveness	Ages	Length
Autism Spectrum Disorders	Intensive Behavioral Treatment	2–12	From 5 weeks to 6 years
	Intensive Communication Training	1–10	From 5 months to 1 year
ADHD	Self-Verbalization Therapy	7–13	Up to 2 weeks
	Behavior Therapy plus Medication	7–11	From 12 weeks to 14 months
	Parent Management Training (PMT)	2–12	6 to 12 weeks
Anxiety/OCD	Cognitive Behavioral Therapy (CBT)	4–18	Up to 6 months
	Exposure Therapy	3–19	Up to 14 weeks
Traumatic Stress	CBT with Parents	2–18	12 to 20 weeks
Depression*	CBT	8–23	4 to 16 weeks
	CBT plus Medication	12–21	12 weeks to 6 months
	CBT with Parents	13–18	8 to 12 weeks
	Family Therapy	10–17	3 to 9 months
Eating Disorders	Family Therapy	11–19	6 to 18 months
	CBT	13–20	6 months
	Family Systems Therapy	11–20	6 months to 1 year
ODD or Disruptive Behavior	PMT	2–15	Up to 2 years depending on the type of therapy
	CBT	9–18	
	Social Skills Training	4–19	
	Multisystemic Family Therapy	10–17	
	PMT and Problem Solving	7–13	
	Assertiveness Training	13–18	
Suicidality	Attachment Based Family Therapy	12–18	12 weeks
Substance Abuse	Family Therapy	6–21	3 weeks to 6 months

* No studies with children under 8 years; however, Parent Child Interaction Therapy Emotion Development (PCIT-ED) has shown promise in younger children.

See the chart at AskDrForrest.com for the most up-to-date research on effective therapies.

Commonly Used Medications for Mental Health

THE SIX BROAD categories of medications listed below are those most commonly used to treat mental health issues. In each category, the list names the most commonly used drugs, but it is not exhaustive. Some medications may not be specifically approved for use with children of a certain age, yet they are sometimes used anyway. Whenever medication is used, the child should be carefully monitored for side effects and efficacy.

Antipsychotics: *Psychosis* is a term used to describe irrational or illogical thought patterns that are not based in reality. People with psychosis often hear voices or have extremely strange ideas (for example, thinking that someone is controlling their mind). Antipsychotic medications work to reduce these symptoms. These kinds of behaviors are often seen in schizophrenia or some severe forms of depression.

Commonly used antipsychotic medications include:

- aripiprazole (Abilify)
- clozapine (Clozaril or Fazaclo)
- ziprasidone (Geodon)
- haloperidol (Haldol)
- thioridazine (Mellaril)
- risperidone (Risperdal)
- quetiapine (Seroquel)
- trifluoperazine (Stelazine)
- chlorpromazine (Thorazine)
- olanzapine (Symbyax or Zyprexa)

Antidepressants: These are medications typically used to treat depression. There are several classes or types (tricyclics, selective serotonin reuptake inhibitor [SSRI], or serotonin norepinephrine reuptake inhibitor [SNRI]). Antidepressants typically used include:

- citalopram (Celexa)
- venlafaxine (Effexor)
- escitalopram (Lexapro)
- fluvoxamine (Luvox)
- paroxetine (Paxil)
- nortriptyline (Pamelor)
- mirtazapine (Remeron)
- fluoxetine (Prozac or Sarafem)
- imipramine (Tofranil)
- sertraline (Zoloft)
- bupropion (Wellbutrin)

Antianxiety: These medications make you feel relaxed or less stressed. Some of them are also used to treat specific phobias. Antianxiety medications typically used include:

- lorazepam (Ativan)
- buspirone (BuSpar)
- fluoxetine (Prozac or Sarafem)
- clonazepam (Klonopin)
- diazepam (Valium, Diastat)
- alprazolam (Xanax)

Mood Stabilizing: These medications help with impulsive or aggressive behavior or the mood swings seen in bipolar disorder. Medications typically used include:

- valproic acid / sodium divalproex (Depakote)
- lithium (Lithobid, Eskalith)
- carbamazepine (Tegretol)

Stimulants and Nonstimulants: These are medications commonly used to treat ADHD. Stimulants include:

- methylphenidate (Concerta, Daytrana, Focalin, Ritalin, Methylin, or Metadate)
- dextroamphetamine (Adderal, Dexedrine)

Nonstimulants include:

- clonodine (Catapres)
- atomoxetine (Strattera)
- guanfacine (Tenex)

Resources for Help

National Crisis Hotlines

- 911 for emergency assistance or 211 for referrals in your area
- Befrienders Worldwide: www.befrienders.org (numbers listed for numerous countries)
- Crisis Textline: Text "LISTEN" to 741-741
- Girls and Boys Town National Hotline: 800-448-3000
- Hopeline: 800-442-HOPE (4673)
- National Suicide Prevention Lifeline: 800-273-TALK (8255) / 775-784-8090
- National Drug and Alcohol Treatment Helpline: 800-662-HELP (4357)
- National Runaway Safeline: 800-RUNAWAY (786-2929)
- Self-Abuse Finally Ends (SAFE): 800-DONTCUT (366-8288)

General Mental Health Information

- American Academy of Child and Adolescent Psychiatry: Facts for Families: www.aacap.org/AACAP/Families_and_Youth/Facts_for_Families/Home.aspx
- American Psychological Association (APA): 800-374-2721; www.apa.org
- Ask Dr. Forrest: www.AskDrForrest.com
- The Child Mind Institute: www.childmind.org
- Mental Health America: 800-969-6MHA (6642); www.mentalhealthamerica.net
- National Academy of Neuropsychology: www.nanonline.org
- National Alliance on Mental Illness: 800-950-NAMI (6264); www.nami.org
- National Federation of Families for Children's Mental Health: http://ffcmh.org
- National Institute of Mental Health: 866-615-6464: www.nimh.nih.gov

- National Mental Health Information Center (SAMHSA): 877-726-4727 and www.samhsa.gov

- REACH Institute: www.thereachinstitute.org

Specific Conditions

Attention Deficit Hyperactivity Disorder

- Free Behavioral Reward Chart Templates: www.freeprintablebehaviorcharts.com

Alcohol and Other Drug Use

- Al-Anon: 888-4ALANON (425-2666); www.al-anon.alateen.org

- National Institute on Drug Abuse : 301-443-1124; www.drugabuse.gov

- Partnership for Drug-Free Kids: 855-DRUGFREE (378-4373); www.drugfree.org

- Substance Abuse and Mental Health Services Administration (SAMHSA): 800-662-HELP (4357); www.samhsa.gov

Alternative Treatments

- NIH Center for Complementary and Alternative Medicine (NCCAM): http://nccam.nih.gov

Autism

- Association of University Centers on Disabilities: www.aucd.org

- NIH Autism Centers of Excellence: www.nichd.nih.gov/research/supported /Pages/ace.aspx#current

Anxiety, Social Phobia, Obsessive-Compulsive Disorder, and Trauma

- Anxiety and Depression Association of America: 240-485-1001; www.adaa.org

- Freedom from Fear: 718-351-1717; www.freedomfromfear.org

- International OCD Foundation: 617-973-5801; www.ocfoundation.org

- National Center for PTSD: www.ptsd.va.gov
- Social Anxiety Association: www.socialphobia.org

Attention-Deficit Hyperactivity Disorder (ADHD)

- Attention Deficit Disorder Association (ADDA): 856-439-9099; www.add.org
- Children and Adults with Attention-Deficit/Hyperactivity Disorder (CHADD): 800-233-4050; www.chadd.org
- Free Behavioral Reward Charts: Empowering Parents: www.empoweringparents.com/free-downloadable-charts
- National Resource Center on ADHD: 800-233-4050; www.help4adhd.org

Bullying

- National Runaway Safeline: 800-RUNAWAY (786-2929); 1800RUNAWAY.org
- Striving to Reduce Youth Violence Everywhere (STRYVE): http://vetoviolence.cdc.gov/stryve
- US government's bullying website: www.stopbullying.gov

Depression, Dysthymia, and Bipolar Disorder

- Depression and Bipolar Support Alliance (DBSA): 800-826-3632; www.dbsalliance.org
- The International Foundation for Research and Education on Depression (iFred); www.ifred.org or www.depression.org

Early Childhood

- Centers for Disease Control and Prevention: www.cdc.gov/
- Early Childhood Technical Assistance Center: http://ectacenter.org/topics/earlyid/earlyid.asp

- ECTA's state-by-state listing of programs: http://ectacenter.org/contact/ptccoord .asp and http://ectacenter.org/search/mapfinder.asp

- Zero to Three: www.zerotothree.org

Eating Disorders

- National Eating Disorders Association (NEDA): 800-931-2237; www.national eatingdisorders.org

- National Association of Anorexia Nervosa and Associated Disorders (ANAD): 630-577-1330; www.ANAD.org

Evidence-Based Interventions

- Clinical Treatment Guidelines: www.guideline.gov

- Effective Child Therapy: http://effectivechildtherapy.com/content /what-evidence-based-practice

- SAMHSA'S National Registry of Evidence-Based Programs and Practices: www.nrepp.samhsa.gov/ViewAll.aspx

Fetal Alcohol Syndrome

- National Organization on Fetal Alcohol Syndrome (NOFAS): 800-66NOFAS; www.nofas.org

Individual Education Plans

- Wrightslaw: www.wrightslaw.com

- Autism Speaks IEP Guide: www.autismspeaks.org

Learning Disabilities

- Learning Disabilities Association of America: www.ldamerica.org

- LD Online: www.ldonline.org

- National Center for Learning Disabilities: www.ncld.org

Obsessive-Compulsive Disorder

- International OCD Foundation: www.ocfoundation.org

Parenting Classes

- The Incredible Years: http://incredibleyears.com/parents-teachers /looking-for-incredible-years-groups/
- The Kazdin Method for Parenting the Defiant Child: http://alankazdin.com /the-kazdin-method-for-parenting-the-defiant-child-with-no-pills-no -therapy-no-contest-of-wills/

Relational Aggression

- The Ophelia Project: www.opheliaproject.org

Screening

- www.ProjectSKIP.com (use the code BOOK1)

Self-Injury (Including Cutting)

- S.A.F.E. Alternatives: http://selfinjury.com
- Young Minds: www.youngminds.org.uk

Substance Abuse

- National Institute of Drug Abuse for Teens: http://teens.drugabuse.gov

Suicide Prevention

- American Foundation for Suicide Prevention: 888-333-2377; www.afsp.org
- Suicide Awareness Voices of Education (SAVE): 952-946-7998; www.save.org

Schizophrenia

- Schizophrenia.com: www.schizophrenia.com

Tourette Syndrome

- National Tourette Syndrome Association: http://tsa-usa.org

Traumatic Brain Injury

- Brain Injury Association of America: 800-444-6443; www.biausa.org

Weight Control

- Weight-Control Information Network; National Institute of Diabetes, Digestive and Kidney Diseases: http://win.niddk.nih.gov/publications/index.htm#public

Insurance Help

- Massachusetts School of Professional Psychology: Insurance Guide: http://msppinterface.org/guides/insurance-guide

- MentalHealth.gov: Health Insurance and Mental Health Services: http://www.mentalhealth.gov/get-help/health-insurance

- National Alliance on Mental Illness (NAMI): Health Coverage: https://www.nami.org/Template.cfm?Section=Health_Care_Reform

- National Conference of State Legislatures (NCSL): http://www.ncsl.org/research/health/mental-health-benefits-state-mandates.aspx

For the most up-to-date list of resources, please visit AskDrForrest.com.

Glossary

anorexia: refusing to consume adequate nutrition out of a powerful and unreasonable fear of becoming overweight.

applied behavior analysis (ABA): using scientific techniques to shape everyday behaviors, based on an understanding of what does or doesn't lead to new behaviors or skills in children. One of the primary tools in ABA is discrete trial training (DTT), which uses intensive drills to prompt or guide a very specific desired behavior and then reinforce it.

assessment: an examination of a person's mental health conducted by a mental health professional. Depending on the type of professional, it will include some or all of the following: pencil-and-paper or computerized tests, checklists, medical and psychological or psychiatric histories, and questions about symptoms, current activities, and academic or work functioning.

attachment theory: describes the impact of a child's relationship with his earliest caregivers on growth and development. If an infant's social and emotional development is to be normal, he needs to develop a warm, nurturing relationship with at least one primary caregiver, a person who is sensitive and responsive to his cues and who consistently provides for his basic comforts. Some theorists believe this attachment sets the tone for our most important relationships for life, because the caregiver's responses to the child lead to the development of patterns of attachment, which, in turn, lead to the models inside the child's head for navigating the world. These will then guide the child's perceptions, emotions, thoughts, and expectations in later relationships. The failure to form a secure attachment has been proven to be a risk factor in later development, and the "disorganized" pattern of attachment is a powerful predictor for serious mental health issues in children. *See also: reactive attachment disorder.*

attention deficit hyperactivity disorder (ADHD): A condition involving certain portions of the brain that help us put the brakes on our behavior, thus enabling us to pay attention and inhibiting our desire to get up and move around. Studies show that ADHD affects areas of the brain (the frontal areas, those involving executive functions) that allow us to evaluate the consequences of our actions, think ahead, stay focused, and control our impulses. The primary symptoms of ADHD are inattention, hyperactivity, and impulsivity.

autism diagnostic observation schedule (ADOS): a crucial assessment for children suspected of having an autism spectrum disorder (ASD). The assessment has four modules designed for children at different ages and language abilities. It uses structured play and other tasks to take a snapshot of the child's eye contact, interactive capabilities, and other skills critical to social interaction that are impaired in an ASD, as well as of the repetitive behaviors characteristic of the disorder.

autism spectrum disorder (ASD): manifests in children through differences in development of thinking, language, behavior, and, most noticeably, social skills. These differences appear before age three and can be diagnosed in children as young as twelve to eighteen months. Some signs can be recognized as early as by the first year. For a diagnosis of an ASD, a child must have a specified number of symptoms in areas involved in social interaction and exhibit a restricted and repetitive range of behaviors, activities, and interests, with stereotypic or repetitive movements and behaviors that have no meaning.

behavior therapy: its goal is to substitute a positive behavior for the behavior that is causing a problem in your child's life.

bipolar disorder (or manic depression): a mood disturbance characterized by extreme alternating episodes of very low energy sadness or hopelessness (depression) and very high energy irritability or explosiveness (mania).

bulimia: grossly overeating (bingeing) and then purging the food by vomiting or using laxatives or some other method to prevent weight gain.

child-parent psychotherapy (CPP): an intervention for children from birth to age five who have experienced at least one traumatic event (such as maltreatment, the sudden or traumatic death of someone close, a serious accident, sexual abuse, or exposure to domestic violence) and who, as a result, are experiencing behavior or mental health problems, which can include post-traumatic stress disorder (PTSD). CPP is designed to support and strengthen the parent-child relationship in order to shore up a child's ability to process the trauma and return to a normal developmental path.

cognitive behavioral therapy (CBT): focuses both on how people act and how they think. In CBT, therapists help children first to identify the thoughts, feelings, and images that precede and accompany the experience of a disturbance, and then to distance themselves from the those thoughts and images.

collaborative problem solving (CPS): CPS views the child's disruptive, explosive behavior as the child's inadequate and inappropriate attempt to solve a problem in his world. The parent or teacher strives to figure out what problem the child is struggling with, and then to assist the child in finding a solution and learning how to solve a problem.

depression: overwhelmingly low mood, low self-esteem, and loss of interest or pleasure in normal daily activities.

developmental delay: a diagnosis based on an ongoing delay in the child's developmental process. There are strict guidelines for the diagnosis, and it is not to be given to children who are temporarily lagging behind in reaching their developmental milestones. A developmental delay can occur in one or many areas, including motor, language, social, or cognitive abilities.

developmental trajectory: the typical path of development that determines what we expect of a child at a certain age, based on what we know about most children's development coupled with this child's history.

developmentally disabled: lifelong disabilities attributable to mental or physical impairments, manifested prior to age eighteen.

diagnostic process: the process used by a mental health professional to work with an individual to understand his symptoms, the history of his illness, its impact on his daily life, and his overall general abilities and daily functioning. The process culminates in clinical findings, which may include a diagnosis and plan for intervention or treatment.

disruptive mood dysregulation disorder (DMDD): severe irritability and an angry mood. The irritability causes frequent, extreme temper outbursts or tantrums when the child is frustrated at home or school. Between these outbursts, the child is angry most of the time.

epigenetics: the study of how genes interact with environmental factors.

evidence-based therapy: therapy that has evidence in the form of scientifically designed research studies that support its effectiveness.

exposure therapy: a type of cognitive behavioral therapy for obsessions, compulsions, and related anxiety disorders during which children receive support while repeatedly doing things that may terrify them by using previously learned coping skills until the fears recede or disappear.

generalized anxiety disorder (GAD): extreme worries or fears about everyday things, even when there is little or no reason to worry about them, that keep children from participating in normal activities such as attending school or making presentations in class.

hyperactivity: too much energy, leaving a person fidgety and unable to sit still.

impulsivity: inability to control behaviors that are inappropriate to the situation or environment.

inhibited/disinhibited behavior: Behavior that is too restricted (inhibited) for the situation or behavior that is over-the-top or too much for the situation (disinhibited).

intellectual disability: difficulties with daily life skills or adaptive functioning and below average intellectual abilities, as formally measured on an intelligence test. *See also: developmentally disabled.*

interpersonal psychotherapy (IPT): a form of cognitive behavioral therapy specifically developed for depression. Within the context of a supportive relationship, it teaches adolescents how to monitor their feelings, understand the link between their emotions and events, improve their communication skills, and solve problems that involve interactions with others.

licensed clinical social worker (LCSW): a social worker trained in talk therapy who helps individuals deal with a variety of problems. Typically has a master's degree (two years beyond college) in social work and has completed a specified number of hours of clinical practice to become licensed in his or her state.

licensed clinical professional counselor (LCPC): another form of licensure for mental health professionals, though the exact title may vary by state (for example, it is also known as "licensed mental health counselor"). The license typically requires a master's degree in counseling and a specific number of hours of clinical practice.

licensed psychologist: see psychologist.

monitoring: documenting your child's progress in the context of his treatment plan. Ask your provider to share the plan with you and work with you to understand the specific goals for the treatment. Once you know the goals and the plan, you will be better prepared to look for signs of progress, such as positive changes in behavior, an ability to manage emotions in different ways, improvement in relationships with friends and siblings, and improvement in grades and school performance. Often you can use objective checklists, such as those at www.ProjectSKIP.com, to compare your child's behavior at two different points in time to see if there has been improvement.

marriage and family therapist (MFT): a therapist licensed by a state on the basis of two years of master's-level course work in therapy and a specified number of hours of clinical practice.

obsessive-compulsive disorder (OCD): the presence of recurrent, intense obsessions (thoughts) or compulsions (behaviors) that interfere with daily functioning.

oppositional defiant disorder (ODD): a repeated pattern of uncooperative, defiant, and hostile behavior toward adult authority figures that seriously interferes with the child's ability to be in school or participate in regular family activities. Symptoms of ODD include, among others, frequent temper tantrums, defiance of and refusal to comply with appropriate adult requests and rules, deliberate attempts to annoy or upset people, irritability, frequent anger and resentment, mean and hateful talk when upset, and revenge-seeking.

panic attack: intense fear that produces physical reactions (such as difficulty breathing) when there is no actual threat or obvious cause.

panic disorder: more than isolated panic attacks before a stressful situation comes to its end, but rather multiple, unforeseen panic attacks. A child may spend hours in persistent fear of additional attacks.

parent-child interaction therapy (PCIT) (or, parent-child attunement therapy for younger toddlers): an evidence-based treatment for conduct-disordered children aged two to twelve that is focused patterns of interaction between parent and child. Parents learn skills that support a nurturing and secure relationship with their child.

parent-directed interaction (PDI): parents learn to use specific behavior-management techniques as they play with their child to shape or guide the child's behavior.

pivotal response therapy (PRT): PRT is focused on producing positive changes in pivotal or fundamental behaviors that are critical for higher-levels skills. Increasing the number of positive pivotal behaviors leads to improvement in communication, social abilities, and a child's skill in monitoring his own behavior.

play therapy: can be used to treat young children with PTSD who are not able to deal with the trauma more directly. The therapist uses games, drawings, and other methods to help children process their traumatic memories.

post-traumatic stress disorder (PTSD): a severe form of an anxiety disorder that can develop after a child experiences an extremely traumatic event. Children and teens may have PTSD, for example, if they have lived through an event that caused someone else severe injury or death, or if they themselves suffered violence or sexual or physical abuse.

present functioning: an individual's performance or behavior at a specific point in time in the present, it is often used to describe symptom levels or psychological test results.

psychiatrist: a mental health professional who is a medical doctor and has completed a four-year residency in psychiatry after medical school. Specialists in child and adolescent psychiatry are also required to complete a two-year fellowship program.

psychological evaluation: provides information about cognitive, emotional, and social functioning. It uses multiple sources of data, including pencil-and-paper tests; teacher and parent reports; behavioral observations; social, academic, and family history; and any medical findings.

psychologist: generally, someone who has completed a doctoral degree and internship training (in some states, also a postdoctoral year of clinical work) and is licensed to practice in a specific state. A psychologist may provide psychological testing and therapy and, in a few states, also has prescription privileges.

randomized clinical trial: the gold standard for research studies. A control group (that does not receive the treatment being studied) and the experimental group (that does receive the treatment) are compared to determine if the treatment truly had an effect.

reactive attachment disorder (RAD): a rare but serious condition in which infants and young children do not establish healthy bonds with parents or caregivers, resulting in their needs failing to be met. A child with reactive attachment disorder is typically neglected, abused, or orphaned.

separation anxiety disorder (SAD): excessive worry beyond what is typical for a child's age over separation from home or from those to whom he is attached.

social phobia (SoP) or social anxiety disorder: a diagnosis applied to children who worry too much in social situations. The signs include extreme anxiousness when meeting or interacting with someone new, excessive distress when speaking in front of a group, avoidance of situations where interactions with unfamiliar people or performances in front of others will be necessary, and extreme misery when having to perform in a social or school situation.

schizophrenia: a serious mental illness that may cause irrational thoughts and behavior. Symptoms may include seeing things or hearing voices that are not real (hallucinations) or bizarre thoughts and ideas (delusions).

structured play group: a group in which social skills are taught to children through modeling and coaching.

talk therapy: talking about oneself to a trained listener.

Tourette syndrome (TS): a form of tic disorder involving motor and vocal tics that occur many times per day, lasting for more than a year.

Notes

Introduction

Difficulties getting solid answers Alan Zarembo, "Autism Boom: An Epidemic of Disease or Discovery?" *Los Angeles Times*, December 11, 2011, www.latimes.com/news/local/autism/la-me-autism-day-one -html-htmlstory.

Fewer than half Linda Radecki et al., "Trends in the Use of Standardized Tools for Developmental Screening in Early Childhood: 2002–2009," *Pediatrics*, 128, no. 1 (2011): 14–19, doi: 10.1542/peds.2010-2180.

Chapter 1: Where to Start When Your Child's Behavior Is Troubling You

behaviors in your child NAMI Southwestern Pennsylvania. "Navigating the Mental Health and Education Systems. A Caregivers' Guide," www .namiswpa.org/documents/pdfs/CAREGIVERS%20GUIDE.pdf.

Assessing the seriousness Lucy Daniels Center, "When to Seek Professional Help," www.lucydanielscenter.org/page/when-to-seek-professional -mental-health-help.

shore up your children's mental and emotional health Australian Government, Department of Health, "Mental Health," www.health.gov.au/internet /main/publishing.nsf/Content/Mental+Health+and+Wellbeing-1.

Chapter 2: Diagnosis, Stigma, and the Clinician's Manual

fraught with controversy Allen Frances, "DSM-5: Where Do We Go from Here?" May 16, 2013, www.huffingtonpost.com/allen-frances/dsm-5 -where-do-we-go-from_b_3281313.html.

explore other classifications Thomas Insel, "Director's Blog: Transforming Diagnosis," National Institute of Mental Health, April 29, 2013, www .nimh.nih.gov/about/director/2013/transforming-diagnosis.shtml.

Chapter 3: Infant and Preschool Mental Health

Selma Fraiberg Selma Fraiberg, *Clinical Studies in Infant Mental Health: The First Year of Life*, with the collaboration of Louis Fraiberg (New York: Basic Books, 1980).

new research is very clear Mo Costandi, "Pregnant 9/11 Survivors Transmitted Trauma to Their Children," *The Guardian* (UK), September 9, 2011, www.theguardian.com/science/neurophilosophy/2011/sep/09 /pregnant-911-survivors-transmitted-trauma.

Yehuda's work Rachel Yehuda et al., "Transgenerational Effects of Posttraumatic Stress Disorder in Babies of Mothers Exposed to the World Trade Center Attacks During Pregnancy," *Journal of Clinical Endocrinology & Metabolism* 90, no. 7 (2005): 4115–18, doi: 10.1210/ jc.2005-0550; Rachel Yehuda et al., "Gene Expression Patterns Associated with Posttraumatic Stress Disorder Following Exposure to the World Trade Center Attacks," *Biological Psychiatry* 66, no. 7 (2009): 708–11, doi: 10.1016/j.biopsych.2009.02.034; Casey Sarapas et al., "Genetic Markers for PTSD Risk and Resilience Among Survivors of the World Trade Center Attacks," *Disease Markers* 30, no. 2–3 (2011): 101–10, doi: 10.3233/DMA-2011-0764.

researchers from the University of Pennsylvania Christopher P. Morgan and Tracey L. Bale, "Early Prenatal Stress Epigenetically Programs Dysmasculinization in Second-Generation Offspring via the Paternal Lineage," *Journal of Neuroscience*, 31, no. 33 (2011): 11748-55, doi: 10.1523/JNEUROSCI.1887-11.2011.

John Bowlby John Bowlby, *Attachment and Loss*, vols. 1–3 (New York: Basic Books, 1969–80).

Mary Ainsworth Mary D. Salter Ainsworth and Silvia M. Bell, "Attachment, Exploration, and Separation: Illustrated by the Behavior of One-Year-Olds in a Strange Situation," *Child Development* 41, no. 1 (1970): 49–67.

typically arises from Mayo Clinic, "Reactive Attachment Disorder. Definition," July 6, 2011, www.mayoclinic.org/diseases-conditions /reactive-attachment-disorder/basics/definition/con-20032126.

The symptoms Ibid.

Joan Luby Joan L. Luby et al., "Preschool Depression: Homotypic Continuity and Course over 24 Months," *Archives of General Psychiatry* 66, no. 8 (2009): 897–905, doi: 10.1001/archgenpsychiatry.2009.97.

little kids can and do get depressed Michael S. Gaffrey et al., "Disrupted Amygdala Reactivity in Depressed 4- to 6-Year-Old Children," *Journal of the American Academy of Child and Adolescent Psychiatry* 52, no. 7 (2013): 737–46, doi: 10.1016/j.jaac.2013.04.009.

DC-0-3R Zero to Three, *Diagnostic Classification of Mental Health and Developmental Disorders of Infancy and Early Childhood*, rev. ed. (Washington, DC: Zero to Three Press, 2005).

Walter Gilliam Walter S. Gilliam, *Prekindergarteners Left Behind: Expulsion Rates in State Prekindergarten Programs*, FCD Policy Brief Series No. 3 (New York: Foundation for Child Development, 2005); www.challengingbehavior.org/explore/policy_docs/prek_expulsion.pdf; Dobbs, Michael; "Youngest Students Most Likely to Be Expelled," *Washington Post*, May 17, 2005, www.washingtonpost.com/wp-dyn/content/article/2005/05/16/AR2005051601201.html.

Incredible Years curriculum The Incredible Years, "The Incredible Years Parenting Programs," 2013, www.incredibleyears.com/programs/parent.

Child-parent psychotherapy Substance Abuse and Mental Health Services Administration, "Child–Parent Psychotherapy (CPP)," January 28, 2014, www.nrepp.samhsa.gov/ViewIntervention.aspx?id=194.

specific methods University of California, San Francisco, Child Trauma Research Program, "Child-Parent Psychotherapy," www.childtrauma.ucsf.edu/resources/index.aspx.

"crack babies" Susan Fitzgerald, "'Crack Baby' Study Ends with Unexpected but Clear Results," Philly.com, July 22, 2013, http://articles.philly.com/2013-07-22/news/40709969_1_hallam-hurt-so-called-crack-babies-funded-study.

made a positive difference Ibid.

Chapter 4: Delayed, Different, Not Fitting In

overall trend is clear Stephen J. Blumberg et al., *Changes in Prevalence of Parent-Reported Autism Spectrum Disorder in School-Aged U.S. Children: 2007 to 2011–2012*, National Health Statistics Report No. 65 (Hyattsville, MD: National Center for Health Statistics, 2013); Autism and Developmental Disabilities Monitoring Network Surveillance Year 2008 Principal Investigators, "Prevalence of Autism Spectrum Disorders—Autism and Developmental Disabilities Monitoring Network, 14 Sites, United States, 2008," *Centers for Disease Control Morbidity and Mortality Weekly Report* 61 (March 30, 2012): 1–19; Autism and Developmental Disabilities Monitoring Network Surveillance Year 2010 Principal Investigators, "Prevalence of Autism Spectrum Disorder among children aged 8 years—autism and developmental disabilities monitoring Network, 11 sites, United States, 2010," *Centers for Disease Control Morbidity and Mortality Weekly Report* 63 (March 28, 2014): Suppl. 2:1–21.

Increase in the diagnosis Ibid.

fewer than 40 percent Beverly A. Pringle et al., *Diagnostic History and Treatment of School-Aged Children with Autism Spectrum Disorder and Special Health Care Needs*, NCHS Data Brief No. 97 (Hyattsville, MD: National Center for Health Statistics, 2012).

red flags Centers for Disease Control and Prevention, "Signs and Symptoms," www.cdc.gov/ncbddd/autism/signs.html.

DSM does not name them separately Susan L. Hyman, "New DSM-5 Includes Changes to Autism Criteria," *AAPNews*, June 4, 2013, http://aapnews.aappublications.org/content/early/2013/06/04/aapnews.20130604-1, doi: 10.1542/aapnews.20130604-1.

Pivotal response therapy Autism Canada Foundation, "Pivotal Response Therapy," www.autismcanada.org/treatments/behav/pivotalresponse.html.

Hyperbaric oxygen chambers Doreen Granpeesheh et al., "Randomized Trial of Hyperbaric Oxygen Therapy for Children with Autism," *Research in Autism Spectrum Disorders* 4 (2010): 268–75, doi: 1016/j.rasd.2009.09.014.

Gluten-Free Diets S. Hyman et al., "The Gluten Free and Casein Free (GFCF) Diet: A Double Blind, Placebo Controlled Challenge Study," paper presented at the International Meeting for Autism Research (IMFAR), Philadelphia, PA, May 2010.

"Recover" from an ASD Molly Helt et al., "Can Children with Autism Recover? If So, How?" *Neuropsychology Review* 18, no. 4 (2008): 339–66.

an important new clue Stoner et al., "Patches of Disorganization in the Neocortex of Children with Autism," *New England Journal of Medicine* 370, no. 13 (2014): 1209–1219. doi: 10.1056/NEJMoa1307491.

Chapter 5: Overactivity and Inattentiveness

Warning Signs National Institute of Mental Health, "Attention Deficit Hyperactivity Disorder," www.nimh.nih.gov/health/topics/attention -deficit-hyperactivity-disorder-adhd/index.shtml; American Academy of Child and Adolescent Psychiatry, "Children Who Can't Pay Attention /Attention-Deficit/Hyperactivity," July 2013, www.aacap.org/aacap /Families_and_Youth/Facts_for_Families/Facts_for_Families_Pages /Children_Who_Cant_Pay_Attention_ADHD_06.aspx.

other tools Ibid.

sluggish cognitive tempo Alan Schwarz, "Idea of New Attention Disorder Spurs Research, and Debate," *New York Times*, April 11, 2014, www .nytimes.com/2014/04/12/health/idea-of-new-attention-disorder-spurs -research-and-debate.html.

sleep disorder Michelle M. Perfect et al., "Risk of Behavioral and Adaptive Functioning Difficulties in Youth with Previous and Current Sleep Disordered Breathing," *Sleep* 36, no. 4 (2013): 517–25, doi: 10.5665/ sleep.2536.

like those observed in ADHD Karen Bonuck et al., "Sleep-Disordered Breathing in a Population-Based Cohort: Behavioral Outcomes at 4 and 7 Years," *Pediatrics* 129, no. 4 (2012): 857–65. doi: 10.1542/ peds.2011-1402.

underdiagnosed in children Firoza Faruqui et al., "Sleep Disorders in Children: A National Assessment of Primary Care Pediatrician Practices and Perceptions," *Pediatrics* 128, no. 3 (2011): 539–46, doi: 10.1542/peds.2011-0344.

lack of confidence Michael J. Breus, "ADHD or Sleep Disorder: Are We Getting It Wrong?" *Psychology Today*, May 1, 2013, www.psychologytoday.com/blog/sleep-newzzz/201305/adhd-or-sleep-disorder-are-we-getting-it-wrong.

Multimodal Treatment Study of ADHD Eugene L. Arnold et al., "NIMH Collaborative Multimodal Treatment Study of Children with ADHD (MTA): Design, Methodology, and Protocol Evolution," *Journal of Attention Disorders* 2, no. 3 (1997): 141–58. doi: 10.177/108705479700200301.

2007, it published new results Peter S. Jensen et al., "3-Year Follow-Up of the NIMH MTA Study," *Journal of the American Academy of Child & Adolescent Psychiatry* 46, no. 8 (2007): 989–1,002, doi: 10.1097/CHI.0b013e3180686d48; Brooke S. G. Molina et al., "The MTA at 8 years: Prospective Follow-Up of Children Treated for Combined Type ADHD in a Multisite Study," *Journal of the American Academy of Child & Adolescent Psychiatry* 48, no. 5 (2009): 484–500.

Debate Over Drugs Shankar Vedantam, "Debate Over Drugs for ADHD Reignites," *Washington Post*, March 27, 2009, www.washingtonpost.com/wp-dyn/content/article/2009/03/26/AR2009032604018.html.

results were not clear-cut William E. Pelham and Gregory A. Fabiano, "Evidence-Based Psychosocial Treatment for ADHD: An Update," *Journal of Clinical Child and Adolescent Psychology* 37, no. 1 (2008): 184–214, doi: 10.1080/15374410701818681.

"If you want something for tomorrow" Vendatam, "Debate Over Drugs for ADHD Reignites."

effective community programs Summit Educational Resources, https://www.summited.org/summer-treatment-program/overview.html.

EEG Geoffrey Mohan, "Brainwave Device to Detect ADHD Approved," *Los Angeles Times*, July 15, 2013, www.latimes.com/news/science/sciencenow/la-sci-sn-brain-wave-adhd-20130715-story.

ADHD explosion Stephen Hinshaw and Richard Scheffler, *The ADHD Explosion: Myths, Medication, Money, and Today's Push for Performance* (New York: Oxford University Press, 2014).

Chapter 6: Anxiety, Fear, Stress, and Obsessive-Compulsive Behaviors

girls are more at risk National Institute of Mental Health, "What Is Anxiety Disorder?" www.nimh.nih.gov/health/topics/anxiety-disorders/index .shtml.

anxiety about social situations Amanda E. Guyer et al., "Amygdala and Ventrolateral Prefrontal Cortex Function during Anticipated Peer Evaluation in Pediatric Social Anxiety," *Archives of General Psychiatry* 65, no. 11 (2008): 1303–12, doi: 10.1001/archpsyc.65.11.1303; National Institute of Mental Health, "Anxious and Health Adolescents Respond Differently to Anxiety-Provoking Situations," November 5, 2008, www .nimh.nih.gov/news/science-news/2008/anxious-and-healthy-adolescents -respond-differently-to-an-anxiety-provoking-situation.shtml.

generalized anxiety disorder Christopher S. Monk et al., "Amygdala and Ventrolateral Prefrontal Cortex Activation to Masked Angry Faces in Children and Adolescents with Generalized Anxiety Disorder," *Archives of General Psychiatry* 65, no. 5 (2008): 568–76, doi: 10.1001/ archpsyc.65.5.568.

panic disorder Mayo Clinic, "Panic Attacks and Panic Disorder." Diseases and Conditions. May 31, 2012, www.mayoclinic.org/diseases -conditions/panic-attacks/basics/definition/con-20020825; National Institute of Mental Health, "What is Panic Disorder?" www.nimh.nih .gov/health/topics/panic-disorder/index.shtml.

Specific Phobias USF Health and Depression and Anxiety Disorders Research Institute, "About Depression and Anxiety." February 28, 2011, http://health.usf.edu/research/dari/about_depression.htm#anxiety.

OCD, ADHD, and Tourette Syndrome Marco A. Grados, Carol A. Mathews, and the Tourette Syndrome Association International Consortium for Genetics, "Latent Class Analysis of Gilles de la Tourette Syndrome Using Comorbidities: Clinical and Genetic Implications," *Biological Psychiatry* 64, no. 3 (2008): 219–25, doi: 10.1016/j. biopsych.2008.01.019.

frequently seen together Carol A. Mathews and Marco A. Grados, "Familiarity of Tourette Syndrome, Obsessive-Compulsive Disorder, and Attention-Deficit/Hyperactivity Disorder: Heritability Analysis in a Large Sib-Pair Sample," *Journal of the American Academy of Child & Adolescent Psychiatry* 50, no. 1 (2011): 46–54, doi: 10.1016/j.jaac.2010.10.004.

PTSD US Department of Veterans Affairs, National Center for PTSD, "PTSD in Children and Teens," January 3, 2014, www.ptsd.va.gov/public/pages/ptsd-children-adolescents.asp.

CAMS Scott Compton et al., "Child/Adolescent Anxiety Multimodal Study (CAMS): Rationale, Design, and Methods," *Child and Adolescent Psychiatry and Mental Health* 4, no. 1 (2010), doi: 10.1186/1753-2000-4-1.

SET-C Deborah C. Beidel et al., "SET-C Versus Fluoxetine in the Treatment of Childhood Social Phobia," *Journal of the American Academy of Child & Adolescent Psychiatry* 46, no. 12 (2007): 1622–32, doi: 10.1097/chi.0b013e318154bb57.

Coping Cat Promising Practices Network, "Coping Cat," www.promisingpractices.net/program.asp?programid=153.

TF-CBT Substance Abuse and Mental Health Services Administration, "Trauma-Focused Cognitive Behavioral Therapy (TF-CBT)," National Registry of Evidence-Based Programs and Practices. www.nrepp.samhsa.gov/viewintervention.aspx?id=135.

EMDR Carol Boulware, "EMDR Therapy—FAQ," EMDR-Therapy, www.emdr-therapy.com/emdr-faq.html.

Chapter 7: Sadness and Loss

diagnosis of depression The Nemours Foundation, "Understanding Depression," http://kidshealth.org/parent/emotions/feelings/understanding_depression.html.

Symptoms of Depression National Institute of Mental Health, "Depression in Children and Adolescents." www.nimh.nih.gov/health/topics/depression/depression-in-children-and-adolescents.shtml; American Academy of Child and Adolescent Psychiatry, "The Depressed Child," www.aacap.org/AACAP/Families_and_Youth/Facts_for_Families/Facts_for_Families_Pages/The_Depressed_Child_04.aspx.

"mood episodes" Janet Wozniak et al., "Mania-Like Symptoms Suggestive of Childhood-Onset Bipolar Disorder in Clinically Referred Children," *Journal of the American Academy of Child & Adolescent Psychiatry* 34, no. 7 (1995): 867–76, doi: 10.1097/00004583-199507000-00010; Myrna M. Weissman et al., "Psychopathology in the Children (Ages 6–18) of Depressed and Normal Parents," *Journal of the American Academy of Child Psychiatry* 23, no. 1 (1984): 78–84, doi: 10.1097/00004583-198401000-00011; Elizabeth B. Weller, Ronald A. Weller, and Mary A. Fristad, "Bipolar Disorder in Children: Misdiagnosis, Underdiagnosis, and Future Directions," *Journal of the American Academy of Child & Adolescent Psychiatry* 34, no. 6 (1995): 709–14, doi: 10.1097/00004583-199506000-00010; Timothy E. Wilens et al., "Patterns of Comorbidity and Dysfunction in Clinically Referred Preschool and School-Age Children with Bipolar Disorder," *Journal of Child and Adolescent Psychopharmacology* 13, no. 4 (2003): 495–505, doi: 10.1089/104454603322724887; Gabrielle A. Carlson and Stephanie E. Meyer, "Phenomenology and Diagnosis of Bipolar Disorder in Children, Adolescents, and Adults: Complexities and Developmental Issues," *Development and Psychopathology* 18, no. 4 (2006): 939–69.

manic episode American Academy of Child and Adolescent Psychiatry, "Bipolar Disorder in Children and Teens," www.aacap.org/AACAP /AACAP/Families_and_Youth/Facts_for_Families/Facts_for_Families _Pages/Bipolar_Disorder_In_Children_And_Teens_38.aspx.

depressive episode National Institute of Mental Health, "Bipolar Disorder in Children and Teens: Easy to Read," www.nimh.nih.gov/health /publications/bipolar-disorder-in-children-and-teens-easy-to-read/index .shtml.

Disruptive Mood Dysregulation Disorder "Disruptive Mood Dysregulation Disorder" May 2013, www.dsm5.org/Documents/Disruptive 20Mood 20Dysregulation 20Disorder 20Fact 20Sheet.pdf.

teachers will notice The Balanced Mind Parent Network, "Fact Sheet: Pediatric Bipolar Disorder," November 27, 2009, www .thebalancedmind.org/learn/library/pediatric-bipolar-disorder.

signs of schizophrenia American Academy of Child and Adolescent Psychiatry, "Schizophrenia in Children," July 2013, www.aacap.org

/AACAP/Families_and_Youth/Facts_for_Families/Facts_for_Families
_Pages/Schizophrenia_In_Children_49.aspx.

grief or bereavement National Cancer Institute, "Grief, Bereavement, and
Coping with Loss (PDQ®) Children and Grief." www.cancer.gov
/cancertopics/pdq/supportivecare/bereavement/Patient/page6.

share several genetic risk factors Alessandro Serretti and Chiara Fabbri.
"Shared Genetics among Major Psychiatric Disorders," *The Lancet* 81,
no. 9875 (2013): 1339–41, doi: 10.1016/S0140-6736(13)60223-8.

behaviors researchers and clinicians Massachusetts General Hospital, School
Psychiatry and Madi Resource Center, "Bipolar Disorder (Manic
Depression)," www2.massgeneral.org/schoolpsychiatry/info_bipolar.asp.

Childhood onset Mayo Clinic, "Childhood Schizophrenia," December 17,
2010, www.mayoclinic.com/health/childhood-schizophrenia/DS00868
/DSECTION =symptoms; Anita Khurana et al., "Childhood-Onset
Schizophrenia: Diagnostic and Treatment Challenges," *Psychiatric Times*
24, no. 2 (February 1, 2007), www.psychiatrictimes.com/schizophrenia
/childhood-onset-schizophrenia-diagnostic-and-treatment-challenges;
NAMI Southwestern Illinois, "Children and Adolescents with Brain
Disorders." http://031e044.netsolhost.com/reference_guide.htm.

IPT John C. Markowitz and Myrna W. Weissman, "Interpersonal
Psychotherapy: Principles and Applications," *World Psychiatry* 3, no. 3
(2004): 136–39.

"Bipolar Disorder in Children and Teens" National Institute of Mental
Health, "Bipolar Disorder in Children and Teens."

Chapter 8: Picky Eating and Eating Too Much

hospitalizations for eating disorders Yafy Zhao and William Encinosa,
Hospitalizations for Eating Disorders from 1999 to 2006, HCUP
Statistical Brief #70 (Rockville, MD Agency for Healthcare Research and
Quality, 2009). www.hcup-us.ahrq.gov/reports/statbriefs/sb70.jsp.

types of eating disorders Katherine Kam, "Eating Disorders in Children
and Teens," WebMD, http://children.webmd.com/features/eating
-disorders-children-teens.

binge eaters are male National Institute of Health, "Males and Eating Disorders," *NIH Medline Plus* 3, no. 2 (2008): 18, www.nlm.nih.gov /medlineplus/magazine/issues/spring08/articles/spring08pg18.html.

anorexia during her life National Institute of Mental Health, "The Numbers Count: Mental Disorders in America," www.nimh.nih.gov/health /publications/the-numbers-count-mental-disorders-in-america/index .shtml.

Symptoms may include Kam, "Eating Disorders in Children and Teens."

Bulimia Ibid.

Obesity American Academy of Child and Adolescent Psychiatry, "Obesity in Children and Teens," March 2011, www.aacap.org/cs/root/facts_for _families/obesity_in_children_and_teens.

80 percent Ibid.

Chapter 9: Bullying and Aggression

bullying is about power US Department of Health and Human Services, "Best Practices in Bullying Prevention and Intervention," 2011, http:// ophp.umdnj.edu/njphtc/AP_-_Public_Health_Policy_files/SBN_Tip_23 20Best 20Practices 20Prevention.pdf.

ODD is a possible diagnosis Mayo Clinic, "Oppositional Defiant Disorder (ODD)," January 6, 2012, www.mayoclinc.org/diseases-conditions /oppositional-defiant-disorder/basics/definition/con-20024559

Symptoms of ODD Ibid; Johns Hopkins Medicine, "Oppositional Defiant Disorder," Health Library. www.hopkinsmedicine.org /healthlibrary/conditions/mental_health_disorders/oppositional _defiant_disorder_90,P02573/; American Academy of Child and Adolescent Psychiatry, "Children with Oppositional Defiant Disorder," www.aacap.org/AACAP/Families_and_Youth/Facts_for_Families /Facts_for_Families_Pages/Children_With_Oppositional_Defiant _Disorder_72.aspx; American Academy of Child and Adolescent Psychiatry, "Frequently Asked Questions," www.aacap.org/AACAP /Families_and_Youth/Resource_Centers/Oppositional_Defiant _Disorder_Resource_Center/FAQ.aspx.

Conduct Disorder American Academy of Child and Adolescent Psychiatry, "Conduct Disorder," http://www.aacap.org/AACAP/Families_and _Youth/Facts_for_Families/Facts_for_Families_Pages/Conduct _Disorder_33.aspx

Dealing with Bullying US Department of Health and Human Services, "Best Practices in Bullying Prevention."

Zero-tolerance policies Amanda Morin, "Does Zero Tolerance Work in Schools?" About.com, http://childparenting.about.com/od /schoollearning/a/does-zero-tolerance-work.htm.

kindergarten class in New York City Corinne Lestch and Rachel Monahan, "Dozens of 4- and 5-Year-Olds Suspended from New City Schools Last Year," *New York Daily News*, November 16, 2012, www.nydailynews .com/new-york/education/dozens-4-5-year-olds-suspended-schools-year -article-1.1203575.

collaborative problem solving The REACH Institute, "Dr. Ross Greene's Model," www.thereachinstitute.org/cps.html.

Chapter 10: Problems with Homework

Types of Problematic Behaviors US Department of Health and Human Services, National Institutes of Health, "What Are the Symptoms of Learning Disabilities?" www.nichd.nih.gov/health/topics/learning /conditioninfo/pages/symptoms.aspx; American Psychiatric Association, "Recent Updates to Proposed Revisions for DSM-5," www.dsm5.org /Pages/RecentUpdates.aspx.

How common American Speech-Language-Hearing Association, "Incidence and Prevalence of Communication Disorders and Hearing Loss in Children—2008 Edition," www.asha.org/research/reports/children.htm.

Dyslexia Margaret Snowling, "Dyslexia as a Phonological Deficit: Evidence and Implications," *Child and Adolescent Mental Health* 3, no. 1 (1998): 4–11, doi: 10.111/1475-3588.00201.

dyscalculia Ronald L. Lindsay et al., "Attentional Function as Measured by a Continuous Performance Task in Children with Dyscalculia," *Journal of Developmental & Behavioral Pediatrics* 22, no. 5 (2001): 287–92;

National Center for Learning Disabilities, "What Is Dyscalculia?" www
.ncld.org/types-learning-disabilities/dyscalculia/what-is-dyscalculia.

Lindamood-Bell Lindamood-Bell Instructional Processes, www
.lindamoodbell.com/research/articles/.

Inspiration.com Institute for the Advancement of Research in Education at
AEL, "Graphic Organizers: A Review of Scientifically Based Research,"
July 2003, www.inspiration.com/sites/default/files/documents/Detailed
-Summary.pdf.

"Learning Disabilities and Disorders" Gina Kemp, Melinda Smith, and
Jeanne Segal, "Helping Children with Learning Disabilities," Helpguide
.org, December 2013, www.helpguide.org/mental/learning_disabilities
_treatment_help_coping.htm.

Chapter 11: Self-Injury, Suicidal Feelings, and Substance Abuse

most people who cut E. David Klonsky and Jennifer J. Muehlenkamp,
"Self-Injury: A Research Review for the Practitioner," *Journal of Clinical
Psychology* 63, (2007): 1045–56, doi: 10.1002/jclp.20412.

Self-injury appears to be more prevalent Andrea L. Barrocas et al., "Rates
of Nonsuicidal Self-Injury in Youth: Age, Sex, and Behavioral Methods
in a Community Sample," *Pediatrics* 130, no. 1 (2012): 39–45, doi:
10.1542/peds.2011-2094.

the following signs American Academy of Child and Adolescent Psychiatry,
"Teen Suicide," July 2013, www.aacap.org/AACAP/Families_and_Youth
/Facts_for_Families/Facts_for_Families_Pages/Teen_Suicide_10.aspx.

suicide attempts are known to parents Anthony R. Pisani et al., "Associations
between Suicidal High School Students' Help-Seeking and Their
Attitudes and Perceptions of Social Environment," *Journal of Youth and
Adolescence* 41, no. 10 (2012): 1312–24, doi: 10.1007/s10964-012
-9766-7.

most adolescents who commit suicide Centers for Disease Control and
Prevention, "Youth Suicide," January 9. 2014, www.cdc.gov
/violenceprevention/pub/youth_suicide.html.

will eventually kill themselves Earl A. Grollman, *Suicide: Prevention,
Intervention, Postvention* (Boston: Beacon Press, 1988).

warning signs Lloyd D. Johnston et al., Secondary School Students, vol. 1 of *National Survey Results on Drug Use from the Monitoring the Future Study 1975–1997* (Bethesda, MD: National Institute on Drug Abuse, 1998); American Academy of Child and Adolescent Psychiatry, "Teens: Alcohol and Other Drugs," July 2013, www.aacap.org/AACAP /Families_and_Youth/Facts_for_Families/Facts_for_Families_Pages /Teens_Alcohol_And_Other_Drugs_03.aspx.

on the rise Ken C. Winters, *Treatment of Adolescents with Substance Use Disorders* (Rockville, MD: Substance Abuse and Mental Health Services Administration, 2003).

NIDA National Institute on Drug Abuse, "Regular Marijuana Use by Teens Continues to Be a Concern" December 19, 2012, www.nih.gov /news/health/dec2012/nida-19.htm.

DSM for drug abuse Patricia A. Harrison, Jayne A. Fulkerson, and Timothy J. Beebe, "DSM-IV Substance Use Disorder Criteria for Adolescents: A Critical Examination Based on a Statewide School Survey," *American Journal of Psychiatry* 155, no. 4 (1998): 486–92.

gateway drug Ralph Tarter et al., "Predictors of Marijuana Use in Adolescents before and after Licit Drug Use: Examination of the Gateway Hypothesis," *American Journal of Psychiatry* 163, no. 12 (2006): 2134–40.

heroin mixed with water National Institute on Drug Abuse, "Regular Marijuana Use by Teens."

The Parents' Role James McIntosh, Fiona MacDonald, and Neil McKeganey, "The Reasons Why Children in Their Pre and Early Teenage Years Do or Do Not Use Illicit Drugs," *International Journal of Drug Policy* 16, no. 4 (2005): 254–61, doi: 10.1016/j.drugpo.2005.05.005; Margarita Tartakovsky, "How to Talk to Your Kids When You Think They're Using Drugs," PsychCentral, http://psychcentral.com/blog /archives/2013/05/02/ how-to-talk-to-your-kids-when-you-think-theyre-using-drugs/.

Treatment for Alcohol Center for Substance Abuse Treatment, *Substance Abuse: Clinical Issues in Intensive Outpatient Treatment*, Treatment Improvement Protocol (TIP) Series No. 47 (Rockville, MD: Substance Abuse and Mental Health Services Administration, 2006).

points to keep in mind Michael D. Newcomb and Peter M. Bentler. "Substance Use and Abuse among Children and Teenagers," *American Psychologist* 44, no. 2 (1989): 242–48; Center for Adolescent Substance Abuse Treatment, "Working with Adolescent Addiction," http:// aiopduke.wordpress.com/.

Chapter 12: The Medical Professionals

master's-degree-level professional Board of Behavioral Sciences (California), "What Is an LPCC? LPCC Scope of Practice—Treatment of Couples and Families," www.bbs.ca.gov/pdf/forms/lpc/lpc_scope_practice.pdf.

Cultural Competence Support for Families of Children with Disabilities, "Guide to Mental Health Services," www.supportforfamilies.org /resourcesmentalhealthguide.html.

Psychoanalytic Therapy Rethink Mental Illness. "Talking Therapies— About." www.rethink.org/diagnosis-treatment/treatment-and-support /talking-treatments/types-of-therapy.

Creative Therapies Ibid.

DBT Ibid.

PCIT Alison Zisser and Sheila M. Eyberg, "Treating Oppositional Behavior in Children Using Parent-Child Interaction Therapy," *Evidence-Based Psychotherapies for Children and Adolescents*, 2nd ed., John R. Weisz and Alan E. Kazdin editors (New York: Guilford, 2010), 179–93.

cognitive behavioral therapy and antidepressants Bruce Chorpita et al., "Evidence-Based Treatments for Children and Adolescents: An Updated Review of Indicators of Efficacy and Effectiveness." *Clinical Psychology: Science and Practice* 18 (2011) 154–172.

Walkup Johns Hopkins Medicine, "Antidepressants Plus 'Talk Therapy' Are Effective Therapy for Teen Depression," http://www.hopkinsmedicine .org/Press_releases/2004/08_17_04.html; P. R. Breggin, "The Proven Dangers of Antidepressants," 2004, http://breggin.com/index.php ?option=com_content&task=view&id=196.

successful partnerships Support for Families of Children with Disabilities, "Guide to Mental Health Services," https://www.supportforfamilies.org /resourcesmentalhealthguide.html.

Chapter 13: Getting Services for Your Child from Your School or State

IDEA Information on IDEA can be accessed through the US Department of Education at http://idea.ed.gov/.

Process D. D. Smith, "Steps in the IEP Process," Education.com, July 20, 2010, www.education.com/reference/article/steps-ndividualized -education-program-IEP.

Part C of IDEA National Dissemination Center for Children with Disabilities, "Questions Often Asked by Parents about Special Education Services," April 2009, www.parentcenterhub.org/resources.

child with a disability Smith, "Steps in the IEP Process."

school's evaluation Ibid.

Independent Educational Evaluation National Dissemination Center for Children with Disabilities, "Right to Obtain an Independent Educational Evaluation." December 2010. http://nichcy.org/schoolage /parental-rights/iee; Education Law Center, "Getting Your Child an Independent Educational Evaluation," https://www.drnpa.org/wp -content/uploads/2012/10/getting-your-child-an-independent -educational-evaluation.pdf.

school's recommendations Kathy McNamara and Constance Hollinger, "Intervention-Based Assessment: Evaluation Rates and Eligibility Findings," *Exceptional Children* 69, no. 2 (2003): 181–93.

Chapter 14: FAQ

children younger than six Jaeah Chung et al., "Medication Management of Preschool ADHD by Pediatric Sub-Specialists: Non-Compliance with AAP Clinical Guidelines," paper presented at the annual meeting of the Pediatric Academic Societies, Washington, DC, May 2013, www .abstracts2view.com/pas/view.php?nu=PAS13L1_1365.5.

spanking Elizabeth T. Gershoff, "More Harm Than Good: A Summary of Scientific Research on the Intended and Unintended Effects of Corporal Punishment on Children," *Law and Contemporary Problems* 73, no. 2 (2010): 31–56.

Epilogue: After Newtown

December 14 Alaine Griffin and Josh Kovner, "Adam Lanza's Medical Records Reveal Growing Anxiety," *Hartford Courant*, June 30, 2013, www.courant.com/news/connecticut/newtown-sandy-hook-school -shooting/hc-adam-lanza-pediatric-records-20130629,0,7137229.story ?page=3.

economic benefits Lynn A. Karoly, M. Rebecca Kilburn, and Jill Cannon. *Early Childhood Interventions: Proven Results, Future Promise.* Washington, DC: Rand Corporation, 2005.

Federal Reserve Bank Arthur J. Rolnick and Rob Grunewald, "Early Intervention on a Large Scale," Quality Counts, January 4, 2007, www .minneapolisfed.org/publications_papers/studies/earlychild/early _intervention.cfm?.

James Heckman The Heckman Equation, http://heckmanequation.org /heckman-equation.

Appendix A: Brain Development 101

fully mature Frontline, "Inside the Teenage Brain," www.pbs.org/wgbh /pages/frontline/shows/teenbrain/work/adolescent.html.

critical periods for development Adapted from Ross A. Thompson and Charles A. Nelson, "Developmental Science and the Media: Early Brain Development," *American Psychologist* 56, no. 1 (2001): 5–15, doi: 10.1037/0003-066X.56.1.5, reprinted with permission.

developmental milestones Center for Disease Control and Prevention, "Developmental Milestones?" www.cdc.gov/ncbddd/actearly /milestones/.

Appendix B: Therapies Found to Be Most Effective for Various Diagnoses

Therapies Bruce F. Chorpita et al., "Evidence-Based Treatments for Children and Adolescents: An Updated Review of Indicators of Efficacy and Effectiveness," *Clinical Psychology: Science and Practice* 18, no. 2 (2011): 154–72, doi: 10.1111/j.1468-2850.2011.01247.x.

PCIT-ED Joan L. Luby, "Treatment of Anxiety and Depression in the Preschool Period," *Journal of the American Academy of Child & Adolescent Psychiatry* 52, no. 4 (2013): 346–358, doi: 10.1016/j.jaac.2013.01.011.

Appendix C: Commonly Used Medications for Mental Health

medications National Institute of Mental Health, "Introduction: Mental Health Medications." Mental Health Medications. www.nimh.nih.gov /health/publications/mental-health-medications/index.shtml.

Bibliography

Books

American Psychiatric Association. *Diagnostic and Statistical Manual of Mental Disorders*. 5th ed. Arlington, VA: American Psychiatric Publishing, 2013.

Bowlby, John. *Attachment and Loss*. 3 vols. New York: Basic Books, 1969–80.

Fraiberg, Selma. *Clinical Studies in Infant Mental Health: The First Year of Life*. With the collaboration of Louis Fraiberg. New York: Basic Books, 1980.

Grollman, Earl. A. *Suicide: Prevention, Intervention, Postvention*. Boston: Beacon Press, 1988.

Hinshaw, Stephen P. and Richard M. Scheffler. *The ADHD Explosion: Myths, Medication, Money, and Today's Push for Performance*. New York: Oxford University Press, 2014.

Johnston, Lloyd D., Patrick M. O'Malley, Jerald G. Bachman, National Institute on Drug Abuse, University of Michigan, and Institute for Social Research. *Secondary School Students*. Vol. 1 of *National Survey Results on Drug Use from the Monitoring the Future Study 1975–1997*. Bethesda, MD: National Institute on Drug Abuse, US Department of Health and Human Services, Public Health Service, National Institutes of Health, 1998.

Karoly, Lynn A., M. Rebecca Kilburn, and Jill Cannon. *Early Childhood Interventions: Proven Results, Future Promise*. Washington, DC: Rand Corporation, 2005.

Zero to Three. *Diagnostic Classification of Mental Health and Developmental Disorders of Infancy and Early Childhood*. Rev. ed. Washington, DC: Zero to Three Press, 2005.

Zisser, Alison and Sheila M. Eyberg. "Treating Oppositional Behavior in Children Using Parent-Child Interaction Therapy." In *Evidence-Based*

Psychotherapies for Children and Adolescents, 2nd ed., edited by John R. Weisz and Alan E. Kazdin, 179–93. New York: Guilford, 2010.

Journals

Ainsworth, Mary D. Salter and Silvia M. Bell. "Attachment, Exploration, and Separation: Illustrated by the Behavior of One-Year-Olds in a Strange Situation." *Child Development* 41, no. 1 (1970): 49–67.

Arnold, L. Eugene, Howard B. Abikoff, Dennis P. Cantwell, C. Keith Conners, Glen R. Elliott, Laurence L. Greenhill, and Karen C. Wells. "NIMH Collaborative Multimodal Treatment Study of Children with ADHD (MTA): Design, Methodology, and Protocol Evolution." *Journal of Attention Disorders* 2, no. 3 (1997): 141–58.

Barrocas, Andrea L., Benjamin L. Hankin, Jami F. Young, and John R. Z. Abela. "Rates of Nonsuicidal Self-Injury in Youth: Age, Sex, and Behavioral Methods in a Community Sample." *Pediatrics* 130, no. 1 (2012): 39–45. doi: 10.1542/peds.2011-2094.

Beidel, Deborah C., Samuel M. Turner, Floyd R. Sallee, Robert T. Ammerman, Lori A. Crosby, and Sanjeev Pathak. "SET-C Versus Fluoxetine in the Treatment of Childhood Social Phobia." *Journal of the American Academy of Child & Adolescent Psychiatry* 46, no. 12 (2007): 1622–32. doi: 10.1097/chi.0b013e318154bb57.

Bonuck, Karen, Katherine Freeman, Ronald D. Chervin, and Linzhi Xu. "Sleep-Disordered Breathing in a Population-Based Cohort: Behavioral Outcomes at 4 and 7 Years." *Pediatrics* 129, no. 4 (2012): 857–65. doi: 10.1542/peds.2011-1402.

Carlson, Gabrielle A. and Stephanie E. Meyer. "Phenomenology and Diagnosis of Bipolar Disorder in Children, Adolescents, and Adults: Complexities and Developmental Issues." *Development and Psychopathology* 18, no. 4 (2006): 939–69.

Chorpita, Bruce F., Eric L. Daleiden, Chad Ebesutani, John Young, Kimberly D. Becker, Brad J. Nakamura, Lisa Phillips, et al. "Evidence-Based Treatments for Children and Adolescents: An Updated Review of Indicators of Efficacy and Effectiveness." *Clinical Psychology: Science and Practice* 18 (2011): 154–72. doi: 10.1111/j.1468-2850.2011.01247.x.

Compton, Scott, John T. Walkup, Anne Marie Albano, John C. Piacentini, Boris Birmaher, Joel T. Sherrill, Golda S. Ginsburg, et al. "Child/ Adolescent Anxiety Multimodal Study (CAMS): Rationale, Design, and Methods." *Child and Adolescent Psychiatry and Mental Health* 4, no. 1 (2010). doi: 10.1186/1753-2000-4-1.

DeRubeis, Robert J., Lois A. Gelfand, Tony Z. Tang, and Anne D. Simons. "Medications Versus Cognitive Behavior Therapy for Severely Depressed Outpatients: Mega-Analysis of Four Randomized Comparisons." *American Journal of Psychiatry* 156 (1999): 1007–13.

Faruqui, Firoza, Jagdish Khubchandani, James H. Price, Dawn Bolyard, and Ramalinga Reddy. "Sleep Disorders in Children: A National Assessment of Primary Care Pediatrician Practices and Perceptions." *Pediatrics* 128, no. 3 (2011): 539–46. doi: 10.1542/peds.2011-0344.

Gaffrey, Michael S., Deanna M. Barch, Janet Singer, Rivfka Shenoy, and Joan L. Luby. "Disrupted Amygdala Reactivity in Depressed 4- to 6-Year-Old Children." *Journal of the American Academy of Child and Adolescent Psychiatry* 52, no. 7 (2013): 737–46. doi: 10 .1016/j. jaac.2013.04.009.

Gershoff, Elizabeth T. "More Harm Than Good: A Summary of Scientific Research on the Intended and Unintended Effects of Corporal Punishment on Children." *Law and Contemporary Problems* 73 (2010): 31–56.

Grados, Marco A., Carol A. Mathews, and the Tourette Syndrome Association International Consortium for Genetics. "Latent Class Analysis of Gilles de la Tourette Syndrome Using Comorbidities: Clinical and Genetic Implications." *Biological Psychiatry* 64, no. 3 (2008): 219–25. doi: 10.1016/j.biopsych.2008.01.019.

Granpeesheh, Doreen, Jonathan Tarbox, Dennis R. Dixon, Arthur E. Wilke, Jeff Bradstreet, and Michael S. Allen. "Randomized Trial of Hyperbaric Oxygen Therapy for Children with Autism." *Research in Autism Spectrum Disorders* 4 (2010): 268–75.

Guyer, Amanda E., Jennifer Y. F. Lau, Erin B. McClure-Tone, Jessica Parrish, Nina D. Shiffrin, Richard C. Reynolds, and Eric E. Nelson. "Amygdala and Ventrolateral Prefrontal Cortex Function during Anticipated Peer Evaluation in Pediatric Social Anxiety." *Archives*

of General Psychiatry 65, no. 11 (2008): 1303–12. doi: 10.1001/
archpsyc.65.11.1303.

Harrison, Patricia A., Jayne A. Fulkerson, and Timothy J. Beebe. "DSM-IV
Substance Use Disorder Criteria for Adolescents: A Critical Examination
Based on a Statewide School Survey." *American Journal of Psychiatry* 155,
no. 4 (1998): 486–92.

Helt, Molly, Elizabeth Kelley, Marcel Kinsbourne, Juhi Pandey, Hilary
Boorstein, Martha Herbert, and Deborah Fein. "Can Children with
Autism Recover? If So, How?" *Neuropsychology Review* 18, no. 4 (2008):
339–66.

Jensen, Peter S., L. Eugene Arnold, James M. Swanson, Benedetto Vitiello,
Howard B. Abikoff, Laurence L. Greenhill, Lily Hechtman, et al. "3-Year
Follow-Up of the NIMH MTA Study." *Journal of the American Academy
of Child & Adolescent Psychiatry* 46, no. 8 (2007): 989–1002. doi:
10.1097/CHI.0b013e3180686d48.

Klonsky, E. David and Jennifer J. Muehlenkamp. "Self-Injury: A Research
Review for the Practitioner." *Journal of Clinical Psychology* 63, (2007):
1,045–56. doi: 10.1002 /jclp.20412.

Lindsay, Ronald L., Terry Tomazic, Melvin D. Levine, and Pasquale
J. Accardo. "Attentional Function as Measured by a Continuous
Performance Task in Children with Dyscalculia." *Journal of
Developmental & Behavioral Pediatrics* 22, no. 5 (2001): 287–92.

Luby, Joan L. "Treatment of Anxiety and Depression in the Preschool
Period." *Journal of the American Academy of Child & Adolescent Psychiatry*
52, no. 4 (2013): 346-358. doi: 10.1016/j.jaac.2013.01.011.

Luby, Joan L., Xuemei Si, Andy C. Belden, Mini Tandon, and Ed
Spitznagel. "Preschool Depression: Homotypic Continuity and Course
over 24 Months." *Archives of General Psychiatry* 66, no. 8 (2009): 897–
905. doi: 10.1001/archgenpsychiatry.2009.97.

Markowitz, John C. and Myrna W. Weissman. "Interpersonal
Psychotherapy: Principles and Applications." *World Psychiatry* 3, no. 3
(2004): 136–39.

Mathews, Carol A. and Marco A. Grados. "Familiarity of Tourette
Syndrome, Obsessive-Compulsive Disorder, and Attention-Deficit/
Hyperactivity Disorder: Heritability Analysis in a Large Sib-Pair

Sample." *Journal of the American Academy of Child & Adolescent Psychiatry* 50, no. 1 (2011): 46–54. doi: 10.1016/j.jaac.2010.10.004.

McIntosh, James, Fiona MacDonald, and Neil McKeganey. "The Reasons Why Children in Their Pre and Early Teenage Years Do or Do Not Use Illicit Drugs." *International Journal of Drug Policy* 16, no. 4 (2005): 254–61. doi: 10.1016/j.drugpo.2005.05.005.

McNamara, Kathy and Constance Hollinger. "Intervention-Based Assessment: Evaluation Rates and Eligibility Findings." *Exceptional Children* 69, no. 2 (2003): 181–93.

Molina, Brooke S. G., Stephen P. Hinshaw, James M. Swanson, L. Eugene Arnold, Benedetto Vitello, Peter S. Jensen, Jeffery N. Epstein, et al. "The MTA at 8 Years: Prospective Follow-Up of Children Treated for Combined Type ADHD in a Multisite Study." *Journal of the American Academy of Child & Adolescent Psychiatry* 48, no. 5 (2009): 484–500.

Monk, Christopher S., Eva H. Telzer, Karin Mogg, Brendan P. Bradley, Xiaoqin Mai, Hugo M. C. Louro, Gang Chen, et al. (2008). "Amygdala and Ventrolateral Prefrontal Cortex Activation to Masked Angry Faces in Children and Adolescents with Generalized Anxiety Disorder." *Archives of General Psychiatry* 65, no. 5 (2008): 568–76. doi: 10.1001/archpsyc.65.5.568.

Morgan, Christopher P. and Tracey L. Bale. "Early Prenatal Stress Epigenetically Programs Dysmasculinization in Second-Generation Offspring via the Paternal Lineage." *Journal of Neuroscience,* 31, no. 33 (2011): 11748-55. doi: 10.1523/JNEUROSCI.1887-11.2011

Newcomb, Michael D. and Peter M. Bentler. "Substance Use and Abuse Among Children and Teenagers." *American Psychologist* 44, no. 2 (1989): 242–48.

Pelham, William E. and Gregory A. Fabiano. "Evidence-Based Psychosocial Treatment for ADHD: An Update." *Journal of Clinical Child and Adolescent Psychology* 37, no. 13 (2008): 184–214. doi: 10.1080/15374410701818681.

Perfect, Michelle M., Kristen Archbold, James L. Goodwin, Deborah Levine-Donnerstein, and Stuart F. Quan. "Risk of Behavioral and Adaptive Functioning Difficulties in Youth with Previous and Current

Sleep Disordered Breathing." *Sleep* 36, no. 4 (2013): 517–25. doi: 10 .5665/sleep.2536.

Pisani, Anthony R., Karen Schmeelk-Cone, Douglas Gunzler, Mariya Petrova, David B. Goldston, Xin Tu, and Peter A. Wyman. "Associations between Suicidal High School Students' Help-Seeking and Their Attitudes and Perceptions of Social Environment." *Journal of Youth and Adolescence* 41, no. 10 (2012): 1312–24. doi: 10.1007/s10964-012 -9766-7.

Radecki, Linda, Nina Sand-Loud, Karen G. O'Connor, Sanford Sharp, and Lynn M. Olson. "Trends in the Use of Standardized Tools for Developmental Screening in Early Childhood: 2002–2009." *Pediatrics*, 128, no. 1 (2011): 14–19. doi: 10.1542/peds.2010-2180.

Sarapas, Casey, Guiqing Cai, Linda M. Bierer, Julia A. Golier, Sandro Galea, Marcus Ising, Theo Rein, et al. "Genetic Markers for PTSD Risk and Resilience Among Survivors of the World Trade Center Attacks." Disease Markers 30, no. 2–3 (2011): 101–10. doi: 10.3233/DMA-2011 -0764.

Serretti, Alessandro and Chiara Fabbri. "Shared Genetics Among Major Psychiatric Disorders." *The Lancet* 81, no. 9875 (2013): 1339–41. doi: 10.1016/S0140-6736(13)60223-8.

Snowling, Margaret. "Dyslexia as a Phonological Deficit: Evidence and Implications." *Child and Adolescent Mental Health* 3, no. 1 (1998): 4–11. doi: 10.111/1475-3588.00201.

Stoner, Rich, Maggie L. Chow, Maureen P. Boyle, Susan M. Sunkin, Peter R. Mouton, Subhojit Roy, Anthony Wynshaw-Boris, Sophia A. Colamarino, Ed S. Lein, and Eric Courchesne. "Patches of Disorganization in the Neocortex of Children with Autism." *New England Journal of Medicine* 370, no 13 (2014): 1209–1219. doi: 10.1056/NEJMoa1307491.

Tarter, Ralph, Michael Vanyukov, Levent Kirisci, Maureen Reynolds, and Duncan B. Clark. "Predictors of Marijuana Use in Adolescents Before and After Licit Drug Use: Examination of the Gateway Hypothesis." *American Journal of Psychiatry* 163, no. 12 (2006): 2,134–40.

Thompson, Ross A. and Charles A. Nelson. "Developmental Science and the Media: Early Brain Development." *American Psychologist* 56, no. 1 (2001): 5–15. doi: 10.1037/0003-066X.56.1.5.

Weissman, Myrna M., Brigitte A. Prusoff, G. Davis Gammon, Kathleen R. Merikangas, James F. Leckman, and Kenneth K. Kidd. (1984). "Psychopathology in the Children (Ages 6–18) of Depressed and Normal Parents." *Journal of the American Academy of Child Psychiatry* 23, no. 1 (1984): 78–84. doi: 10.1097/00004583-198401000-00011.

Weller, Elizabeth B., Ronald A. Weller, and Mary A. Fristad. "Bipolar Disorder in Children: Misdiagnosis, Underdiagnosis, and Future Directions." *Journal of the American Academy of Child & Adolescent Psychiatry* 34, no. 6 (1995): 709–14. doi: 10.1097/00004583-199506000-00010.

Wilens, Timothy E., Joseph Biederman, Peter Forkner, Jeff Ditterline, Mathew Morris, Hadley Moore, Maribel Galdo, et al. "Patterns of Comorbidity and Dysfunction in Clinically Referred Preschool and School-Age Children with Bipolar Disorder." *Journal of Child and Adolescent Psychopharmacology* 13, no. 4 (2003): 495–505. doi: 10.1089/104454603322724887.

Wozniak, Janet, Joseph Biederman, Kathleen Kiely, J. Stuart Ablon, Stephen V. Faraone, Elizabeth Mundy, and Douglas Mennin. "Mania-Like Symptoms Suggestive of Childhood-Onset Bipolar Disorder in Clinically Referred Children." *Journal of the American Academy of Child & Adolescent Psychiatry* 34, no. 7 (1995): 867–76. doi: 10.1097/00004583-199507000-00010.

Yehuda, Rachel, Guiqing Cai, Julia A. Golier, Casey Sarapas, Sandro Galea, Marcus Ising, Theo Rein, et al. "Gene Expression Patterns Associated with Posttraumatic Stress Disorder Following Exposure to the World Trade Center Attacks." *Biological Psychiatry* 66, no. 7 (2009): 708–11. doi: 10.1016/j.biopsych.2009.02.034.

Yehuda, Rachel, Stephanie Mulherin Engel, Sarah R. Brand, Jonathan Seckl, Sue M. Marcus, and Gertrud S. Berkowitz. "Transgenerational Effects of Posttraumatic Stress Disorder in Babies of Mothers Exposed to the World Trade Center Attacks During Pregnancy." *Journal of Clinical*

Endocrinology & Metabolism 90, no. 7 (2005): 4115–18. doi: 10.1210/
jc.2005-0550.

Newsletters/Presentations/Reports

Autism and Developmental Disabilities Monitoring Network Surveillance Year 2008 Principal Investigators. "Prevalence of Autism Spectrum Disorders—Autism and Developmental Disabilities Monitoring Network, 14 Sites, United States, 2008." Surveillance Summaries. *Centers for Disease Control Morbidity and Mortality Weekly Report* 61 (March 30, 2012): 1–19.

Autism and Developmental Disabilities Monitoring Network Surveillance Year 2010 Principal Investigators. "Prevalence of Autism Spectrum Disorder among children aged 8 years—autism and developmental disabilities monitoring Network, 11 sites, United States, 2010." *Centers for Disease Control Morbidity and Mortality Weekly Report* 63 (March 28, 2014): Suppl. 2:1-21.

Blumberg, Stephen J., Matthew D. Bramlett, Michael D. Kogan, Laura A. Schieve, Jessica R. Jones, and Michael C. Lu. *Changes in Prevalence of Parent-Reported Autism Spectrum Disorder in School-Aged U.S. Children: 2007 to 2011–2012.* National Health Statistics Report No. 65. Hyattsville, MD: National Center for Health Statistics, 2013.

Center for Substance Abuse Treatment. *Substance Abuse: Clinical Issues in Intensive Outpatient Treatment.* Treatment Improvement Protocol (TIP) Series No. 47. Rockville, MD: Substance Abuse and Mental Health Services Administration, 2006.

Chung, Jaeah, Suzanne Sunday, David Meryash, Alyson Gutman, and Andrew Adesman. "Medication Management of Preschool ADHD by Pediatric Sub-Specialists: Non-Compliance with AAP Clinical Guidelines." Paper presented at the annual meeting of the Pediatric Academic Societies, Washington, DC, May 2013.

Gilliam, Walter S. *Prekindergarteners Left Behind: Expulsion Rates in State Prekindergarten Programs.* FCD Policy Brief Series No. 3. New York: Foundation for Child Development, 2005. www.challengingbehavior .org/explore/policy_docs/prek_expulsion.pdf.

Hyman, S., P. A. Stewart, T. Smith, J. Foley, U. Cain, R. Peck, D. D. Morris, and H. Wang. "The Gluten Free and Casein Free (GFCF) Diet: A Double Blind, Placebo Controlled Challenge Study." Paper presented at the International Meeting for Autism Research (IMFAR), Philadelphia, PA, May 2010.

Johns Hopkins Medicine. "Antidepressants Plus 'Talk Therapy' Are Effective Therapy for Teen Depression." Press release, August 17, 2004. http://www.hopkinschildrens.org/newsDetail.aspx?id=2242.

Khurana, Anita, Arastou Aminzadeh, Jeff Q. Bostic, and Caroly Pataki. "Childhood-Onset Schizophrenia: Diagnostic and Treatment Challenges." *Psychiatric Times* 24, no. 2 (February 1, 2007). www.psychiatrictimes.com/schizophrenia/childhood-onset-schizophrenia-diagnostic-and-treatment-challenges.

Morin, Amanda. "Does Zero Tolerance Work in Schools?" School-Age Children. About.com. http://childparenting.about.com/od/schoollearning/a/does-zero-tolerance-work.htm.

National Institute of Health. "Males and Eating Disorders." *NIH Medline Plus* 3, no. 2 (2008): 18. www.nlm.nih.gov/medlineplus/magazine/issues/spring08/articles/spring08pg18.html.

Pringle, Beverly A., Lisa J. Colpe, Stephen J. Blumberg, Rosa M. Avila, and Michael D. Kogan. *Diagnostic History and Treatment of School-Aged Children with Autism Spectrum Disorder and Special Health Care Needs.* NCHS Data Brief No. 97. Hyattsville, MD: National Center for Health Statistics, 2012.

Rolnick, Arthur J. and Rob Grunewald. "Early Intervention on a Large Scale." Quality Counts, January 4, 2007. www.minneapolisfed.org/publications_papers/studies/earlychild/early_intervention.cfm?.

Winters, Ken C. *Treatment of Adolescents with Substance Use Disorders.* Rockville, MD: US Department of Health and Human Services, Public Health Service, Substance Abuse and Mental Health Services Administration, Center for Substance Abuse Treatment, 2003.

Zhao, Yafy and William Encinosa. *Hospitalizations for Eating Disorders from 1999 to 2006.* HCUP Statistical Brief #70. Rockville, MD: Agency for Healthcare Research and Quality, 2009. www.hcup-us.ahrq.gov/reports/statbriefs/sb70.jsp.

Newspapers

Breus, Michael J. "ADHD or Sleep Disorder: Are We Getting It Wrong?"
Psychology Today. May 1, 2013. www.psychologytoday.com/blog/
sleep-newzzz/201305/adhd-or-sleep-disorder-are-we-getting-it-wrong.

Costandi, Mo. "Pregnant 9/11 Survivors Transmitted Trauma to Their
Children." Neurophilosophy (blog). *The Guardian* (UK). September 9,
2011. www.theguardian.com/science/neurophilosophy/2011/sep/09
/pregnant-911-survivors-transmitted-trauma.

Dobbs, Michael. "Youngest Students Most Likely to Be Expelled."
Washington Post. May 17, 2005.

Fitzgerald, Susan. "'Crack Baby' Study Ends with Unexpected but Clear
Results." Philly.com. July 22, 2013. http://articles.philly.com/2013-07
-22/news/40709969_1_hallam-hurt-so-called-crack-babies-funded
-study.

Frances, Allen. "DSM-5: Where Do We Go from Here?" The Blog. Huff
Post Science. May 16, 2013. www.huffingtonpost.com/allen-frances/dsm
-5-where-do-we-go-from_b_3281313.html.

Griffin, Alaine and Josh Kovner. "Adam Lanza's Medical Records Reveal
Growing Anxiety." *Hartford Courant*. June 30, 2013. www.courant.com
/news/connecticut/newtown-sandy-hook-school-shooting/hc-adam
-lanza-pediatric-records-20130629,0,7137229.story?page=3.

Hyman, Susan L. "New DSM-5 Includes Changes to Autism Criteria."
AAP News, June 4, 2013. doi: 10.1542/aapnews.20130604-1.

Lestch, Corinne and Rachel Monahan. "Dozens of 4- and 5-Year-Olds
Suspended from New City Schools Last Year." *New York Daily News*.
November 16, 2012. www.nydailynews.com/new-york/education
/dozens-4-5-year-olds-suspended-schools-year-article-1.1203575.

Mohan, Geoffrey. "Brainwave Device to Detect ADHD Approved." *Los
Angeles Times*. July 15, 2013. www.latimes.com/news/science
/sciencenow/la-sci-sn-brain-wave-adhd-20130715.

Schwarz, Alan. "Idea of New Attention Disorder Spurs Research, and
Debate." *New York Times*. April 11, 2014. www.nytimes.com/2014
/04/12/health/idea-of-new-attention-disorder-spurs-research-and-debate
.html.

Vedantam, Shankar. "Debate over Drugs for ADHD Reignites." *Washington Post.* March 27, 2009. www.washingtonpost.com/wp-dyn/content /article/2009/03/26/AR2009032604018.html.

Zarembo, Alan. "Autism Boom: An Epidemic of Disease or Discovery?" *Los Angeles Times.* December 11, 2011. www.latimes.com/local/autism/la-me -autism-day-one-html-htmlstory.html.

Websites

American Academy of Child and Adolescent Psychiatry. "Bipolar Disorder in Children and Teens." No. 38. Facts for Families Pages. Last updated December 2008. www.aacap .org/AACAP/AACAP/Families_and_Youth /Facts_for_Families/Facts_for_Families_Pages/Bipolar_Disorder_In _Children_And_Teens_38.aspx.

———. "Children with Oppositional Defiant Disorder." No. 72. Facts for Families Pages. Reviewed July 2013. www.aacap.org/AACAP/Families _and_Youth/Facts_for_Families/Facts _for_Families_Pages/Children _With_Oppositional_Defiant_Disorder_72.aspx.

———. "Children Who Can't Pay Attention/Attention-Deficit/ Hyperactivity." No. 6. Facts for Families Pages. Last updated July 2013. www.aacap.org/aacap/Families_and_Youth/Facts_for_Families/Facts _for_Families_Pages/Children_Who_Cant_Pay_Attention_ADHD_06 .aspx.

———. "Conduct Disorder." http://www.aacap.org/AACAP/Families_and _Youth/Facts_for_Families/Facts_for_Families_Pages/Conduct_Disorder _33.aspx.

———. "The Depressed Child." No. 4. Facts for Families Pages. Last updated July 2013. www.aacap.org/AACAP/Families_and_Youth/Facts _for_Families/Facts_for_Families_Pages/The_Depressed_Child_04.aspx.

———. "Facts for Families." Facts for Families. www.aacap.org/AACAP /Families_and _Youth/Facts_for_Families/Home.aspx.

———. "Frequently Asked Questions." Bullying Resource Center. www .aacap.org/AACAP /Families_and_Youth/Resource_Centers /Oppositional_Defiant_Disorder_Resource _Center/FAQ.aspx.

————. "Obesity in Children and Teens." No. 79. Facts for Families Pages. March 2011. www.aacap.org/cs/root/facts_for_families/obesity_in _children_and_teens.

————. "Schizophrenia in Children." No. 49. Facts for Families Pages. July 2013. www.aacap.org/AACAP/Families_and_Youth/Facts_for_Families /Facts_for_Families_Pages/Schizophrenia_In_Children_49.aspx.

————. "Teens: Alcohol and Other Drugs." No. 3. Facts for Families Pages. Last updated July 2013. www.aacap.org/AACAP/Families_and _Youth/Facts_for_Families/Facts_for_Families_Pages/Teens_Alcohol _And_Other_Drugs_03.aspx.

————. "Teen Suicide." No. 10. Facts for Families. Updated July 2013. www.aacap.org /AACAP/Families_and_Youth/Facts_for_Families/Facts _for_Families_Pages/Teen _Suicide_10.aspx.

American Psychiatric Association. "Recent Updates to Proposed Revisions for DSM-5." DSM-5 Development. www.dsm5.org/Pages /RecentUpdates.aspx.

American Speech-Language-Hearing Association. "Incidence and Prevalence of Communication Disorders and Hearing Loss in Children—2008 Edition." www.asha.org/research/reports/children.htm.

Australian Government, Department of Health. "Mental Health." Last modified November 7, 2013. www.health.gov.au/internet/main /publishing.nsf/Content/Mental+Health+and+Wellbeing-1.

Autism Canada Foundation. "Pivotal Response Therapy." www .autismcanada.org/treatments /behav/pivotalresponse.html.

The Balanced Mind Parent Network. "Fact Sheet: Pediatric Bipolar Disorder." November 27, 2009. www.thebalancedmind.org/learn /library/pediatric-bipolar-disorder.

Board of Behavioral Sciences (California). "What Is an LPCC? LPCC Scope of Practice—Treatment of Couples and Families." www.bbs.ca .gov/pdf/forms/lpc/lpc_scope_practice.pdf.

Boulware, Carol. "EMDR Therapy—FAQ." EMDR-Therapy. www.emdr -therapy.com/emdr-faq.html.

Breggin, P. R. "The Proven Dangers of Antidepressants." *Psychiatric Drug Facts with Dr. Peter Breggin*. 2004. http://breggin.com/index.php ?option=com_content&task=view&id=196.

Center for Adolescent Substance Abuse Treatment. "Working with Adolescent Addiction." Adolescent Intensive Outpatient Program. http://aiopduke.wordpress.com/.

Centers for Disease Control and Prevention. "Signs and Symptoms." Last updated December 26. 2013. www.cdc.gov/ncbddd/autism/signs.html.

Centers for Disease Control and Prevention. "Youth Suicide." Injury Center: Violence Prevention. Last updated January 9. 2014. www.cdc .gov/violenceprevention/pub /youth_suicide.html.

Center for Disease Control and Prevention. Last updated: January 27. 2014. "Developmental Milestones?" www.cdc.gov/ncbddd/actearly /milestones/.

"Disruptive Mood Dysregulation Disorder." May 2013. www.dsm5.org /Documents /Disruptive%20Mood%20Dysregulation%20Disorder%20 Fact%20Sheet.pdf.

Education Law Center, "Getting Your Child an Independent Educational Evaluation," https://www.drnpa.org/wp-content/uploads/2012/10 /getting-your-child-an-independent-educational-evaluation.pdf.

Frontline. "Inside the Teenage Brain." www.pbs.org/wgbh/pages/frontline /shows/teenbrain/work/adolescent.html.

Hoecker, Jay L. "Is Chelation Therapy an Effective Autism Treatment?" Diseases and Conditions. July 9, 2013. www.mayoclinic.com/health /autism-treatment/AN01488

The Incredible Years. "The Incredible Years Parenting Programs." 2013. www.incredibleyears.com/programs/parent.

Insel, Thomas. "Director's Blog: Transforming Diagnosis." National Institute of Mental Health. April 29, 2013. www.nimh.nih.gov/about /director/2013/transforming-diagnosis.shtml.

Institute for the Advancement of Research in Education at AEL. "Graphic Organizers: A Review of Scientifically Based Research." Inspiration Software. July 2003. www.inspiration.com/sites/default/files/documents /Detailed-Summary.pdf.

James Heckman: The Heckman Equation. http://heckmanequation.org /heckman-equation.

Johns Hopkins Medicine. "Oppositional Defiant Disorder." Health Library.
www.hopkinsmedicine.org/healthlibrary/conditions/mental_health
_disorders/oppositional_defiant_disorder_90,P02573/.

Kam, Katherine. "Eating Disorders in Children and Teens." Children's
Health. WebMD. Reviewed on April 14, 2007. http://children.webmd
.com/features/eating-disorders-children-teens.

Kemp, Gina, Melinda Smith, and Jeanne Segal. "Helping Children with
Learning Disabilities." Helpguide.org. Last updated December 2013.
www.helpguide.org/mental/learning _disabilities_treatment_help
_coping.htm.

Lifepath Systems. "EDI—Is This Typical Development?" www
.lifepathsystems.org/is-this-typical.

Lindamood-Bell Instructional Processes. Research Articles. www
.lindamoodbell.com/research/articles/.

Lucy Daniels Center. "When to Seek Professional Help." March 31, 2009.
www.lucydanielscenter.org/page/when-to-seek-professional-mental
-health-help.

Massachusetts General Hospital, School Psychiatry and Madi Resource
Center. "Bipolar Disorder (Manic Depression)." www2.massgeneral.org
/schoolpsychiatry/info_bipolar.asp.

Mayo Clinic. "Childhood Schizophrenia." Diseases and Conditions.
December 17, 2010. www.mayoclinic.com/health/childhood
-schizophrenia/DS00868/DSECTION=symptoms.

———. "Oppositional Defiant Disorder (ODD)." Diseases and
Conditions. January 6, 2012. www.mayoclinc.org/diseases-conditions
/oppositional-defiant-disorder/basics/definition/con-20024559.

———. "Panic Attacks and Panic Disorder." Diseases and Conditions.
May 31, 2012. www.mayoclinic.org/diseases-conditions/panic-attacks
/basics/definition/con-20020825.

———. "Reactive Attachment Disorder. Definition." Diseases and
Conditions. July 6, 2011. www.mayoclinic.org/diseases-conditions
/reactive-attachment-disorder/basics/definition/con-20032126.

NAMI Southwestern Pennsylvania. "Navigating the Mental Health and
Education Systems. A Caregivers' Guide." https://www.namiswpa.org
/documents/pdfs/CAREGIVERS%20GUIDE.pdf.

NAMI Southwestern Illinois. "Children and Adolescent with Brain Disorders." http://031e044.netsolhost.com/reference_guide.htm.

National Cancer Institute. "Grief, Bereavement, and Coping with Loss (PDQ®) Children and Grief." www.cancer.gov/cancertopics/pdq /supportivecare/bereavement/Patient/page6.

National Center for Learning Disabilities. "What Is Dyscalculia?" www .ncld.org/types-learning-disabilities/dyscalculia/what-is-dyscalculia.

National Dissemination Center for Children with Disabilities. "Questions Often Asked by Parents about Special Education Services." April 2009. nichcy.org/wp-content/uploads /docs/lg1.pdf. [The National Dissemination Center for Children with Disabilities is no longer in operation as of September 30, 2013. The website and all its free resources will remain available until September 30, 2014.]

———. "Right to Obtain an Independent Educational Evaluation." December 2010. http://nichcy.org/schoolage/parental-rights/iee.

National Institute on Drug Abuse. "Regular Marijuana Use by Teens Continues to Be a Concern." December 19, 2012. www.nih.gov/news /health/dec2012/nida-19.htm.

National Institute of Mental Health. "Anxious and Healthy Adolescents Respond Differently to Anxiety-Provoking Situations." November 5, 2008. www.nimh.nih.gov/news/science-news/2008/anxious-and-healthy -adolescents-respond-differently-to-an-anxiety-provoking-situation .shtml.

———. "Attention Deficit Hyperactivity Disorder." www.nimh.nih.gov /health/topics/attention-deficit-hyperactivity-disorder-adhd/index.shtml.

———. "Bipolar Disorder in Children and Teens: Easy to Read." www .nimh.nih.gov/health/publications/bipolar-disorder-in-children-and -teens-easy-to-read/index.shtml.

———. "Depression in Children and Adolescents." www.nimh.nih.gov /health/topics/depression/depression-in-children-and-adolescents.shtml.

———. "Introduction: Mental Health Medications." Mental Health Medications. www.nimh.nih.gov/health/publications/mental-health -medications/index.shtml.

———. "The Numbers Count: Mental Disorders in America." www.nimh
.nih.gov/health/publications/the-numbers-count-mental-disorders-in
-america/index.shtml.

———. "What Is Anxiety Disorder?" Anxiety Disorders. www.nimh.nih
.gov/health/topics/anxiety-disorders/index.shtml.

———. "What is Panic Disorder?" www.nimh.nih.gov/health/topics
/panic-disorder/index.shtml.

The Nemours Foundation. "Understanding Depression." KidsHealth.
http://kidshealth.org/parent/emotions/feelings/understanding
_depression.html.

New York University Child Study Center. "Fact Sheet." www.aboutourkids
.org/files/pages/assests/fact_sheet.pdf.

Promising Practices Network. "Coping Cat." Last reviewed October 2006.
www.promisingpractices.net/program.asp?programid=153.

The REACH Institute. "Dr. Ross Greene's Model." www.thereachinstitute
.org/cps.html.

Rethink Mental Illness. "Talking Therapies—About." www.rethink.org
/diagnosis-treatment/ treatment-and-support/talking-treatments/about.

Smith, D. D. "Steps in the IEP Process." Education.com. Updated July 20,
2010. www.education.com/reference/article/steps-ndividualized
-education-program-IEP.

Substance Abuse and Mental Health Services Administration. "Child-
Parent Psychotherapy (CPP)." National Registry of Evidence-Based
Programs and Practices. Last updated January 28, 2014. www.nrepp
.samhsa.gov/ViewIntervention.aspx?id=194.

———. "Trauma-Focused Cognitive Behavioral Therapy (TF-CBT)."
National Registry of Evidence-Based Programs and Practices. Last
updated January 28, 2014. www.nrepp.samhsa.gov/viewintervention
.aspx?id=135.

Summit Educational Resources. https://www.summited.org/summer
-treatment-program/overview.html.

Tartakovsky, Margarita. "How to Talk to Your Kids When You Think
They're Using Drugs." World of Psychology. PsychCentral. Last reviewed
May 2013. http://psychcentral.com/blog/archives/2013/05/02/how-to
-talk-to-your-kids-when-you-think-theyre-using-drugs/.

Support for Families of Children with Disabilities. "Guide to Mental Health Services." https://www.supportforfamilies.org /resourcesmentalhealthguide.html

US Department of Education. "Building the Legacy: IDEA 2004." http:// idea.ed.gov/.

US Department of Health and Human Services. "Best Practices in Bullying Prevention and Intervention." 2011. http://ophp.umdnj.edu/njphtc /AP_-_Public_Health_Policy_files/SBN_Tip_23%20Best%20Practices %20Prevention.pdf.

US Department of Health and Human Services, National Institutes of Health. "What Are the Symptoms of Learning Disabilities?" www.nichd .nih.gov/health/topics/learning/conditioninfo/pages/symptoms.aspx.

US Department of Veterans Affairs. "PTSD in Children and Teens." PTSD: National Center for PTSD. Last updated January 3, 2014. www .ptsd.va.gov/public/pages/ptsd-children-adolescents.asp.

University of California, San Francisco, Child Trauma Research Program. "Child-Parent Psychotherapy." www.childtrauma.ucsf.edu/resources /index.aspx.

USF Health and Depression and Anxiety Disorders Research Institute. "About Depression and Anxiety." Last modified February 28, 2011. http://health.usf.edu/research/dari/about_depression.htm#anxiety.

Index